DISCARDED

POVERTY, INEQUALITY AND
RURAL DEVELOPMENT

CASE-STUDIES IN ECONOMIC DEVELOPMENT

General Editor: David Greenaway, Professor of Economics,
University of Nottingham

Published

Poverty, Inequality and Rural Development

Case-Studies in Economic Development, Volume 3

Edited by

Tim Lloyd
Lecturer in Economics
University of Nottingham

and

Oliver Morrissey
Lecturer in Economics
University of Nottingham

St. Martin's Press

First published in Great Britain 1994 by
THE MACMILLAN PRESS LTD
Houndmills, Basingstoke, Hampshire RG21 2XS
and London
Companies and representatives
throughout the world

A catalogue record for this book is available
from the British Library.

ISBN 0–333–58502–X

Printed in Great Britain by
Ipswich Book Co Ltd
Ipswich, Suffolk

First published in the United States of America 1994 by
Scholarly and Reference Division,
ST. MARTIN'S PRESS, INC.,
175 Fifth Avenue,
New York, N.Y. 10010

ISBN 0–312–12099–0

Library of Congress Cataloging-in-Publication Data
Poverty, inequality, and rural development / edited by Tim Lloyd and
Oliver Morrissey.
p.   cm.
Includes bibliographical references (p.   ) and index.
ISBN 0–312–12099–0
1. Rural poor—Developing countries—Case studies.   2. Rural
development—Developing countries—Case studies.   3. Agriculture-
-Economic aspects—Developing countries—Case studies.
4. Developing countries—Rural conditions—Case studies.   I. Lloyd,
Tim.   II. Morrissey, Oliver.
HC59. 72.P6P684   1994
362.5 ' 09173 ' 4—dc20   93–47023
                                                              CIP

Contents

General Editor's Foreword

As anyone who has taught development economics to undergraduates will be aware, case-study material is very important. It is a medium which helps highlight the key role of country-specific factors (such as institutional constraints) in explaining particular processes or episodes. The problem from a teaching perspective however, is that once one has crammed all the analytical material we regard as essential into a programme of lectures, there is precious little time available for the study of particular cases. In the light of this, some years ago the Centre for Research in Economic Development and International Trade (CREDIT) at the University of Nottingham initiated a programme of development seminars designed to fill this gap. We were helped in this venture by Maxwell Stamp plc, a leading economic consultancy firm with extensive experience in developing countries. They generously supported our programme, allowing us to bring in outside speakers with specialist knowledge.

The Maxwell Stamp Lectures have turned out to be an invaluable teaching resource to students and faculty alike. Out of these Lectures has grown *Case-Studies in Economic Development*. This is a five-volume series which we hope will prove useful to students and teachers of development economics. The cases are arranged thematically. The first volume focused on *Policy Adjustment in Africa*. Like the second volume *Topics in Policy Appraisal*, this volume is thematic rather than region-specific. We settled upon *Poverty and Inequality* because these are defining characteristics of developing countries, and are areas where there is no shortage of excellent work under way. As General Editor I am personally very pleased with the way things have worked out in this volume. Tim Lloyd and Oliver Morrisey have done an excellent job in carefully editing the papers, as well as setting the scene. The papers themselves cover issues relating to the causes of poverty, government intervention in its alleviation and the pattern of inequality. The case-studies themselves include China, Bangladesh, Côte d'Ivoire and Mauritania. I found them informative and stimulating and I hope others find them equally rewarding.

A number of people who have been involved in this project deserve thanks. First, the volume editors for steering this through to publication. Second, Oliver Morrisey who takes responsibility within CREDIT for organising the Maxwell Stamp Lectures. Last, but by no means least, Maxwell Stamp plc for their generous sponsorship of the Lectures. I hope they will be widely used as a teaching aid.

David Greenaway
CREDIT, University of Nottingham

Preface

The contributions to this edited volume emerged from a series of seminars in development economics given to students at the University of Nottingham between 1990 and 1992, which were sponsored by Maxwell Stamp plc. We would like to express our gratitude to Maxwell Stamp for facilitating the organisation of the seminar programme, without which there would have been no material from which to conceive this volume.

We are of course especially grateful to the individual contributors. Not only were they willing and able to come to Nottingham and present a seminar to our students, but they were also willing and diligent in preparing their contributions to this volume (which in some cases were only tentatively related to the actual subject of their seminar). We endeavoured to select from some twenty seminars over three years those that would contribute to the theme of rural development, and commend the authors in tailoring their contributions to the theme. Poverty afflicts more than a fifth of the world's population, the majority in rural areas, and we hope this volume can contribute to our understanding of the process of rural development and to the design and implementation of policies to alleviate poverty.

Finally, a general thanks to all those who have made this volume possible, notably staff at Macmillan. In particular, we should register the support and encouragement of David Greenaway who initiated the series of *Case-Studies in Economic Development*, of which this is the third volume.

Tim Lloyd
Oliver Morrissey

Notes on the Contributors

David Burch is Senior Lecturer in the Division of Science and Technology, Griffith University, Brisbane, Australia.

Harold Coulombe is Research Associate with the Development Economics Research Centre (DERC) in the Department of Economics, University of Warwick.

Lawrence Haddad is Senior Economist with the International Food Policy Research Institute, Washington, DC.

John Hoddinott is Research Officer with the Centre for the Study of African Economies (CSAE) and Research Lecturer of Trinity College, Oxford.

John Knight is Senior Research Officer with the Centre for the Study of African Economies (CSAE) and a Fellow of St Edmund Hall, Oxford.

Peter Lanjouw is an economist in the Policy Research Department of the World Bank, Washington, DC.

John Lingard is Senior Lecturer in the Department of Agricultural Economics and Food Marketing, University of Newcastle.

Tim Lloyd is Research Fellow in the Centre for Research in Economic Development and International Trade (CREDIT) and a Lecturer in Economics, University of Nottingham.

J. Allister McGregor is Research Fellow in the Centre for Development Studies and Lecturer in Development Studies, University of Bath.

Andrew McKay is Research Fellow in the Centre for Research in Economic Development and International Trade (CREDIT) and a Lecturer in Economics, University of Nottingham.

Oliver Morrissey is Assistant Director in the Centre for Research in Economic Development and International Trade (CREDIT) and a Lecturer in Economics, University of Nottingham.

Wendy Olsen is Lecturer in Social Research Skills, Departments of Sociology at Salford University and Lancaster University (joint appointment).

Robert Read is Lecturer in Economics in the Management School, Lancaster University.

1 Introduction

Tim Lloyd and Oliver Morrissey

Poverty alleviation would be widely accepted as the single most important ultimate objective of development. There would be much less agreement on the policies appropriate to achieving this objective. Some of the relevant considerations are addressed and appraised in the contributions to this volume. Poverty is a major problem in itself, and is inextricably linked to many other economic, social, political and environmental problems observed in the modern world. The *World Development Report 1990* took poverty as its theme. After noting the rapid progress of developing countries over 1965–85 in terms of economic growth rates and improvements in social indicators, the editors comment that 'it is all the more staggering – and all the more shameful – that more than one billion people in the developing world are living in poverty . . . struggling to survive on less than $370 a year' (World Bank, 1990, p. 1). Roughly speaking, more than a fifth of the world's population live in absolute poverty; of these almost half live in South Asia, and about one-fifth are in Sub-Saharan Africa; in both cases the poor account for about half the population. While urban poverty and squalor is not to be ignored, it remains true that the poor are predominantly resident in rural areas: over 80 per cent of the poor in Asia and Sub-Saharan Africa live in rural areas, and even for most of the relatively urbanised Latin American countries more than half the poor live in rural areas (World Bank, 1990, p. 31).

The focus of this volume is on rural development, which is taken to have the objectives of designing and implementing strategies to reduce rural poverty, increase rural incomes and ultimately reduce rural inequality. The first four chapters address issues and evidence in the measurement of poverty and inequality. Lanjouw describes a methodology that allows comparisons and rankings to be made; Coulombe and McKay focus on the measurement of poverty from household expenditure surveys; Haddad and Hoddinott focus on intra-household income distribution; and Knight provides evidence on inequality in China, and how it has been affected by recent economic reforms.

The remaining five chapters consider particular strategies for rural

1

development. Both McGregor and Olsen address aspects of rural credit, comparing the performance of formal sector and informal providers; Lingard provides an extensive discussion of technical change in agriculture; Burch also focuses on agricultural production, but takes the case of contract farming; finally, Read addresses an international dimension of rural development, examining the problems that can arise for a small economy heavily reliant on a single crop produced by peasant farmers when market demand conditions change significantly. Thus, the course of this volume is from measurement issues to case studies, and from a focus on households to rural agriculture to the international dimension. In the process, a number of lessons for rural development strategies emerge, although there are no 'universal' solutions.

The nine contributions are each independent case-studies. Thus, the later case-studies are not applications of the measurement issues discussed in the early chapters. In fact, all of the early chapters provide applications as well as discussions of measurement issues. On the other hand, all contributions share the broad theme of rural development (issues and strategies) and reflect a wide range of approaches: Chapters 2 and 5 represent statistical analyses; Chapters 3, 4 and 8 include econometric applications; Chapters 6, 7, 9 and 10 are essentially in the tradition of institutional economic analysis. Furthermore, most of the issues addressed here featured in *World Development Report 1990*, even including the effect of the Single European Market on bananas (World Bank, 1990, p. 22).

Peter Lanjouw presents the Stochastic Dominance Framework as a unified methodology for the measurement and ranking of inequality, poverty and welfare over time. The novelty of the technique lies in its recognition and incorporation of the links between these three dimensions of living standards, in contrast to more conventional approaches which typically treat them as separate issues requiring independent investigation. In addition, the technique is shown to encompass alternative measures of inequality, poverty and welfare that are frequently based on widely divergent assumptions and/or embody a variety of distributional and value judgements. As a result, dominance statements are likely to command widespread support, unlike many alternative measures of living standards. However, by its very nature, such an encompassing framework incurs a cost in terms of the frequency with which unambiguous statements can be made. Nevertheless, a situation in which dominance is not observed is useful, since it reinforces the fact that a contradictory result exists if an alternative measure were used. Following a useful discussion of its limitations, the approach is applied to data from Palanpur, India, for 1957/58, 1962/63, 1974/75 and 1983/84. The results suggest that while poverty is unambiguously lowest in 1974/75, and welfare unambiguously highest, it is more difficult to provide clear rankings for the other periods. The evidence on inequality defies clear rankings because of the difficulties of weighting alternative tails of the distribution. The chapter demonstrates the usefulness of the approach for comparing measures of living standards and implicitly suggests that poverty measures are easier to rank than inequality measures. The study also demonstrates the paucity of evidence supporting the contention that poverty has been reduced over a 25-year period, despite apparent improvements in the village economy. In addition, the evidence for 1974/75 highlights the vulnerability of rural households to external shocks, and the evidence over the whole period indicates how difficult it is to achieve effective rural development.

Harold Coulombe and Andrew McKay address the problems inherent in measuring poverty and use data from the Mauritania Living Standards Survey to present a detailed analysis of the incidence of poverty (the proportion of population below the poverty line) and its depth (the extent of poverty among the poor). Poverty is widespread in Mauritania: about half the households can be classed as having living standards below the poverty line and the majority of these poor households reside in rural areas. While some 40 per cent of urban households are classified as poor, almost 70 per cent of rural households are below the poverty line. The principal aim of this study is to identify the factors that are associated with poverty and quantify their impact using econometric techniques. The results reveal a strong rural–urban differential in living standards, with rural households more likely to be both poor and poorer than their urban counterparts. In addition, a strong positive correlation between education and household standard of living is identified, particularly in non-agricultural households, where the level of educational attainment is often a precondition for employment. However, even within agricultural households education is shown to be positively related with living standard, reflecting as the authors suggest, that better educated households are more likely to adopt 'Green Revolution' technologies. These results for education are consistent with Knight's results for China and signal the importance of education in any poverty alleviation strategy.

The results also bear out the influence of demographic factors in determining living standards, particularly household size and the number of children which are both negatively related to living standards, although interestingly, this relationship is reversed for agricultural households, which appear to benefit from an increase in household size, at least up to a certain threshold, an inference that reflects the productive contribution of family labour on the farm. Evidence of this sort underscores the fact that attempts to limit population growth as part of a future development strategy may well be frustrated by the predominance of agricultural production in developing countries.

The effects of any rural development policy aimed at increasing welfare and reducing poverty, especially if directed towards women and children, depends crucially on how resources are allocated within the household. Evidence from Asia suggests strong discrimination against women, and especially female children, although the evidence for Africa is less conclusive. **Lawrence Haddad and John Hoddinott** apply 'outlay equivalent analysis' to Ivorian household expenditure data to assess whether discrimination exists in Côte d'Ivoire. The approach identifies the effect of an additional child on expenditure on adult goods. Any child should have an income effect but if a male child leads to a greater reduction in expenditure on adult goods than a female child, that is evidence of discrimination against female children. In general, the study finds no evidence of discrimination against females in Côte d'Ivoire, although there is some evidence that own children are favoured over foster children. The authors suggest that the absence of discrimination in the African case may be due to the practice of bridewealth in which the parents of a bride receive payment as compensation for the loss of a valuable worker and as a result are reluctant to discriminate against daughters. This contrasts nicely with the Asian experience where discrimination is commonplace, reflecting, in part, the fact that a dowry has to be paid to the groom's parents.

This study casts light on the distribution of resources within households and suggests that resources within the household are allocated with efficiency criteria in mind. As such, the study has implications for the debate on poverty alleviation. In particular, relatively equitable intra-household allocation implies that policies can be targeted on the household and on increasing incomes, rather than directly targeting individuals within the group, which can be more costly.

Approximately one-fifth of the world's population, and its poor, live in China and while this is a relatively good ratio for a poor country (World Bank, 1990, p. 29) it nevertheless represents a very large absolute number. Western researchers have only recently gained access to detailed data on income distribution in China. **John Knight** presents some results from a recently completed large survey. China is particularly interesting as one might expect a communist regime to have a relatively low degree of inequality, and one would like to examine the effect on income distribution of the market reforms gradually introduced since 1978. Knight reveals that although there has been a high degree of equity *within* urban and rural areas, there has been a large rural–urban divide, with urban wages considerably higher, so that overall equity has not been as great as may have been expected. The rural reforms introduced from 1978 were successful in increasing rural incomes and reducing rural poverty. While there may have been an increase in inequality within rural areas, the rural–urban divide was reduced and overall equity rose. However, the introduction of market reforms in urban areas from 1984 restored the rural–urban divide. Overall, then, China has relatively low poverty but is not exceptionally egalitarian. Furthermore, market reforms seem to be reducing poverty at the cost of increased inequity.

The trade-off between poverty alleviation and inequality should not really be taken as surprising, as Kuznets long ago hypothesised that growth would initially lead to increasing inequality, although the degree of inequality may begin to fall after some critical level of income has been achieved. The chapter also demonstrates the importance of differential access to education; boys are favoured over girls (suggesting that China exhibits the pattern of sex discrimination that Haddad and Hoddinott report has been found in other parts of Asia), and this is particularly acute when urban and rural areas are compared. This highlights the importance of investing in human capital, and is also indicative of the role education can play in determining inequality: Knight's analysis provides evidence that inhabitants of rural areas had less access to education, reflecting relative poverty (rural–urban inequality) and is a feature borne out in Coulombe and McKay's study of Mauritania. Private sector wage differentials have increased significantly since the market reforms, which should ultimately be reflected in higher wages for the better educated. The evidence on rural–urban inequality that emerges from a number of these early chapters supports that view that an effective scheme to alleviate rural poverty should focus on expanding the opportunities available to the rural poor themselves. One important way to achieve this is to promote agricultural development.

The World Bank (1990, pp. 65–9) identified the central importance of improving access to credit in policies to reduce rural poverty and expand agricultural output. **Allister McGregor** provides a case study

of the evolution of the formal sector rural credit market in Bangladesh. Facilitating and increasing the access of the rural poor to credit
is recognised as a central plank in any strategy to promote rural development and alleviate rural poverty. McGregor shows that a successful scheme must provide rural borrowers with reliable access to
credit on an on-going basis since the rural poor need the security of
a relationship that guarantees access to credit when it is needed. Thus,
the relationship must provide access and security over time. In Bangladesh, the government became involved in the provision of rural credit
since independence in 1972. However, the banks were not used to
working with the rural poor, who were perceived as being unable to
deal properly with banks, and acted through intermediaries who disbursed loans on a patronage basis. Default rates were very high, and
the scheme became a costly failure. A number of non-governmental
organisations (NGOs), such as the Grameen Bank, began working with
the rural poor from the early 1970s. Like many NGOs providing credit,
the approach was to build a relationship among borrowers and between borrowers and the NGOs. Their participatory approach, with
close contact and monitoring, is time-intensive for NGO staff, but has
nonetheless been successful, by the criteria of very low default rates
and very rapid expansion of the (profitable) provision of credit to the
rural poor.

   Wendy Olsen also examines credit relations, focusing on the role
of credit in the exchange relations of small farmers and merchants in
two Indian villages. Credit facilities offered by merchant money-lenders
to small farmers are found to act as an informal tie between the two
parties. Once indebted to a merchant money-lender, farmers are required to sell their cash crop production on the merchant's demand
and as a result, this leads to sales of cash crops at low prices: so
called distress sales. Moreover, credit acts as a tie that pervades other
aspects of exchange, such that an indebted farmer would also be required to purchase household provisions and retail goods from the
same merchant throughout the year, typically at prices higher than
elsewhere. This feature of *interlocking transactions* strengthens the tie,
since default on the loan would prevent farmers from obtaining such
goods and credit facilities in the future. The study finds evidence of
distress sales for groundnuts, a major source of cash income, but not
for paddy, which was mostly used for own consumption. Rational
storage and sale timing decisions can explain why small farmers sell
to merchants at low prices, although much of the stability of the relationship derives from the merchant's monopsonistic power in an emerg-

ing capitalist village economy. The evidence presented suggests that it is very difficult for the farmer-borrower to break out of the dependency relationship due to interlocking transactions and the absence of effective competition from banks. Whilst the existing credit arrangements are not necessarily exploitative, the study highlights the need for increased competition in rural credit markets and offers a number of important lessons for formal bank-administered credit schemes in rural areas.

Agricultural technology is crucial to rural development. While all forms of technology are intended to increase output and, through growth, reduce poverty, different forms have different distributional effects. **John Lingard** reviews the impact of the Green Revolution technologies in the Philippines. While the high-yielding seed varieties were viewed initially as scale neutral and land-augmenting, so that labour use should actually increase, this did not always result. To the extent that the adoption of new technology favoured large farmers, concentration of land ownership increased and this induced mechanisation. Consequently, the end result was labour-saving mechanisation and increased inequity in land ownership. The study shows that mechanisation was not a significant determinant of cropping intensity or yield, but rather, farmers adopted mechanisation to reduce costs by substituting for labour and the incentive to do so often resulted from input price distortions due to government policies. The net effect on labour's share of income is difficult to determine, but Lingard does identify the complex ways in which technical change can affect distribution, output growth and rural poverty. An appreciation that final outcomes are critically dependent upon the economic, physical, social and political environment that technologies take root in is a theme that runs throughout the chapter and is exemplified by a case study of a mechanical reaper that was introduced to Filipino rice farmers in the 1980s. In particular, the case-study offers a warning of the dangers that may be encountered when promoting capital intensive technologies in surplus labour economies.

Thailand could be classified as a relatively successful dynamic economy with a flourishing agricultural sector, which still accounts for almost a fifth of national income; it is one of the world's largest exporters of rice and has relatively low food import needs. Nevertheless, about 70 per cent of the population live in rural areas and the majority of these are poor (World Bank, 1990). Rural development, and government policies towards agriculture as a livelihood, are clearly important. **David Burch** addresses this issue through a case-study of the growth of contract farming in Thailand. Such farming arises where farmers grow under contract (often quite specific regarding quality of crop, timing and method of production, purchase price and quantity taken) to agribusiness companies, often multinational. While contract farming can benefit farmers, providing a guaranteed outlet and, at least, a stable price, it is subject to criticisms. Peasant farmers find themselves in a dependency relationship where companies control the production process, farmers' margins are squeezed and cash crops are favoured over (local) food crops.

Thailand has emerged as a, if not *the*, major Asian exporter of processed foods, much of it produced under contract. From the perspective of rural development, two problems emerge. First, the export crops have often displaced basic food production for the local market; the volume of cereal food imports increased in the 1980s and in 1988 Thailand received a significant volume of cereal food aid (World Bank, 1990, p. 184). Second, the state's involvement has been increasingly interventionist, farmers have limited discretion over accepting contracts, and limited choice over what to produce and for whom. Although the state cited the goals of raising farm incomes and rural employment in promoting contract farming, the measures imposed have favoured the position of agribusiness rather than of farmers. While contract farming may benefit farmers in the short run, Burch suggests that contract farming does little to alleviate rural poverty or to promote rural development in the long run.

Robert Read highlights the important role exports can play in determining rural incomes, and the vulnerability of small states largely reliant on a single crop. The four Windward Islands are small and poor, largely undiversified and heavily dependent on agriculture; bananas alone account for some fifty per cent of export earnings, equivalent to 15 per cent of GDP, and employ some 40 per cent of the labour force. The world market for bananas is dominated by the large-scale plantations, so-called Dollar Area bananas, whose products are cheaper than those produced by smallholders. Preferential access to the EC, in particular Britain, has sustained the smallholder banana industry in the Windwards, but this is now under serious threat. As part of the favourable treatment of Africa, Caribbean and Pacific (ACP) states under the Lomé Convention, the Banana Protocol allowed EC countries to subject Dollar Area bananas to import quotas and tariffs while permitting free access to certain producers. In effect, Britain guaranteed a market to Windward bananas at prices well above the world level which is a form of 'trade-as-aid', perhaps preferable to direct aid grants. The Single Market implies a liberalisation of heavily protected markets and easier access, on similar terms, to Dollar Area bananas which, being cheaper, are likely to increase their market share. Windward exporters can anticipate losing both market share and volume of sales, with a detrimental impact on rural incomes. While favoured trade access has worked fairly well as a means of assisting the Windwards, it may no longer be feasible and increased aid may be needed to compensate the islands if they lose export markets.

The contributions to this volume are intended to provide introductory reading for students in areas not often addressed in textbooks and/or in material that is not always readily accessible to students (either because it is published in disparate outlets, often research monographs or reports, or because it is technically advanced). They are also intended to contribute to our understanding of the problems of rural development. We hope both objectives have been met through the combination of papers on technical and measurement issues and those on the experiences within particular countries which require detailed knowledge and fieldwork. Unfortunately, the conclusions from these studies may not imbue the reader with optimism. A quarter of a century of development in a village in India has yielded little clear evidence of reduced poverty and increased welfare (Chapter 2); although the market reforms in China have led to rapid growth, the poverty ratio may not be any less and inequality is rising (Chapter 5). Many of the policies advocated for development do not appear to have been implemented effectively: bank credit schemes have at least been inefficient, have apparently done little to alleviate poverty and have probably increased inequality (Chapters 6 and 7); mechanisation associated with the Green Revolution in the Philippines has done little to reduce poverty and may have increased inequality (Chapter 8); contract farming is of questionable benefit to peasants (Chapter 9); even the benefits the Winward Islands have gained through preferential access to the UK market may well be lost as a result of changes within the European Community (Chapter 10).

If one looks for the lessons from these studies, however, all is clearly not bad news. Investment in human capital and education is clearly a most important factor in promoting development and reducing inequality (Chapters 3 and 5). The positive findings for intra-household allocation in Côte d'Ivoire are encouraging, and suggest that the benefits of development strategies will be spread and may therefore be more effective (Chapter 4). Furthermore, even if government provision of rural credit has not been successful, informal markets often prove efficient and NGOs are effective providers (Chapters 6 and 7).

Finally, preferential trade access, which could be posited as an alternative to aid (one might want to consider which approach costs the consumer more) can be effective in facilitating and supporting rural development. Poverty remains a major problem, but there are strategies to alleviate rural deprivation and these involve a reorientation towards rural development. Only through an evaluation of past episodes can we learn the lessons necessary for effective rural development in the future.

Reference

World Bank (1990), *World Development Report 1990*, Washington DC: Oxford University Press for The World Bank.

2 Living Standards in a North Indian Village: An Analysis within the Stochastic Dominance Framework[1]

Peter Lanjouw

2.1 INTRODUCTION

This chapter focuses on the measurement of poverty, inequality and welfare within a unified framework of analysis. It examines these issues on the basis of income data from a North Indian village (Palanpur) collected through four separate surveys in 1957/58, 1962/63, 1974/75 and 1983/84.[2] The paper seeks to fulfil two objectives: first, an exposition of how the stochastic dominance approach to measurement can be readily implemented within a small village study context; and second, to shed some light on the interlinked paths traced out by poverty, inequality and welfare over time in the village of Palanpur. We begin with a brief description of the village, followed by an outline of the methodology to be adopted.

The Village Economy

Palanpur is located in the district of Moradabad in western Uttar Pradesh. The four surveys involved the extensive collection of detailed information on family structure, occupation, land ownership and cultivation, production, incomes, assets and related variables. The village is surrounded by open fields covering about 400 acres. At the beginning of the last survey (which covered the agricultural year 1983/84), the village numbered 960 inhabitants, divided into 143 households. Hindus represented 87 per cent of the village population and Muslims 13 per cent. The three largest castes in the village are Thakur (traditionally warriors), Murao (a cultivating caste) and Jatab (a scheduled caste).

Despite the recent expansion of employment opportunities outside the village, facilitated by a nearby railway line, agriculture remains the main source of economic activity in Palanpur. Land is cultivated through family labour, wage labour or tenancy arrangements. About 30 per cent of the total village land is leased. While fixed-rent leasing does occur, the principal contractual arrangement is share-cropping. Sales of land occur infrequently and usually as a consequence of distress. Other important markets in Palanpur are the labour and credit markets. The labour market within the village consists largely of casual wage labour and households involved in such agricultural labour are typically very poor. Wage rates tend to be uniform across villagers but do vary over time. The credit market in Palanpur can be broadly divided into four segments: (1) interest free credit from friends or relatives; (2) low-interest credit from state institutions, including rural banks and a local Credit Cooperative; (3) commercial credit from urban goldsmiths and pawnbrokers; and (4) high-interest credit from village money-lenders. Generally, better-off households are able to obtain cheaper credit, while the poorest households find it hard to borrow from sources other than village money-lenders.

The economy of Palanpur changed radically from the late 1950s to the mid-1980s. Three factors played a major role in this transformation. First, the village population nearly doubled, from 528 in 1957/58 to 960 in 1983/84. The rapid growth of population accentuated pressure on land and increased the incentive for economic diversification and involvement in the wider economy. Second, substantial technological change took place in agriculture. This involved an intensified use of modern inputs such as fertilisers, motorised irrigation devices, and new seed varieties, and, correspondingly, large increases in productivity. Average wheat yields in Palanpur have approximately tripled over the study period (see Table 2.1). Third, employment opportunities outside the village, mainly in nearby towns, expanded very substantially. These jobs contributed around one-third of total village income in the mid-1980s, compared with less than one-tenth in the 1950s. This is partly due to the expansion of outside employment opportunities, and partly to the comparatively rapid increase in real wages for these occupations.

Methodology for Evaluating Living Standards

The use of income as a measure of living standards raises several issues which have received widespread attention in the literature (Sen, 1992, presents a useful survey of a number of these issues). Income, as it is measured from the Palanpur data, does not reflect many of the components of living standards which should be included in a comprehensive measure. A more satisfactory indicator would take into account not only earnings but also health, disutility of labour, the consumption of public goods, wealth, life style, etc. Lanjouw and Stern (1990) rank households in Palanpur on the basis of apparent prosperity, thereby incorporating these less quantifiable aspects. However, this is possible for one survey year only, and at best can allow only an ordinal ranking of the village population into deciles.

In a setting such as Palanpur where villagers share a common environment and common access to public goods, differences between individuals in terms of the ability to translate commodity command into welfare are largely based on income. Unlike in situations where data are drawn from more widely dispersed or differentiated environments, income is a useful indicator of living standards in Palanpur.

The conventional approach taken in the literature on the measurement of income inequality, poverty and welfare is to treat them as separate problems which can be investigated independently. The measurement of these three aspects of living standards has generated a vast literature and a large number of different measures have been proposed. However, the conclusions which arise from the implementation of any particular measure may carry little weight if we disagree with its embodied assumptions. In addition, the chosen measure for say, poverty, may conflict with that chosen for measuring some other aspect of living standards such as inequality. While the conceptual linkages have been widely recognised and explored, only recently has there been a growing recognition in the measurement literature of the many linkages between welfare, inequality and poverty. This has prompted a number of researchers to adopt approaches to measurement which take explicit account of such linkages (see, for example, Atkinson, 1970, 1987; Foster and Shorrocks, 1988; Shorrocks, 1983; and Sen, 1976). This chapter draws on an approach originally developed in Atkinson (1970) which makes possible the evaluation of living standards without the need to restrict oneself to specific measures and their embodied assumptions.

The framework adopted here takes as its bench-mark an aggregate 'living-standards function' which is assumed to be an additively separable function of the incomes of individuals in Palanpur. Also assumed is that this function is non-decreasing in income and that it is continuous. Within this framework attention can be confined to questions of poverty by paying attention only to those villagers whose incomes are below some designated upper bound. If our concern is with inequality we examine the incomes of all villagers in this function, but we normalise by village average income so that our focus is entirely on the dispersion of incomes as opposed to their levels. Finally, if our concern is with welfare in the village we focus on the level of all incomes in the village and their dispersion at the same time.

The procedure followed here is to assess the relative standard of living in Palanpur in different survey years on the basis of how our living-standards function compares between the years. Atkinson (1970, 1987), discusses two frameworks within which one can compare living-standards functions. The first consists of examining for Lorenz dominance and is so-called because it employs the Lorenz curve when comparing distributions of mean-normalised income (for the purpose of evaluating inequality). This approach has been extended by Shorrocks (1983) who introduced the 'generalised' Lorenz curve and showed that it could be used to make welfare comparisons of distributions which have different mean incomes. The second, and closely related, framework within which we can compare living-standards functions, and the one employed in this study, is the stochastic dominance framework. This approach (also denoted the 'primal' approach) does not involve comparing distributions of income using Lorenz curves, but rather compares cumulative distribution functions, or alternatively 'deficit' curves (where a deficit curve is the integral of a cumulative distribution function). This second approach is better suited for our purposes because it more readily permits us to consider poverty as well as inequality and welfare, with only minimal redirection necessary as we turn from one aspect to another.

The two analytical tools described above have been developed to permit comparisons of distributions which command the support of people with differing views and distributional judgements. We describe specific classes of living-standards functions and say that one distribution dominates another if it is preferred for all living-standards functions belonging to a specific class. These classes of living-standards functions can be very wide, such that sharply divergent distributional viewpoints may be represented within a class. Where we find that one distribution dominates another for such a class of living-standards functions, we can be confident that our dominance judgement is likely to command widespread support.

The outline of this chapter is as follows. Section 2.2 describes the framework of stochastic dominance and Section 2.3 addresses some of its limitations. The stochastic dominance approach is applied to the Palanpur data for the four survey years in Section 2.4. An attempt is made to arrive at some overall evaluation of living-standards on this basis. The detailed knowledge of circumstances in the village during the four survey years is invoked to assess the extent to which the stochastic dominance approach is successful. Section 2.5 offers some concluding observations.

2.2 THE STOCHASTIC DOMINANCE APPROACH

The framework of stochastic dominance was originally explored in relation to welfare economics by Atkinson (1970) and we begin by drawing together some results he presented in his 1970 and 1987 papers. Assume a standard of living function, S, which is additively separable, so that the aggregate standard of living can be written as an integral:

$$S = \int_b^{Z^{max}} S\,(Y, Z^{max})\, f\,(Y)\, dY \qquad (2.1)$$

defined over the distribution, with distribution function $f(Y)$, with which one is concerned. The distribution function is assumed to be normalised by population size, i.e. $F(Z^{max}) = 1$, where $F(.)$ is the cumulative distribution, so that S may be seen as per-capita living-standards. No other restrictions need be placed on S, other than that it be continuous and non-decreasing in Y. One can consider Y as either income or income divided by the mean. The parameter b is the lower bound of income such that $F(b) = 0$ and Z^{max} is the upper income bound of the segment of the distribution one is interested in.

Our notation allows us to interpret S as a welfare, an inverse-poverty or an inequality measure. If we are looking at *welfare*, and Y is our income measure, then Z^{max} will be no lower than the maximum income of the distributions being compared, i.e. we are looking at the entire income range. If we are examining *poverty*, Y is again income but Z^{max} will be typically below the maximum income (although this need not be the case) and can be thought of here as the upper bound on the set of possible poverty lines one is prepared to consider. In other words, we are examining a truncated distribution. Finally, if we are looking at *inequality*, Y will not be income, but will be mean-normalised income, and Z^{max} here will refer to the highest income in the population we are considering, normalised by the mean income. While inequality could be studied over a complete or truncated distribution, in practice it is normally used as a tool of analysis for complete distributions, and we follow that convention here.

It is possible to show that all particular forms of S which satisfy our assumptions (additive separability, non-decreasing and continuous) will show an improvement, or at least no deterioration, in living-standards in moving from distribution f^* to f if and only if

$$\Delta F(Z) \leq 0 \qquad \text{for all } Z \in [0, Z^{max}]$$
$$\text{where } \Delta F(Z) = \int_{b}^{Z^{max}} (f(Y) - f^*(Y))\, dY \qquad (2.2)$$

If this condition holds, then there is said to be first-order stochastic dominance up to Z^{max} and this can be very easily checked because it involves simply comparing the two cumulative distribution functions. If the first lies nowhere above the other and it lies at least somewhere below the second, then first-order stochastic dominance of the first distribution over the second holds. In simple terms, this implies that for each and every income level Z up to Z^{max} there is no point at which the cumulative share of income enjoyed by those at Z or less is higher for the first distribution than for the second. Figure 2.1 provides a hypothetical example. If Z^* were taken as the highest poverty line which we would allow, then distribution B has first-order stochastic dominance (up to Z^*) over distribution A because its cumulative distribution lies everywhere below that for A. However, if the highest poverty line were Z^{*max} in Figure 2.1, then, first-order dominance would no longer hold. This is because curves A and B intersect below Z^{*max}.

If one is prepared to make the additional assumption that $S(Y, Z^{max})$ is (weakly) concave as a function of Y, i.e. that increases in income carry less weight in the living-standards evaluation at higher levels of income, then one can use a condition of second-order stochastic dominance to show that all particular forms of S will show an improvement, or at least no worsening, in moving from distribution $f^*(Y)$ to $f(Y)$ if and only if

$$\Delta G(Z) \leq 0 \qquad \text{for all } Z \in [0, Z^{max}]$$

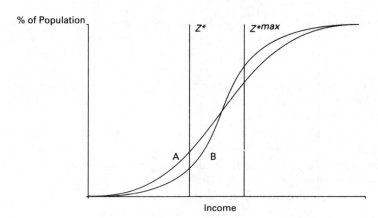

Figure 2.1   *Cumulative distributions*

where,

$$\Delta G(Z) = \int_{b}^{Z^{max}} (F(Y) - F^*(Y)) \, dY \qquad (2.3)$$

Note that first-order implies second-order stochastic dominance but not vice versa. Checking for second-order stochastic dominance is also straightforward and involves drawing 'deficit' curves by integrating over the cumulative distribution functions for income. An example is provided in Figure 2.2, with deficit curves derived from the distributions illustrated in Figure 2.1. A distribution will second-order stochastic dominate another if over the whole range of incomes in the distribution its deficit curve lies nowhere above the deficit curve of the other, and it lies at least somewhere below. In other words, at no (income) point (on the horizontal axis) is a lower income associated with a relatively greater area under $F(.)$ for $F(B)$ compared with $F(A)$. As can be seen from Figure 2.2, while we did not have first order stochastic dominance of distribution B over A up to a poverty line such as Z^{*max}, the deficit curves for these two distributions do not intersect up to this higher poverty line. At all income levels up to Z^{*max} distribution B lies below A, and hence there is second order stochastic dominance of B over A up to (at least) Z^{*max}.

Atkinson (1970) shows that if we have two distributions with equal mean income for which $f(Y)$ could have been reached from $f^*(Y)$ by a sequence of mean-preserving transfers of income from a person with income Y_1 to a person with a lower income Y_2, then $f(Y)$ dominates

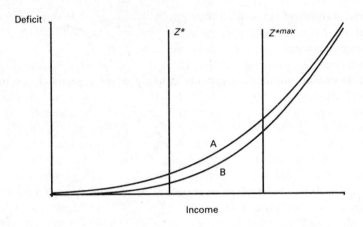

Figure 2.2   *Deficit curves*

$f^*(Y)$ under the second-order stochastic dominance criterion. In other words the distribution functions $f(Y)$ and $f^*(Y)$ would be distributed over the same mean income, but the tails on $f^*(Y)$ would be fatter than on $f(Y)$. It can be seen that first-order stochastic dominance is a more restrictive requirement than second-order stochastic dominance because any intersection of two cumulative distribution functions excludes the possibility of the first-order stochastic dominance. However, as long as the area under the intersecting cumulative distribution function F (which is what the deficit curve represents) is always smaller than the area under distribution function F^*, F would still stochastically dominate in a second-order sense. For this to be possible (although it is not sufficient) the dominating cumulative distribution function must cross the other from below if they intersect only once (as in Figure 2.1). Where the curves intersect more than once the dominating cumulative distribution function must cross the other from below at the first intersection.

Consistent with our earlier remarks, let us say that, if Y is defined as income, we have *poverty-domination* (for the poverty line Z^{max}) if domination (of whatever order) holds up to $Z^{max} \leq \max(Y^{max}, Y^{*max})$. Note that if we have such poverty-dominance then one distribution will dominate the other not only at Z^{max} but at any poverty line up to and including Z^{max}. *Welfare-domination* is obtained if domination holds up to $Z^{max} \geq \max(Y^{max}, Y^{*max})$. If Y is mean-normalised income we will have *inequality-domination*.[3]

These results are important. From each of the perspectives of poverty, inequality and welfare they provide necessary and sufficient conditions for agreement over measures embodying possibly widely divergent assumptions. For a discussion of this in relation to inequality measures see Atkinson (1970). In relation to poverty the conditions of stochastic domination provide conditions for agreement not only over different poverty measures, but they also permit statements to be made about poverty even where there might not be agreement about where to draw a specific poverty line (Atkinson, 1987).[4] We noted above that in the example of Figure 2.1 there was no first order dominance of distribution B over A at a poverty line such as Z^{*max}. This means that if one were to measure poverty at that line using conventional summary measures, there would be at least two poverty measures which would rank distributions A and B differently. For example, while a head-count index would rank B as having greater poverty, some other measure, which put a lot of weight on the extent of poverty (associated with the distance below the poverty line), would rank A as having greater poverty. Considering the two cumulative distribution functions in Figure 2.1, it is easy to see that a first-order dominance ranking would obtain for any poverty line up to the level of income at which A and B intersect. For any poverty line up to that level rankings based on different poverty measures will always agree, but beyond it there will be disagreement unless we are prepared to restrict the class of permissable poverty measures.

Domination up to Z^{max} is also domination up to any poverty line less than Z^{max}. Of course there is a cost, namely that a stochastic dominance ordering will generally be a partial one. But even so, this approach provides a useful starting point, and is employed in Section 2.4.

2.3 THE LIMITATIONS OF STOCHASTIC DOMINANCE

While we advocate the use of second-order stochastic dominance rather than generalised Lorenz dominance as a criterion for judgements on living-standards, there are weaknesses in the stochastic dominance framework (which are also evident in the generalised Lorenz framework). For one distribution to dominate another it is a necessary, but not sufficient, condition that its mean and its minimum income be no lower than those of the other distribution. If we examine two deficit curves at $\max(Y^{max}, Y^{*max})$ the ranking of distributions we obtain will be the same as if we had examined the means of the two distributions (although we must remember that a deficit curve is *ranked* higher than another if it lies *below the other*). Similarly, our ranking of two deficit curves at min(Y^{min}, Y^{*min}) will be identical to the ranking we obtain if we only look at the two minimum incomes. If this necessary condition is met we will say that *mean-minimum dominance* obtains. This has a very natural interpretation, as focus on the two variables, mean and minimum, spans the range of possible concerns with distribution, namely from a zero weight (in which case only the mean matters) to a weight approaching infinity (where we focus exclusively on the least advantaged, as in the Rawlsian approach).

The sensitivity of stochastic dominance measures to the minimum income may give cause for concern. One must distinguish two problems. The first is one of measurement. It is very hard to ascertain anyone's income, let alone that of the poorest. In particular, the reported minimum income will be very sensitive to decisions made concerning cleaning the data. One way to get round the measurement problem may be to widen the income bands for relative frequency groups. For example, one may be prepared to believe that if someone's income is reported as 20 rupees, it is certainly no more than 100 rupees. However, this could result in the loss of much valuable distributional information.

This problem of measurement is of immediate relevance to the Palanpur data. The income figures calculated, while quite detailed, are not exhaustive, nor were they calculated with exactly the same precision for each survey year. There are several components of income which could not be accurately assessed, notably illegal income and income earned from money-lending. In addition, the quality of the data collected in the two earlier survey years is not as high as that of the data collected in 1974/75 and 1983/84. Both of these factors might make one question the reliability of the actual minimum income figure obtained for any one year.

A second problem is conceptual. Do we really want to accommodate the full range of viewpoints, including those of strict Rawlsians? Say that we could measure income perfectly. If one distribution had incomes which were double those of another, except for the minimum income which was ever so slightly less, would we really want to refrain from ordering the former distribution as superior in welfare terms? Related to this sensitivity to minimum income is the broader problem of what we call 'slight rejection'. The stochastic dominance criteria do not distinguish between a strong and weak rejection of dominance. One distribution may record dominance over one half of the income distribution, and not over the other; another may record

Table 2.1 *Broad indicators of economic change in Palanpur*

	1957/58	*1962/63*	*1974/75*	*1983/84*
Population	528	585	757	960
Number of households	100	106	112	143
Village real income (Rs)	85,176	88,935	208,001	186,402
Real income per capita (Rs)	161.3	152.0	274.8	194.2
Minimum income per capita (Rs)	21.5	9.67	54.5	−41.0
Maximum income per capita (Rs)	713.1	1115.8	1085.9	494.1
Gini coefficient for income	0.336	0.390	0.253	0.307
Price index (1960/61=1.00)	1.07	0.98	3.78	5.28
Agricultural wages (1960/61=100)	123	100	123	158
Food purchasing power (kg wheat/day)	2.5	2.3	3.1	5.0
Index of off-farm real wages	n.a	100	122	193
Wheat yields, actual kg per bigha	40	40	114	97
Wheat yields, normal kg per bigha	40/50	50	100	150/160

Notes
1. n.a = not available
2. The price index is the consumer price index for agricultural labourers (CPIAL), which is taken from the *Bulletin of Food Statistics* for the relevant years. See Lal (1976) for the price index for 1957/58 and 1962/63.
3. One acre = 6.4 bighas
4. Normal wheat yields correspond to the expected yield for Palanpur ex-ante to the respective year's harvest.

dominance over 99 per cent. In both cases the same verdict of dominance-failure will be recorded. But the welfare significance of the former is likely to be much greater than that of the latter, and more robust to small changes in the data.

2.4   POVERTY, INEQUALITY AND WELFARE DOMINANCE IN PALANPUR

We now turn to an application of the stochastic dominance methodology to income data collected in Palanpur in the four survey years between 1957 and 1984. Where conclusions are drawn regarding poverty, inequality or welfare, it is important to remember that these will be dependent on the extent to which we are satisfied that income represents living-standards. For quick reference, Table 2.1 provides a broad overview of economic change in Palanpur for the survey years. The population of the village nearly doubled over the 26-year interval, and village real income also increased significantly. Although real income in either of the earlier two years was at best only about 50 per cent of village income in the later two years (due to the income-enhancing impact of technological change in agriculture and the spread of off-farm employment), income in 1983/84 was less than in 1974/75. This is the consequence of poor harvests for both the *rabi* (winter) and *kharif* (summer) seasons in Palanpur during the later survey year. Per capita real income in the four survey years did not follow a monotonic path either, with the lowest average incomes recorded in the two earliest survey years, and the highest per capita income obtaining in 1974/75.

Figure 2.3 provides graphical depictions of the distribution functions of income in the four survey years, following smoothing using a kernel smoothing technique.[5] In Figure 2.3 the unit of analysis is individual per capita income obtained by allocating to each individual in a household their household per capita income. In Figure 2.3 the unit of analysis is individual per capita income obtained from dividing household income by household size and then attributing to each household member his or her per capita income. This measure is appropriate to the evaluation of living-standards because it reflects household size not only when establishing household per capita income, but also in the weighting of these per capita incomes in the distribution of income. This weighting assures that if one sums up all individual per capita incomes, total village income would obtain. In contrast, summing household per capita income would provide us with village average income.

Stochastic Dominance and Poverty

The traditional approach to measuring poverty in a village such as Palanpur would entail specifying a poverty line below which people would be considered poor. For India as a whole, Dandekar and Rath (1971) have proposed a poverty line based on nutritional requirements of Rs 15 per person per month (at 1960/61 prices). Taking relative prices between Uttar Pradesh and India as a whole in 1963/64, a poverty line of Rs 11.3 obtains for Uttar Pradesh in 1960/61 prices. In annual terms this corresponds to Rs 136 per person, and for convenience, we will call this level of income the 'official' poverty line. In arriving at this poverty line, numerous assumptions have been made, explicitly or implicitly. One of the attractions of the stochastic dominance approach is that one is not obliged to commit oneself to a particular

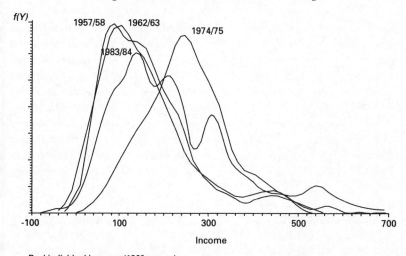

Figure 2.3 *Probability density functions*

poverty line and, in fact, where rankings are possible they will occur over all poverty lines up to a specified upper limit. Although it is of interest to measure poverty up to this official poverty line for bench-mark purposes, we will also consider poverty over all poverty lines up to 1.5 times and two times the conventional poverty line.

Turning first to an examination for first-order stochastic dominance, we present in Figure 2.4 the cumulative distribution functions for real individual incomes in the four survey years, with reference lines representing the official poverty line of Rs 136 as well as another representing Rs 204, or 1.5 times the official poverty line. A third reference line is drawn where the cumulative distribution functions are truncated at Rs 272, or two times the official poverty line. From Figure 2.4 it is clear that the cumulative distribution function for 1974/75 lies nowhere above the functions for the three other years, so we can state that poverty, measured by a wide range of poverty measures including the head-count ratio, is lowest in that year. On the basis of the official poverty line, and reading off from Figure 2.4, just over 10 per cent of the population of Palanpur were poor in 1974/75, about 35 per cent in 1983/84 but around 50 per cent of the population were poor in the earlier two survey years. Even at 1.5 times the official poverty line, poverty in 1974/75 was below 30 per cent, while for the other three survey years it ranged between 55 per cent and 75 per cent.

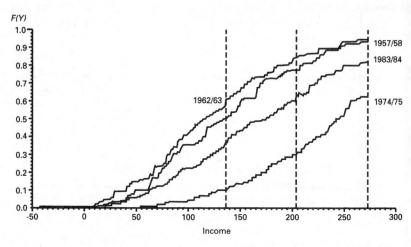

Real individual income per capita (1960 rupees)

Figure 2.4   *Cumulative distribution functions for incomes below* Z^{max}

Measuring poverty using the head-count ratio as in Figure 2.4, although widely practised, has been criticised by numerous commentators (see for example Sen, 1976, and Atkinson, 1987). The head-count measure ignores the distance of a particular individual from the poverty line and in this way neglects important issues associated with the degree of destitution. Similarly, a disequalising transfer from one individual below the poverty line to a somewhat richer individual also below the poverty line could lead to a reduction in the head-count measure of poverty, because the transfer recipient might cross the poverty line as a result of the transfer.

If we are prepared to confine ourselves to a class of poverty measures which does not include the headcount ratio, but which does include the poverty gap and related measures, we can make use of the second-order stochastic dominance result described in Section 2.2. We stated that a distribution will dominate a second distribution if the deficit curve (the integral of the cumulative distribution function) for the first lies everywhere on or below the deficit curve for the second distribution, up to the upper bound of income (Z^{max}) which we will accept as the poverty line. Figure 2.5 presents such deficit curves drawn for the four survey years up to the income level of twice the official poverty line. We can see that the deficit curve for 1974/75 lies no-

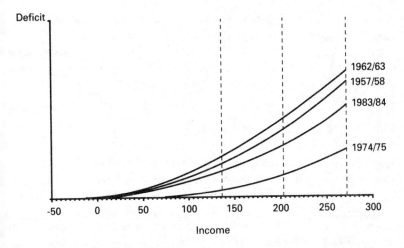

Real individual income per capita (1960 rupees)

Figure 2.5 *Poverty-deficit curves for incomes below Z^{max}*

where above the deficit curves of the other survey years. We could have already concluded this point from Figure 2.4, as the cumulative distribution function for 1974/75 was also below that of all other survey years. As first order stochastic dominance is a sufficient condition for second order stochastic dominance, we know that the deficit curve for 1974/75 will lie below the other curves as well.

From Table 2.1 we can see that the minimum income recorded in 1983/84 is lower than for all other survey years. This means that 1983/84 cannot dominate, neither first order nor second order, any of the other distributions. Although the deficit curve for 1983/84 appears to lie well below the 1957/58 and 1962/63 curves, in fact at very low incomes the 1983/84 curve lies slightly above the other two curves and therefore we cannot conclude that all poverty measures in the class we are considering will rank poverty as lower in 1983/84 than in the two earlier survey years. At least one of the measures in the class will consider poverty in 1983/84 to be greater than the two earlier surveys. This point emphasises the observation that the stochastic dominance approach does not always give a full ranking. We can clearly rank 1974/75 above the other survey years, but are unable to do the same with 1983/84. Comparing the 1957/58 and 1962/63 deficit curves, we know that the latter survey year cannot dominate the former because the lowest income in 1962/63 was Rs 9.67 while in 1957/58 it was Rs 21.5. As the deficit curve for 1962/63 lies on or above the curve for 1957/58 over the whole range of incomes up to and including twice the official poverty line (Figure 2.5), the earlier survey year poverty dominates the latter (recalling that poverty-dominance refers to the situation where the dominating distribution has lower poverty than the other).

Stochastic Dominance and Inequality

Without the need to substantially redirect our attention, the approach we are taking also allows us to evaluate the distribution of income in the four survey years. When we wish to consider this aspect of living-standards we can utilise the results of stochastic dominance by considering deficit curves over the whole range of incomes. Because we are specifically concentrating on income inequality, we normalise all incomes by their respective means. The focus on mean-normalised income allows us to rank one distribution as being more equally distributed (over a wide range of inequality measures) if its deficit curve lies nowhere above the deficit curves of the distributions with which it is being compared, i.e. if the first distribution second-order dominates all other distributions. In the focus on inequality we do not work with first-order stochastic dominance because we need to invoke the assumption of (weak) concavity in our class of living-standards functions in order to be able to compare distributions which have the same mean. When we examine for first-order stochastic dominance, the only three restrictions on our standard of living function which we allow are additive separability, continuity, and non-decreasing in income. On the basis of these assumptions we are unable to rank distributions which have the same mean but which have diverging distributions.

It is best to compare deficit curves presented in the form of differences between the deficit curve for a bench-mark year against those for the other years. This approach is taken because comparing actual deficit curves for mean-normalised incomes is visually difficult due to the range of normalised income and the magnitude of the differences between the deficit curves. The deficit curves would appear to lie on top of each other. Figure 2.6 shows the differences between the deficit curve for 1983/84 and those for the other survey years. If the difference is always positive, then the 1983/84 year is being dominated. Equally if the difference between two deficit curves is always negative, then 1983/84 dominates the distribution with which it is being compared. We can see in Figure 2.6 that the difference curve compar-

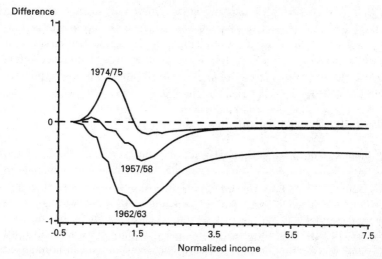

Figure 2.6 *Differences between deficit curves for mean-normalised incomes (taking 1983/84 incomes as a benchmark)*

ing 1983/84 and 1974/75 clearly lies above the reference line (0) over the lower range of normalised income. Beyond a mean normalised income of around 1.5, however, the 1983/84 deficit curve lies below the 1974/75 curve, and consequently the difference curve becomes negative. This implies that incomes in 1983/84 would be considered more *equally* distributed than incomes in 1974/75 by measures very sensitive to transfers among the rich, i.e. measures that place greater emphasis on equality between the rich, and therefore the 1983/84 survey year is not dominated by 1974/75.

The difference curves for 1962/63 and 1957/58 lie largely below the reference line, but do lie above it over a small part of the normalised income range. Although the 1962/63 difference curve does not perceptibly lie above the zero reference line, we know it has a higher minimum income and therefore *must* cross the reference line from above at least once. We are therefore unable to rank 1983/84 higher than those two survey years, and can state that there will be at least one summary measure of income inequality (such as a Rawlsian approach placing the greatest emphasis on the poorest) which would consider incomes in 1983/84 as distributed more unequally than the earlier survey years. Because the difference curves for the two earlier survey years lie above the reference line at low values of the normalised income range, we can see that inequality measures which are very sensitive to transfers among the poor would be likely to rank 1983/84 below the first two survey years. Similar comparisons of difference curves, as in Figure 2.6, but with different survey years as bench-marks, allow us to conclude that income inequality in 1974/75 was lower than in 1962/63 and similarly that 1957/58 inequality dominates 1962/63.

Stochastic Dominance and Welfare

In Figure 2.7 we present cumulative distribution curves for incomes in the four survey years. This is essentially the same as Figure 2.4 except that for the purpose of welfare evaluations we now consider the curves over the entire income range. In Figure 2.7 we can see that the cumulative distribution curve for 1974/75 lies everywhere below the curves for the other years. This means that we can rank 1974/75 as higher in terms of welfare than the other years, even if we are only prepared to make very unrestrictive assumptions on the form of welfare function to be used. As first order dominance is a sufficient condition for second-order dominance, 1974/75 will continue to dominate if we make further restrictions on the welfare function.

The cumulative distribution functions for the other three survey years intersect at several points, and we are therefore unable to extend our ordering any further, unless we are prepared to make the additional assumption of welfare increasing at a decreasing rate with income. If we examined deficit curves for the four survey years over the entire income range we are considering, we would be able to extend our ranking a bit further. Income in 1983/84 cannot welfare dominate any other survey years because it has the lowest minimum income recorded for all four years. However, we saw in Figure 2.5 that up to an income level as high as Rs 272, the deficit curve for 1957/58 was below that for 1962/63. We know, moreover, that 1957/58 also has a mean-minimum dominance over 1962/63 (a necessary, but not sufficient requirement for dominance over the whole distribution). These two factors suggest that there could be second-order stochastic dominance of 1957/58 over 1962/63, and when deficit curves are drawn over the entire distribution of incomes for these two years, it turns out that indeed this is the case. Hence, for all welfare functions which have the property of weak concavity not only does 1974/75 dominate all other survey years, but 1957/58 dominates 1962/63.

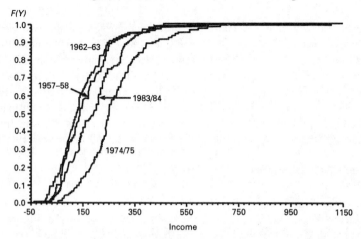

Real individual income per capita (1960 rupees)

Figure 2.7 *Cumulative distribution functions for incomes*

2.5 CONCLUSION

This chapter was written with two objectives in mind. The first is an exposition of a specific methodology which permits the analysis of poverty, inequality and welfare within a unified framework. It has the additional advantage of not being prey to criticisms that conclusions are based on specific implicit assumptions or judgements. To recapitulate briefly, we began with a simple presentation of the stochastic dominance approach as providing a unified framework for the study of welfare, poverty and inequality. We then turned to some of the weaknesses implicit in the second-order stochastic dominance framework, in particular the problem of 'slight rejection', of which the sensitivity of stochastic dominance results to the minimum incomes being compared is a particularly acute example.

The second objective was to apply this methodology to the Palanpur data, to demonstrate not only the practical simplicity of this approach but also to provide an organised examination of poverty, inequality and welfare during the four survey years. Given the important caveat that we are prepared to accept the use of current income as our sole proxy for living-standards, several conclusions can be drawn. Ultimately it is the success of the stochastic dominance approach in allowing us to draw such conclusions that determines its usefulness.

Poverty in Palanpur was unambiguously lowest during the 1974/75 survey year. This is true not only over almost all poverty measures available (including the head-count ratio) but over all poverty lines that one could specify. Similarly, poverty in 1957/58 was unambiguously lower than in 1962/63 for all poverty lines up to two times the official poverty line. Dominance of 1957/58 over 1983/84 was not observed, however. Nor was it possible to poverty rank 1983/84 and 1962/63. There will be poverty measures, and poverty lines, that will lead to different conclusions whenever we compare poverty in these paired survey years. The observation that our poverty ordering over the four years is only partial is not without interest. It cautions us against accepting rankings based on a specific poverty measure or poverty line, because such rankings might easily be overturned if we were to choose an alternative poverty measure or select a different poverty line.

Income was unambiguously more equally distributed in 1974/75 and 1957/58 than in 1962/63. A wide class of inequality measures, including the Gini coefficient, would be in agreement with this conclusion. However, we would not be able to command such agreement everywhere when comparing other survey years. Incomes in the 1983/84 survey year would be considered more unequally distributed than the two earlier survey years by inequality measures which put much weight on the distribution of incomes among the very poor, but more equally distributed if one chose other inequality measures. Inequality measures which were extremely sensitive to transfers among the rich would find incomes in both 1983/84 and 1957/58 to be more equally distributed than in 1974/75 while other measures would conclude the reverse.

Welfare evaluations, which consider not only the distribution but also average incomes, were also unable to achieve a full ordering. While 1974/75 emerges as clearly dominating the other three survey years, the 1983/84 survey year cannot dominate the earlier survey years because the lowest minimum income was recorded in that year. Of the two earlier survey years, the former (1957/58) welfare dominates the latter (1962/63).

If we split the four years into two pairs, with the earlier two distinguished from the later two by the introduction of new agricultural technologies in the mid-1960s, and the expansion of outside employment opportunities in the early 1970s, then there is some evidence to support the assertion that living-standards have risen between the two pairs. However, within each pair of years, there is a suggestion that living standards in the earlier year were higher than in the later year. This is particularly striking when we compare 1974/75 with 1983/84. Whether the apparent decline in living standards between 1974/75 and

1983/84 (unambiguous for poverty and overall welfare, although not inequality) represents a trend, or whether further agricultural intensification combined with inter-sectoral transfer of labour towards outside employment will be able to offset the impact of population growth and a fixed quantity of land, is an important question which merits further research.

Notes

1. This chapter has benefited from comments provided by Anthony B. Atkinson, Frank Cowell, Stephen Howes, Jean Olson Lanjouw, Jean Philippe Platteau and Nicholas Stern. I am also grateful for the helpful comments and suggestions from the editors of this volume. All errors remain my own.
2. The first survey was organised by the Agricultural Economics Research Centre at the University of New Delhi and conducted by S.S. Tyagi (Sr); the results are analysed in Ansari (1964). The second survey was a follow-up by the same Centre. The 1974/75 survey was conducted by Christopher Bliss, Nicholas Stern and S.S. Tyagi (Jr) and the results are reported in Bliss and Stern (1982). The final survey was directed by the same researchers in collaboration with Jean Drèze; the intensive fieldwork in 1983/84 was conducted by Drèze, Tyagi and Naresh Sharma. The data have been extensively analysed, especially those from the last survey. See, for example, Lanjouw and Stern (1990); Drèze, Lanjouw and Sharma (1990) and Lanjouw (1992).
3. Note that while such scale-neutrality is widely regarded as an attractive property in the measurement of inequality, it is not essential that differences in mean incomes be ignored when making inequality comparisons.
4. Second-degree dominance, however, is not strong enough to ensure the same ranking by the Sen poverty index or the head-count ratio, because neither satisfies the Dalton principle that a disequalising transfer from a poor person to a richer person cannot reduce poverty. In the case of the head-count ratio, poverty falls if the recipient is moved above the poverty line. In the case of the Sen index, where the weights on the poverty gap reflect the number of poor people, it is possible that the index will register a reduction in poverty should the recipient move out of poverty.
5. The kernel smoothing technique used is the Epanechnikov kernel utilised by Deaton (1989). The author is grateful to Angus Deaton for his programme and advice on the calculations.

References

Ansari, N. (1964), 'Palanpur: A Study of Its Economic Resources and Economic Activities', Continuous Village Surveys No. 41, Agricultural Economics Research Centre, University of Delhi.

Atkinson, A. (1970), 'On the Measurement of Inequality', *Journal of Economic Theory*, 2(3), 244–263.

Atkinson, A. (1987), 'On the Measurement of Poverty', *Econometrica*, 55 (4), 749–763.

Bliss, C. and Stern, N. (1982), *Palanpur: the Economy of an Indian Village*, Oxford: Oxford University Press.

Dandekar, V. and Rath, N. (1971), *Poverty in India*, Poona: Indian School of Political Economy.

Deaton, A. (1989), 'Rice Prices and Income Distribution in Thailand: a Non-Parametric Analysis', *Economic Journal*, 99, 1–37.

Drèze J.P., Lanjouw, P. and Sharma, N. (1990), 'Credit in a North Indian Village', mimeo, STICERD, London School of Economics.

Foster, J.E. and Shorrocks, A.F. (1988), 'Poverty Orderings', *Econometrica*, 56, 173–177.

Lal, D. (1976), 'Agricultural Growth, Real Wages and the Rural Poor in India', *Economic and Political Weekly*, Review of Agriculture, XI (26), A47–A61.

Lanjouw, P. and Stern, N. (1990), 'Poverty in Palanpur', *World Bank Economic Review*, 5(1), 23–55.

Lanjouw, P. (1992), *Inequality, Poverty and Mobility: the Experience of a North Indian Village*, PhD thesis, London School of Economics.

Sen, A.K. (1976), 'Poverty: an Ordinal Approach to Measurement', *Econometrica*, 44, 219–231.

Sen, A.K. (1992), *Equality and Diversity*, Oxford: Oxford University Press.

Shorrocks, A.F. (1983), 'Ranking Income Distributions', *Economica*, 50, 3–17.

3 The Causes of Poverty: A Study Based on the Mauritania Living Standards Survey 1989–90

Harold Coulombe and Andrew McKay

3.1 INTRODUCTION

Given that poverty is ultimately a problem at the individual or household level, an understanding of its nature and causes can only properly be developed at the micro-economic level. In any given social and economic environment, poverty will affect different households to different extents, these differences reflecting differences in the resources at their command, in the constraints they face and in their economic behaviour. To understand and specify more precisely the nature and relative importance of these various factors requires an analysis at the individual household level, which in turn requires the availability of a detailed household survey data set containing information on the economic and socio-economic characteristics of households and their members.

The present study of Mauritania is made possible by the second year results of the Mauritania Living Standards Survey (Enquête Permanente sur les conditions de vie des ménages en Mauritanie) conducted by the National Statistical Office in 1989/90. Along with the first year results of the same survey, this data set has already been used as the basis for the construction of a descriptive profile of poverty in Mauritania (McKay and Ould Houeïbib, 1992). Such an analysis, drawing on a rich data set, provides a detailed characterisation of poverty and of poor households, looking at aspects such as the regional and socio-economic distribution of poverty, employment and the pattern of basic needs fulfilment. The intention of this paper is to build on this descriptive analysis, analysing the causes of poverty in Mauritania. This is done using regression techniques to analyse the factors influencing both the incidence and the depth of poverty, relating each of these as dependent variables to household characteristics. Conventional statistical tests of significance enable the important causes of poverty to be identified.

The principal aim of the present study is therefore the examination of the *causes* of poverty in Mauritania. Firstly, however, some information is given on the methods used to measure poverty at the conceptual level (Section 3.2) and on the data set used (Section 3.3). After a summary description of the regional and socio-economic pattern of poverty in Mauritania (Section 3.4) the main analysis of its causes is presented in Section 3.5. The concluding Section 3.6 attempts an evaluation of the results, including an assessment of possible priorities for poverty alleviation policy.

3.2   THE MEASUREMENT OF HOUSEHOLD WELFARE AND POVERTY

Before proceeding to an analysis of the nature and causes of poverty in Mauritania, it is first necessary to arrive at a definition of poverty which is both theoretically defensible and operationally useful. To do this requires the following three logically distinct steps:

(i)   the identification of a suitable metric for the measurement of individual welfare;
(ii) the identification, on the basis of the same metric, of an appropriate value which demarcates the poor from the non-poor (the poverty line); and
(iii) the choice of an index of poverty which can conveniently capture its different dimensions.

Measurement of Household Welfare

The first of these steps is probably the most difficult given that the concept of welfare is both multidimensional and subjective. It is multidimensional in that many of its different aspects (e.g. the different dimensions of 'basic needs' fulfilment) are not conveniently reducible to a single numéraire. It is subjective, given the standard problem of interpersonal comparison of utility. However, notwithstanding these problems, it is generally argued (e.g. Deaton, 1980; Deaton and Muellbauer, 1980) that money metric utility measures represent the best basis for measuring welfare at the individual level.[1]

Money metric welfare measurement requires the availability of suitable data on incomes and/or consumption expenditures. However, careful attention needs to be paid to the appropriate definition of income and expenditure (Johnson, McKay and Round, 1990). In particular, at the theoretical level the conventional money metric approach implicitly presupposes that transactions take place within the market system. Hence, in the context of a developing country, in which a significant volume of transactions occur outside the market system (e.g. subsistence consumption, wage payment in kind), it is important that values be imputed for such transactions at an appropriate price and included in the money metric welfare measure.

An important practical issue is that data on incomes and expenditure are typically collected, at least partially, at the *household* level rather than at the level of each *individual*, reflecting the importance of income sharing and public goods within the household. The implication of this is that it is only possible to satisfactorily measure income or expenditure (viewed as the basis for money metric utility measures) at the household level. However, in general, households differ significantly in their size and composition. Given that the ultimate interest is in the welfare of the individual, it is important that such differences in size and composition be taken into account, since they imply that a different level of household consumption is needed in order to attain the same average individual welfare level. The theoretically preferred way of doing this is to divide household income or expenditure by the number of 'equivalent adults' in the household in question, defined according to an appropriate country-specific adult equivalence scale (Deaton and Muellbauer, 1980, 1986). In practice, however, as in the present case, such equivalent scales frequently do not exist and analysts are often forced to use per capita values of income or expenditure as the basis of their welfare measure; this is likely to underestimate the relative welfare status of households with a large proportion of young children among their members, plus that of large households given that household level economies of scale have not been allowed for. Moreover, another problem with this approach based on household level income or expenditure is that, by implicitly treating all members equally, it takes no account of intra-household inequality in individual consumption levels relative to needs, a factor which may be important in practice.[2]

An additional aspect of the differences in 'needs' across households relates to the prices they face, prices which may differ over space (for example, according to region of residence) or time (in a survey conducted over a period of time). This is equally relevant to imputed transactions valued at market prices as to explicit market transactions. Given these differences, it is therefore necessary that the income or expenditure measure be deflated by an appropriate cost of living index capturing these two dimensions of price variation, thereby expressing income or expenditure in the constant prices of a reference region in a reference time period. For this purpose a Laspeyres index, calculated as follows, will suffice

$$C_{rt} = \sum_{i=1}^{n} w_{i11} \frac{p_{irt}}{p_{i11}} \qquad (3.1)$$

where p_{irt} is the price of commodity i ($i = 1, \ldots, n$) in region r ($r = 1, \ldots R$) and time period t ($t = 1, \ldots, T$), p_{i11} is the price of the same commodity in the reference region ($r = 1$) and time period ($t = 1$), w_{i11} is the share of total expenditure in the reference region and time period accounted for by commodity i, and C_{rt} is the cost of living index for region r and time period t.

In summary then, the preferred measure of household welfare would be one based on total household income or expenditure per equivalent adult, expressed in the constant prices of a reference region and time period, and would include a valuation of appropriate imputed transactions in the measure of income or expenditure. As regards the choice between income and expenditure, the latter is generally preferred because it represents a better approximation of permanent income and because it is typically more easily measured in practice; as explained in the following section, this convention has also been followed here.

Choice of a Poverty Line

Given this welfare measure, and assuming an absolute concept of poverty (as opposed to a relative one), the poverty line is defined as the lowest value of the welfare measure which permits an individual to obtain a 'minimum subsistence standard of living'. The problem of course arises in defining this minimum subsistence level. It is more difficult with regard to non-food commodities than with regard to food commodities. In the latter case, a minimum food expenditure can in principle be defined on the basis of information on the minimum required intakes of key nutrients (calories, proteins etc.) as estimated by the World Health Organisation for example, plus information on the nutrient contents of available food commodities. Additional factors, such as taste and availability of food commodities, can also be taken into account in the determination of the food poverty line (Altimir, 1982). However, in the case of non-food commodities, it is even more difficult to specify objectively a minimum required consumption basket. Anand (1983) discusses various possible approaches in the context of determining an absolute poverty line for Malaysia; in practice, as in the determination of a poverty line for the United States (Orshansky, 1965), the problem is often circumvented by specifying a minimum required level of non-food expenditure as a fixed multiple of the minimum required food expenditure, the multiple being determined by the relative importance of food and non-food expenditure in the consumption basket of low income groups. Obviously, as well as its arbitrary nature, there is also an element of circularity in such an approach.

The determination of a poverty line in this way, besides involving a large number of not entirely satisfactory assumptions, also requires that a large amount of information be available, in particular with reference to the average nutrient contents of local foods and the minimum required nutrient intakes, the latter likely to be different according to ethnic group, gender and occupation. For this reason studies of poverty often use more short-cut approaches to defining a poverty line, for example, defining it, in absolute or relative terms, based on a statistical parameter of the observed welfare distribution, such as a certain fraction of the mean or a particular percentile point (Anand, 1983; Kanbur, 1990; Boateng et al., 1992). Another possibility is to use a poverty line defined for other, comparable, low income countries converted into a local currency value at an appropriate conversion factor. As an example of the latter approach, based on estimated absolute poverty lines for several countries, the World Bank (1990) has defined two standard poverty lines at levels of $370 and $275 per person and per year, in constant 1985 prices. In the absence of information on the nutrient content of commodities in Mauritania, and given the arbitrariness of poverty lines based on statistical parameters of the observed welfare distribution, these World Bank poverty lines will be used in order to define a poverty line for Mauritania for use in this study.

Poverty Indices

Having defined the welfare measure (y_i for individual i) and the poverty line (z), it remains to define a convenient means of summarising the principal dimensions of poverty in a country. Essentially, two aspects are of interest: the *incidence* and the *depth* of poverty. The former is conveniently summarised as the proportion of individuals in the population of interest who are poor, and the latter by the mean proportion by which the welfare level of the poor falls short of the poverty line. Both of these may be derived as special cases of the by now widely used P_α indices of poverty proposed by Foster, Greer and Thorbecke (1984) which are defined as follows

$$P_\alpha = \frac{1}{n} \sum_{i=1}^{q} \left(\frac{z - y_i}{z}\right)^\alpha \tag{3.2}$$

where individuals have been ranked from the poorest ($i = 1$) to the richest ($i = $ n, where n is the population size), where q is the number of economic units defined to be poor and α is a parameter reflecting the weight placed on the welfare levels of the poorest among the poor. The incidence of poverty (the proportion of the population defined to be poor; $P_0 = q/n$) is obtained for the special case $\alpha = 0$, whereas the depth of poverty may be defined as P_1/P_0.

In the case in which welfare is measured at the household level and/ or in which prices differ between households, the P_α index should be calculated as follows

$$P_\alpha = \frac{1}{\sum_{i=1}^{n} w_i} \sum_{i=1}^{q} w_i \left(\frac{z - y_i}{z}\right)^\alpha \tag{3.3}$$

where w_i is a measure of the needs of household i, calculated as the product of its size and the cost of living index it faces (both measured in the same way as in calculating y_i), y_i is household welfare, and q is the number of *households* defined to be poor. In the analysis that follows (3.3) is used to calculate P_α.

3.3 DATA

The present study is based on the results of the second year of the Mauritania Living Standards Survey (MLSS), which was conducted by Mauritania's Office National de la Statistique (ONS) in 1989–90. The principal objective of the MLSS is to provide information which can help in assessing the effects of the structural adjustment programme which the country has been undertaking since 1985 and hence in guiding interventions to alleviate poverty and to rectify the adverse effects of the adjustment programme. It is a multipurpose household survey collecting information on expenditure and income, as well as on many other dimensions of household behaviour including subsistence consumption, health, education, housing, migration, fertility and economic activities. The survey was conducted in the context of the World Bank's Living Standards Measurement Study (LSMS) project and the structure of the questionnaire follows the standard LSMS model (Grootaert, 1986). Separate questionnaires were used to collect data on market prices of key food and non-food commodities and on community level characteristics.

In the tradition of LSMS, the sample design is a self-weighting, stratified, two-stage cluster sample of 1600 households, selected from the sedentary population. In the first stage, around 100 area units were selected with probability proportional to the number of dwelling units. The area units, based on the listing prepared for the 1987 population census, were divided into four strata: 'Nouakchott City', 'Other Towns', 'Rural River' and 'Other Rural'. The second stage consisted of a random draw from a complete listing of all the dwelling units in the area units. Scott and Amenuvegbe (1989) provide a more detailed description of the sampling frame.

In principle, the data collected by the MLSS are sufficient to enable the estimation of both household income and household expenditure, either of which can serve as the basis of a money metric household welfare measure. While both were estimated following the methodology set out by Johnson, McKay and Round (1990), total household expenditure has been preferred for the construction of the welfare measure for both theoretical reasons (see Section 3.2) and practical reasons (greater accuracy).[3] The measure of total expenditure includes market purchases of food and non-food items, an imputation for domestic consumption of the output of household level production activities (valued at market prices), expenditure in cash and kind on remittances and other transfers, and an imputed consumption of wage income paid in kind.

This measure of expenditure was expressed in constant prices by deflating it with a cost of living index capturing price variations over space (using the four strata previously referred to). This index was calculated as a Laspeyres index based on the results of the price survey along with expenditure weights derived from the household survey. However, the available price data only covered a small number of commodities, and in particular very few non-food commodities; the consequence of the latter point was that it was not possible to allow for regional differences in the price of non-food items in the index. A further problem was the small number of price observations due to items not being available in all clusters. While the resulting uncertainty regarding the accuracy of the cost of living index does suggest the need to analyse the sensitivity of the results to the precise choice of cost of living index, in fact the resulting index does not indicate major inter-regional differences in prices. The resulting real expenditure measure expressed on a per capita basis was used for the welfare indicator at the household level, in the absence of a suitable adult equivalent scale for use in Mauritania.

Similarly, no country-specific poverty line is available for Mauritania, and the estimation of such a line would have required data beyond those available for this study. Instead, therefore, a poverty line has been selected based on the lower of the two general lines used by the World Bank in the 1990 *World Development Report*, which was $275 per person and per year in constant prices of 1985. Allowing for inflation of 17.7 per cent between 1985 and 1988 (the first year in which this survey was conducted) and a conversion rate of $1 = 75 Uguiya (UM), this implies a poverty line in local currency of UM 24400 in constant 1988 prices.

Obviously such a poverty line can be criticised as being arbitrary. The essential point is again to ensure that the pattern of poverty is not highly sensitive to the precise choice of the poverty line. In a study of this nature the ultimate interest is less in the extent of poverty in the country as a whole, but rather in its distribution by region, socio-economic group, and other household characteristics. This latter type of information is of most value both for policy purposes and for examining the causes of poverty. To enable robust conclusions to be drawn, it is necessary that the distribution of poverty according to these characteristics should not be greatly altered by reasonable changes in the level of the poverty line.

3.4 DESCRIPTIVE ANALYSIS OF POVERTY IN MAURITANIA

Having defined and estimated the measure of household level welfare and a poverty line as described in the previous section, it is possible to estimate values of poverty indices. As a precursor to the discussion of the causes of poverty in the following section, this section focuses on a descriptive analysis of the pattern of poverty in Mauritania based on its incidence and depth. Note that the interest here is less in the overall dimensions of poverty in the country as a whole, especially given the arbitrary nature of the poverty line, but rather in the pattern of poverty across different groups of households. The latter is likely to be much less sensitive to the exact position of the poverty line (a contention which can be tested empirically and which is indeed supported for this data set). Further, such information is of much greater interest in understanding the causes of poverty, and for identifying policy measures for poverty alleviation.

For the purposes of this paper two separate criteria are used to identify groups of households: region of residence and principal economic activity. Five regional groups are identified, based initially on an urban–rural distinction. The urban households are further disaggregated between those resident in the main economic centres (covering the non-peripheral areas of Nouakchott, and the cities of Nouadhibou and Zouerate) and those resident in other urban areas (including those in the *kebbas* or peripheral areas of Nouakchott); the rural households are disaggregated between those living in the valley of the River Senegal in the south ('rural-river'), those resident in the area to the east of the River Senegal which borders on Mali and Senegal ('rural-east'), and those resident in the vast expanse – mostly desert – of the rest of the country ('rural-centre'). Cutting across this regional classification is the socio-economic classification based on the principal economic activity of the household (gauged with reference to all household members, not just the head). The distinction is initially made between households primarily engaged in wage employment, households primarily self-employed, and non-working households, each of these being further disaggregated into two groups to give the following six socio-economic groups: public sector wage employees, private sector wage employees, agricultural self-employed households, non-agricultural self-employed households, unemployed households and non-active households (the distinction between these last two being that in the unemployed households at least one member searched for a job in the week preceding the survey interview).

Based on these definitions, the distribution of the sample by region of residence and socio-economic group is presented in Table 3.1. The largest number of households are engaged in self-employment activities, but also there is a significant proportion of non-working households; some of these non-working households may however have members of their families working elsewhere who may send them remittances, but are classified here as part of another household. The small cell sizes which arise in many cases when the two criteria are combined should be noted in interpreting the values of the poverty indices by region and socio-economic group, which are presented in

Table 3.1   *Distribution of households by socio-economic group and region*

Region	Socio-economic group						
	Unemployed	Non-active	Public employees	Private employees	Indep. agric.	Indep. business	All
Main Econ.							
Centres	25	22	114	58	3	54	276
Other urban	65	45	87	59	28	118	402
Rural-river	12	17	12	16	135	14	206
Rural-east	16	36	12	27	221	44	356
Rural-centre	27	44	27	28	129	37	292
Mauritania	145	164	252	188	516	267	1532

Table 3.2   *Incidence of poverty (P_0) by socio-economic group and region*

Region	Socio-economic group						
	Unemployed	Non-active	Public employees	Private employees	Indep. agric.	Indep. business	All
	P_0	P_0	P_0	P_0	P_0	P_0	P_0
Main econ.							
centres	0.05	0.17	0.09	0.07	*0.00	0.14	0.10
Other urban	0.37	0.38	0.37	0.51	0.68	0.30	0.40
Rural-river	0.80	0.83	0.66	0.83	0.55	0.45	0.61
Rural-east	0.64	0.62	0.71	0.60	0.71	0.38	0.65
Rural-centre	0.66	0.33	0.21	0.50	0.61	0.21	0.49
Mauritania	0.43	0.42	0.27	0.43	0.63	0.28	0.44

Note: *less than 10 observations.

the same format in Tables 3.2 and 3.3.

As discussed in Section 3.2, the P_0 poverty index represents the incidence of poverty, that is the proportion of households, weighted by needs, lying below the poverty line. Table 3.2 gives the value of P_0 for each combination of region and socio-economic group. Given the World Bank suggested poverty line of $275 per person and per year in 1985 dollars, 44 per cent of the Mauritanian population were below the poverty line in 1989–90. Looking at regional incidence of poverty, households in the main economic centres, with a value of P_0 of 10 per cent, are by far the least likely to be considered poor, followed by the other urban households at about 40 per cent and the rural regions at between 49 per cent (rural-centre) and 65 per cent (rural-east). Looking at the pattern of poverty by socio-economic group, the agricultural self-employed households are, by far, the worst off.

Table 3.3 *Depth of poverty (P_1/P_0) by socio-economic group and region*

Region	*Socio-economic group*						
	Unemployed	*Non-active*	*Public employees*	*Private employees*	*Indep. agric.*	*Indep. business*	*All*
	P_1/P_0	P_1/P_0	P_1/P_0	P_1/P_0	P_1/P_0	P_1/P_0	P_1/P_0
Main econ. centres	0.13	0.19	0.36	0.14	*–	0.13	0.24
Other urban	0.36	0.35	0.37	0.27	0.37	0.36	0.34
Rural-river	0.41	0.37	0.28	0.42	0.55	0.46	0.48
Rural-east	0.51	0.70	0.55	0.46	0.51	0.45	0.52
Rural-centre	0.51	0.48	0.44	0.61	0.54	0.23	0.52
Mauritania	0.42	0.45	0.38	0.38	0.52	0.35	0.46

Note: * less than 10 observations.
– not defined.

As expected, the households in which most of the income is from employment in the public sector are least likely to be below the poverty line, followed closely by the households engaged in non-farm self-employment. The remaining socio-economic groups are mid-way between. Therefore the agricultural self-employed households in rural regions are the group most likely to have a standard of living below the poverty line, a conclusion which is unlikely to change even taking into account the concerns expressed above about the undervaluation of home-produced food.

For the same breakdown, Table 3.3 presents the ratio P_1/P_0, which can be interpreted as the average income gap for the group of households lying below poverty line. For the country as a whole, the depth of poverty stands at 0.46 implying that the average income of households below the poverty line is just over half the poverty line income level. The regional pattern for P_1/P_0 is broadly similar to that for P_0 except that there is no significant difference between the three rural regions. Again, the agricultural self-employed households represent the most disfavoured group, followed closely by the households defined as non-active and unemployed.

In conclusion, the households mainly engaged in agricultural self-employment activities in rural regions (33 per cent of the sample) are more likely to be considered as poor (measured by P_0) than those in other groups, and if they are poor, their deprivation is on average more acute (measured by P_1/P_0). However we should not forget the group of 'non-active' households, which in spite of having a relatively low incidence of poverty nevertheless has one of the two highest measures of the depth of poverty, which strongly suggests the existence of a high level of heterogeneity within that group. Along with the other socio-economic groups, the last two will be the objects of further and more detailed scrutiny in the next section using multivariate analysis.

3.5   THE CAUSES OF POVERTY IN MAURITANIA

The tables presented in the previous section indicate the existence of important regional and socio-economic patterns in poverty in Mauritania. However, in order to understand the causes of poverty it is necessary to examine the association between the characteristics of individual households and their poverty status. In particular, it is of interest to look at those characteristics which are likely to be important determinants of household incomes and of their 'needs'. The causes of poverty are then identified as those factors which cause households to have low income levels (proxied by consumption in this context) relative to their needs.

Methodology and Specification

Among the factors potentially influencing a household's poverty status, some will be of relevance to all households (e.g. demographic factors) whereas others will be specific to a subgroup of households defined according to their economic activity status. For this reason, the analysis of the causes of poverty is conducted at the level of four separate, mutually exclusive and exhaustive groups of households, based on the socio-economic disaggregation previously used, distinguishing households who are predominantly working as employees (whether in the public or private sectors), households who are primarily engaged in agricultural self-employment, households mainly engaged in non-farm self-employment, and non-working households (including both the unemployed and non-active households). The aggregation of the six groups previously used to four here is justified on the basis of the relative similarity within the groups which are combined, and on the need to avoid small sample sizes in the analysis which follows.

In addition to region and socio-economic group, household size and composition might potentially be of relevance for the determination of the poverty status. *Ceteris paribus*, larger households will need a larger total income than smaller households to maintain the same living-standard. For a given household size, it would be expected that households with a higher proportion of members who are children or elderly (and so a higher dependency ratio in general) are more likely to be poor than those for which this proportion is lower. Indeed, the distinction between the old and children may be relevant (because of differences in the resources which they may be able to contribute to household level activities – especially domestic activities – or because of differences in their consumption needs), and the proportion of those in the age of activity who are actually active is also likely to influence a household's poverty status. Further, the characteristics of the household head, including gender, ethnic group and marital status, may also be important for the determination of household welfare for reasons related to both supply and demand side factors.[4] In general, each of the factors discussed in this paragraph are potentially relevant irrespective of the economic activity status of the household, although this is not to say that these factors are equally important for all groups.

With regard to the group-specific factors, the predominant interest is in those factors which influence the level of total household income, and hence of household consumption. In the case of households in wage employment the type of factors which might be relevant would be those included in a typical earnings function, except that in this case the interest is in total earnings over an annual period, and at the household level. The former difference means that it may be appropriate to take account of the number of hours worked in the year to distinguish, for example, those involved in seasonal work from others. The fact that the analysis is at the household level causes certain difficulties given that many of the typically relevant variables can only be defined at the *individual* level (e.g. level of education, number of hours worked, sector of employment). The approach taken has been to define such variables for the main income earner of the household (the economic head). This will undoubtedly reduce the fit of the equation relative to that which would be obtained for an earnings function at the individual level but in this particular case the interest is not in individual wage rates but in the total purchasing power of the household in question.

The problems of relating individual level characteristics to household level incomes are slightly less serious in the case of households engaged in self-employment activities, given that these typically involve household members working together as a unit within a narrowly defined range of activities. While human capital variables are still relevant – and are again defined for the most active household member employed in the activity in question – in general, the interest is in estimating a household level profit function for the activity in question, in which income is related to household level variables, including *inter alia* measures of fixed and variable input use, sector of activity and technology. In the case of agricultural self-employment activities, relevant variables available in the questionnaire include land size; land type (irrigated or not); tenure status; use of on-farm and off-farm labour inputs; use of fertiliser, insecticides and extension services; extent of commercialisation; use of large equipment such as tractors. All other self-employment activities are considered as a group. It is, however, important to consider the sector of activity (e.g. commerce, services, industry) as an explanatory variable. Other relevant available variables include measures of the size (number of people working, number employed), permanence (number of months of operation, whether the enterprise occupies a fixed site) and formality of the enterprise (whether employees have a contract or not), and the value of its capital assets.

For non-working households, the only possible sources by which they can sustain themselves are rental income, income from transfers and borrowing/dissavings. Thus the explanatory variables for this type of household should be measures of the access of households to these different mechanisms: whether they have any rental income or own any significant assets, whether they have close relatives elsewhere who send them remittances, whether they have any savings or have taken out any loans. Such variables are crude and imperfect measures; they are in principle available from the questionnaire, but given their sensitivity, are probably among the least accurate variables collected.

These variables have been used to examine the determinants of poverty status of an individual household. As previously noted, two aspects of poverty are generally of interest: its incidence and its depth. Reflecting these two dimensions of interest, two types of regression have been estimated here: one for the factors determining whether a household is poor or not (associated with incidence), the results of which are reported in Table 3.4, and a second for the determination of the standard of living (associated with depth), reported in Table 3.5. In the former case the dependent variable is therefore dichotomous, indicating whether a household is poor or not relative to the poverty line previously defined. Given the dichotomous dependent variable, estimation by ordinary least squares (OLS) is inappropriate and consequently, the probit estimation method is used instead. The dependent variable takes the value of unity if the household is not poor and zero if it is poor. The predicted value of the regression is therefore the estimated probability that a household of given characteristics is not poor. Given that probit estimation is inherently non-linear, the marginal effect of each explanatory variable on the probability that the household is not poor is not constant but depends on the position within the distribution (see Maddala, 1983). However, for any household the magnitude of the coefficients can be taken as measures of the relative influence of the different explanatory variables on the probability that the household is not poor. Hence the larger the coefficient, the greater is the effect of the explanatory variable on the probability that the household has a living-standard greater than or equal to the poverty line.

The second regression is conducted for all households, poor and non-poor, with the logarithm of the living-standards measure as the dependent variable. This may be viewed as a straightforward transformation of the proportion by which the living-standard is inferior to the poverty line (that is, the depth of poverty).[5] Given that the dependent variable is continuous, OLS estimation may be used and given that it is expressed in logarithmic form, the coefficients give the proportionate effect of each explanatory variable on the living-standard.

The definition of the explanatory variable in each case is such that a positive coefficient indicates that the variable in question has a positive influence on the household's living-standard. In general, it would be expected that the observed effects of the explanatory variables would be similar in the two different types of regression equation; a variable which has a significant positive influence on the probability that a household is non-poor would also be expected to have a positive significant influence on the standard of living more generally, and conversely. Note, however, that it is possible to have exceptions to this if, for example, a given variable only has an influence on the living-standard up to a certain threshold. Such a variable might influence the probability that a household has a living-standard above the poverty line, but may not influence the level of the living-standard beyond this.

Econometric Results: All Households

The resulting estimates are presented as equation (5) in Tables 3.4 (the incidence of poverty equation) and 3.5 (the living-standard equation) in the appendix to this chapter. These equations reinforce the pattern displayed by the poverty indices presented in the previous section, which indicated the existence of strong influences of region of residence and socio-economic group on poverty status, whether incidence or depth. In terms of regions, a very strong urban–rural differential is observed, and within the urban areas living-standards are significantly higher in the main economic centres than in the other cities. Even in these poorer urban regions living-standards are around 40 per cent higher than in rural areas, *ceteris paribus*.[6] Within rural areas there is some evidence that households in the rural-centre locality are less affected by poverty and have higher living-standards than those in the other rural areas.

In terms of socio-economic group, households engaged in non-farm self employment activities have a significantly lower probability of being poor and a significantly higher living-standard than those in the other groups, other things being equal; apart from this there is no other significant difference according to socio-economic group. These regressions qualify in some respects the conclusions suggested by the poverty indices presented in the previous section. This had suggested that agricultural households were much poorer than other groups, and that it was the public sector employees, rather than the non-farm self-employed, who were the least affected by poverty. Once other factors are taken into account some of the differences suggested by a bivariate table become insignificant in a multivariate analysis, as a result of differences in other characteristics between the households in question.

Among the other explanatory variables, demographic factors and the level of education of the household head appear to have the most significant influence on the two dimensions of poverty. Household size has a significant negative influence both on the living-standard of a household and on the probability that this latter exceeds the poverty line; for a given household size, both the proportion of members who are children and the proportion of those aged over 65 have similar negative effects. While these effects may be exaggerated by the non-utilisation of an adult equivalence scale in calculating the welfare measure, in general, increases in either of these demographic factors have the effect of increasing a household's 'needs' more than they increase the resources available to it. The education level of the household head has a significant positive influence on the dependent variable in both regressions, this effect being significant both for traditional (Koranic) and modern school, but being quantitatively largest for those having attended six years or more of modern school. It is this strong education effect which explains why in the multivariate analysis households engaged in non-farm self-employment activities appear to be richer than those engaged in wage employment in the public sector; the latter have much higher education levels than the former, but, for a given level of education, households engaged in non-farm self-employment are richer than public sector employees.

Somewhat surprisingly, there is no evidence of a significant effect of technical training or apprenticeship in either regression and these variables have been dropped from the final specification. This could be interpreted as reflecting measurement difficulties given the ill-defined and non-standardised nature of these variables, especially, perhaps, difficulties in measuring the 'quality' or appropriateness of such training or apprenticeship.

There is some evidence that households whose head is divorced or widowed are more likely to be poor and have lower living-standards than those whose head is married. On the other hand there is no evidence that female-headed households are significantly poorer than male-headed households. While the ethnic group variable is significant, with the Moors apparently having a higher probability of being poor than the other groups, no great weight should be placed on this, given that the non-Moor groups have been significantly – and apparently systematically – undersampled due in part to the large numbers of them with no fixed dwelling or working as resident domestic servants.

Finally, there is evidence for a seasonal effect on living-standards, with those households interviewed between November and May having significantly lower living-standards than those interviewed in the period June–August (the wet season). This pattern is surprising given that the main harvest occurs towards the end of the calendar year. It may be that at this time subsistence consumption increases in importance within households; however, this is the component of household expenditure which is likely to be most underestimated.

Econometric Results: Socio-economic Group Level Equations

Turning to the group-specific regression equations (equation numbers (1), (2), (3) and (4) in Tables 3.4 and 3.5 of the appendix), it may be noted that whilst it is likely that many of the factors which are significant for the entirety of households will also be significant at the group level, this need not necessarily be the case for all groups. Here, the level of education is an important determinant of the living-standards within the groups of agricultural households and households in wage employment and it is also positively associated with living-standards for the group of non-working households. However, education does not seem to have a significant influence on the living-standards of households engaged in non-farm self-employment.[7]

The education effect is particularly strong for those who have attended six years or more of modern school. This important influence of education may well be due to the importance of human capital in determining earnings levels, but could also reflect a screening process based on education in allocating well paid jobs (Knight and Sabot, 1990). Unfortunately it is not possible to discriminate between these two hypotheses with the available data set. For agricultural households, however, the distinction between those with traditional education and those with modern education seems to be less important than the distinction between those with some education and those with none. A positive association between education level and agricultural productivity has been found in several studies in other countries (Lockheed et al., 1980). One factor may be that more educated households are more receptive to using modern inputs such as improved quality seeds or fertiliser.

For non-working households it is difficult to argue that education is a direct determinant of their living-standards in the same way as for the two groups considered above. In fact, the level of education and training of households in this group is surprisingly high, especially among the non-poor, suggesting the presence of many well-educated households who are currently voluntarily unemployed, such that they are searching for a new job and/or not prepared to accept any job. According to this argument, education, rather than being a direct and immediate determinant of living-standards may rather be an indicator of households who have had well-paid jobs in the past or who have advantageous backgrounds, either of these factors enabling them to support a period of voluntary unemployment.[8]

Demographic factors continue to have a significant influence on poverty within each of the four socio-economic groups, most particularly household size and the proportion of children. The proportion of members older than 65 years has much less significant influence at the group level than in aggregate; this is predominantly because the households with a relatively high proportion of elderly members are to be found disproportionately in the relatively poor socio-economic group of non-working households. An interesting exception to the general pattern of demographic influences on poverty is observed in the agricultural households. From equation (3) of Table 3.5 the living-standard of this group is observed to depend inversely on household size, on the proportion aged less than 15 years and on the proportion aged over 65 years, as for other groups. However, in the poverty incidence regression (equation (3) of Table 3.4) the reverse pattern is observed. This suggests that up to a certain threshold, an increase in household size, for example, has a beneficial effect on living-standards. Beyond this threshold the beneficial effect from having an increased number of people to work on the family farm is outweighed by the increased burden on consumption that these additional members represent.

Marital status is a significant factor for some groups, with households whose head is divorced or widowed being significantly poorer among the wage employee and agricultural household groups. While the ethnic group variable is sometimes significant, the same reservations stated above apply, and the gender of the household head is never a significant explanatory variable.

Of the group-specific explanatory variables included in the regressions, few appear to be statistically significant. For example, in non-working households, the value of transfers received does not significantly influence either the probability of being non-poor or the living-standard. However, the possession of formal sector savings and the presence of a loan is significantly associated with higher welfare levels, although only the latter significantly influences the probability that a non-working household is non-poor. Several other variables included in earlier specifications representing other possible mechanisms by which non-working households might sustain themselves turned out to be insignificant throughout, and so are not reported here. This difficulty in finding significant relationships may reflect the difficulties in collecting accurate data on these types of variables. Further, in the cases of borrowing and transfers, the direction of the relationship may be positive for some households (who have relatively high consumption levels as a direct result of the transfer or loan) but negative for others (who, for example, try to take out loans or who receive transfers from relatives or elsewhere precisely because they are very poor). In any case, it is difficult to see from the survey data how many of these non-working households sustain themselves, and it seems clear that there is considerable non-reporting of income sources for this group.

For the group of households working as employees no significant difference is observed between those in the public and those in the private sectors. It seems that the differences suggested by the poverty indices in the preceding section are fully accounted for by differences in the other characteristics of the households, notably in education levels which are higher among public sector employees than private sector employees. Working in the formal sector is observed to have a significant influence on living-standards and on the probability of being non-poor. This variable is likely to be strongly associated with education levels, education generally being a requirement for access to formal sector jobs; however, it is still significant in its own right even though the education variables are included in the equation. Overall it seems that, among the factors considered here, education has the most important influence on the living-standard of those in wage employment; however the extent to which this is a reflection of the effect of education on productivity remains an open question.

For agricultural households it is possible to define the largest number of group-specific explanatory variables, although in practice many of these turn out to be insignificant (including many variables not present in the final specification reported here). There is, however, a strong positive influence of the following variables on both welfare levels and on the probability of being non-poor:

(i)   herding as opposed to cultivating crops,
(ii) cultivating land collectively,
(iii) employed hired labour, and
(iv) the use of extension services.

That the third and fourth factors are significant is understandable, identifying as they do the larger scale cultivators. The influence of the first factor should be qualified by the consideration that the nomads, who engage in herding but who are potentially very poor, are excluded from the sample.

Land area has a significant positive influence on living-standards in the rural-centre region; the absence of a significant land size effect in the other rural regions is almost certainly a consequence of very large variations in land quality. Surprisingly, however, the use of irrigated land does not significantly influence living-standards. Given the Mauritanian climate, the use of irrigated land would appear to be an important determinant of living-standards, as irrigation would enable cultivation throughout the year; it may be that the effect of irrigation is being picked up by other explanatory variables included in the equation. Also surprisingly, there is no strong evidence that commercial farmers (that is, those who sell some or all of their output) have higher living-standards than subsistence farmers. Finally, it is of interest to note that the variables capturing the use of fertiliser and insecticide are insignificant at the 5 per cent level in both regressions (and anyway with perverse signs), possibly due to the inability to distinguish effects according to the crop in question.

For those self-employed in non-agricultural activities, the variables which seem to have the most significant effects would seem to be measures of the permanence of the enterprise in question (whether it occupies fixed premises, the number of months of operation). According to the sector of activity, households with enterprises in the commerce sector have significantly higher welfare levels than those in the reference sector (construction); there are no other significant effects according to the sector of activity.

In summary, many of the group-specific factors which *a priori* might have been considered important turn out not to be significant in practice. To some extent, this may reflect difficulties in defining an appropriate explanatory variable based on the survey data which corresponds *precisely* to the factor in question. Also, it may reflect the fact that we have been forced to use consumption rather than income as the dependent variable; consumption is obviously not perfectly correlated with income, and anyway will in general be financed by incomes derived from more than one source. Had the data permitted it, the preferred approach would have been to relate income from each source (wage employment, agricultural self-employment income, etc.) to the specific explanatory variables. A further problem may be the endogenity of some of the explanatory variables.

Besides region and socio-economic group, education and demographic factors are observed to have the most consistently significant influence on a household's living-standard. The importance of demographic factors is easily understood. The importance of education is also not surprising, but the analysis conducted here does not permit us to identify the precise mechanisms through which education influences living standards. One possibility is that the education level influences many of the specific factors included in the socio-economic group level equations (such as input usage for agricultural households). If this is true it might explain why some of the group-specific factors turn out to be insignificant in regression equations in which education variables are also included; it would also mean that the equation would be affected by a simultaneity bias. To analyse the validity of this hypothesis would require a much more detailed simultaneous equation approach.

3.6   CONCLUSIONS

This study has sought to identify some of the key contributory causes of poverty in Mauritania at the household level. There have been a number of potentially important factors which it has not been possible to take into account in this analysis, notably factors relating to community-level variables (such as infrastructure) in view of the weaknesses of the data collected by the community surveys. This is unfortunate, as such factors are likely to be important in rural areas, where, for example, inaccessibility of the locality may have a significant negative influence on living-standards. Nonetheless, in spite of this and other omissions, a number of factors have been identified. The use of multivariate analysis has confirmed a number of the strong effects associated with region of residence and socio-economic group which had been suggested by the bivariate analysis. Within socio-economic groups, education level and demographic factors are overall the most important influences on poverty status, though it is likely that these factors also influence a household's living-standard more generally by influencing their employment status and hence the socio-economic group to which they belong. Some influences of poverty status which are socio-economic group specific are also identified, primarily in the case of self-employed households (such as permanence of the enterprise for the non-farm self-employed, scale of the operation for the agricultural self-employed).

This study has focused on the causes of poverty at the micro-economic level, and it is only at this level that one can properly capture the complexity of the phenomenon. However, for a complete understanding of the causes of poverty it is also necessary to understand the role of sectoral, macro-economic and global factors in determining the micro-economic outcomes. In the present policy environment in Africa, the issue of the impact of structural adjustment on poverty (and consequently of the design of poverty-sensitive macro-economic policy) is of particular interest. Such an investigation has unfortunately been beyond the scope of this paper.

Nevertheless, the results of the regression analysis do provide important general information about the pattern and causes of poverty in Mauritania, which is of value in working out at least some of the key priorities of a poverty alleviation strategy. In the long-run, clear priorities are to increase access to education, in particular at the primary level, and to reduce the rate of population growth, these two objectives being potentially complementary. These longer-run objectives have clear implications for public spending priorities now. More immediately, attention needs to be paid to the reduction in urban–rural inequalities, given that poverty in Mauritania is disproportionately a rural phenomenon and given that such inequalities are ultimately an important contributory factor to urban poverty as well (through the migration induced as a result). In terms of economic activity, the priority socio-economic groups should be the poor among the group of non-working households, and households engaged in small-scale agricultural cultivation in general.

Appendix

Table 3.4 *Results from PROBIT analysis*

| | Socio-economic group | | | | |
	(1) Without job	(2) Employee	(3) Indep. agric.	(4) Indep. Business	(5) All
urban-rich	1.811	2.120		1.293	1.573
	(.000)	(.000)		(.034)	(.000)
urban-poor	0.969	0.784		0.851	0.584
	(.005)	(.020)		(.120)	(.000)
urban			−0.348		
			(.503)		
rural-east	−0.401	0.185	−0.204	0.185	−0.117
	(.278)	(.639)	(.398)	(.750)	(.362)
rural-centre	0.220	0.848	−0.193	0.828	0.297
	(.541)	(.023)	(.472)	(.156)	(.025)
rural-river	–	–	–	–	–
Koranic	0.295	0.494	0.476	0.701	0.419
	(.120)	(.021)	(.032)	(.005)	(.000)
school 1–5	0.670	0.698	0.892	0.559	0.444
	(.240)	(.073)	(.370)	(.389)	(.058)
school 6+	1.550	1.082	0.762	0.729	0.924
	(.004)	(.000)	(.213)	(.295)	(.000)
none	–	–	–	–	–
March	−0.566	−0.462	0.222	−0.500	−0.271
	(.103)	(.183)	(.531)	(.219)	(.061)
September	−0.924	0.151	0.230	−0.202	−0.103
	(.001)	(.531)	(.256)	(.514)	(.289)
December	−0.820	−0.104	−0.711	−0.546	−0.446
	(.002)	(.694)	(.005)	(.097)	(.000)
June	–	–	–	–	–

continued

Table 3.4 *continued*

	(1) Without job	(2) Employee	(3) Indep. agric.	(4) Indep. Business	(5) All
		Socio-economic group			
single	−0.700 (.089)	−0.086 (.900)	0.096 (.863)	7.336 (.999)	0.009 (.969)
widow(er)	−0.142 (.635)	−1.028 (.012)	−0.490 (.093)	−0.296 (.449)	−0.198 (.139)
divorced	−0.265 (.377)	−0.608 (.071)	−0.312 (.379)	0.118 (.756)	−0.282 (.040)
married	−	−	−	−	−
female	0.412 (.144)	0.082 (.771)	0.150 (.522)	0.171 (.550)	0.163 (.138)
Moor	0.807 (.024)	−0.196 (.470)	−0.441 (.100)	0.901 (.035)	−0.336 (.008)
young	−0.890 (.028)	−1.365 (.002)	1.406 (.003)	−0.917 (.091)	−0.818 (.000)
elderly	−0.342 (.349)	−0.623 (.563)	2.374 (.006)	−1.995 (.082)	−0.522 (.028)
household size	−0.131 (.013)	−0.135 (.000)	0.095 (.015)	−0.059 (.237)	−0.095 (.000)
unemployed	0.074 (.707)				0.047 (.741)
non-active					0.001 (.996)
public employee					0.172 (.223)
private employee					0.092 (.484)
indep. business					0.502 (.000)
indep. agric.					−
transfer	8.9E−6 (.274)				
saving	7.602 (.999)				
loan	0.347 (.081)				
government		−0.374 (.140)			
state		−0.319 (.297)			

continued

Table 3.4   *continued*

	(1) Without job	(2) Employee	(3) Indep. agric.	(4) Indep. Business	(5) All
		Socio-economic group			
society		−0.636 (.072)			
individual		−			
formal		0.474 (.044)			
herder			2.103 (.011)		
both			0.548 (.008)		
cultivator			−		
owner			0.690 (.386)		
fertiliser			−1.437 (.093)		
insecticide			−0.326 (.538)		
irrigation			1.287 (.166)		
dieri			0.460 (.127)		
consult			0.842 (.012)		
collective			0.396 (.033)		
commercial			0.118 (.572)		
hired-labour			1.175 (.011)		
area			−0.021 (.245)		
area-river			0.013 (.503)		
area-east			0.019 (.291)		
area-centre			0.022 (.288)		
no. month				0.067 (.015)	
contract				5.459 (.999)	
fixed				0.352	

continued

Table 3.4　*continued*

| | Socio-economic group | | | | |
	(1) Without job	(2) Employee	(3) Indep. agric.	(4) Indep. Business	(5) All
(.160)					
commerce				0.675	
				(.220)	
service				−0.002	
				(.997)	
industry				0.135	
				(.821)	
other				1.217	
				(.245)	
construction				−	
labour				0.013	
				(.775)	
number of observations	309	440	325	238	1532

Note: The figures in parentheses give the level of significance at which the corresponding coefficient is significantly different from zero, according to a chi-squared test. For example, a value of 0.10 indicates significance at the 10 per cent level, etc.

Table 3.5　*Results from WELFARE analysis*

| | Socio-economic group | | | | |
	(1) Without job	(2) Employee	(3) Indep. agric.	(4) Indep. Business	(5) All
urban-rich	0.731	0.809		0.603	0.945
	(.002)	(.000)		(.027)	(.000)
urban-poor	0.331	0.323		0.121	0.447
	(.130)	(.049)		(.640)	(.000)
urban			−0.091		
			(.715)		
rural-east	−0.648	−0.056	−0.022	−0.166	−0.073
	(.006)	(.772)	(.855)	(.552)	(.395)
rural-centre	−0.159	0.197	−0.095	0.180	0.197
	(.492)	(.279)	(.506)	(.519)	(.028)
rural-river	−	−	−	−	−
Koranic	0.415	0.254	0.316	0.099	0.291
	(.001)	(.010)	(.005)	(.357)	(.000)

Table 3.5 *continued*

| | Socio-economic group | | | | |
	(1) Without job	(2) Employee	(3) Indep. agric.	(4) Indep. business	(5) All
school 1–5	0.296 (.386)	0.321 (.036)	0.419 (.463)	0.342 (.179)	0.359 (.007)
school 6+	0.912 (.000)	0.454 (.000)	0.426 (.155)	0.151 (.563)	0.549 (.000)
none	–	–	–	–	–
March	−0.327 (.107)	−0.040 (.758)	−0.001 (.995)	−0.205 (.247)	−0.136 (.120)
September	−0.481 (.003)	0.116 (.287)	0.146 (.174)	0.049 (.727)	−0.022 (.732)
December	−0.337 (.034)	0.021 (.853)	−0.254 (.041)	−0.179 (.220)	−0.152 (.025)
June	–	–	–	–	–
single	−0.580 (.023)	−0.101 (.560)	−0.297 (.315)	0.055 (.849)	−0.164 (.196)
widow(er)	−0.109 (.558)	−0.029 (.882)	−0.414 (.007)	−0.269 (.159)	−0.202 (.023)
divorced	−0.118 (.532)	−0.380 (.005)	−0.170 (.336)	−0.080 (.621)	−0.262 (.002)
married	–	–	–	–	–
female	0.181 (.301)	−0.058 (.656)	−0.025 (.839)	−0.014 (.914)	0.075 (.292)
Moor	−0.011 (.961)	−0.046 (.636)	−0.329 (.019)	−0.336 (.032)	−0.285 (.000)
young	−0.784 (.002)	−0.600 (.001)	−0.911 (.000)	−0.285 (.217)	−0.527 (.000)
elderly	−0.314 (.181)	−0.846 (.044)	−0.912 (.020)	−0.621 (.230)	−0.410 (.009)
household size	−0.042 (.185)	−0.073 (.000)	−0.053 (.007)	−0.062 (.004)	−0.063 (.000)
unemployed	−0.018 (.878)				0.014 (.880)
non-active					0.010 (.914)
public employee					0.126 (.153)
private employee					0.061 (.473)
indep. business					0.351 (.000)

continued

Table 3.5 *continued*

	(1) Without job	(2) Employee	(3) Indep. agric.	(4) Indep. Business	(5) All
	Socio-economic group				
indep. agric.					–
transfer	3.9E−6 (.420)				
saving	0.614 (.091)				
loan	0.291 (.018)				
government		−0.128 (.257)			
state		0.031 (.806)			
society		−0.025 (.858)			
individual		–			
formal		0.348 (.001)			
herder			0.763 (.036)		
both			0.175 (.106)		
cultivator			–		
owner			0.050 (.881)		
fertiliser			−0.349 (.333)		
insecticide			−0.374 (.168)		
irrigation			0.408 (.296)		
dieri			0.122 (.406)		
consult			0.280 (.116)		
collective			0.207 (.031)		
commercial			0.071 (.514)		
hired-labour			0.549 (.007)		
area			0.016		

Table 3.5 *continued*

| | Socio-economic group | | | | |
	(1) *Without job*	(2) *Employee*	(3) *Indep. agric.*	(4) *Indep. business*	(5) *All*
area-river			(.035) −0.015		
area-east			(.054) −0.015		
area-centre			(.053) −0.008		
no. month			(.366)	0.024	
contract				(.072) 0.575	
fixed				(.314) 0.082	
commerce				(.453) 0.450	
service				(.060) 0.218	
industry				(.414) 0.136	
other				(.608) −0.104	
construction				(.804) −	
labour				0.011	
R^2-adjusted	0.26	0.41	0.25	(.485) 0.21	0.29
number of observations	309	440	325	238	1532

Note: The figures in parentheses give the level of significance at which the corresponding coefficient is significantly different from zero, according to a *t* test. For example, a value of 0.10 indicates significance at the 10 per cent level, etc.

Definition of variables

urban-rich	= 1, if household lives in Nouakchott (non-peripheral areas), Nouadhibou or Zouerate
	= 0, if not.
urban-poor	= 1, if household lives in another urban region
	= 0, if not.
urban	= 1, if household lives in an urban region

continued

Table 3.5   Definition of variables, continued

	= 0, if not.
rural-east	= 1, if household lives in the rural-east region
	= 0, if not.
rural-centre	= 1, if household lives in the rural-centre region
	= 0, if not.
rural-river	= 1, if household lives in the rural-river region
	= 0, if not.
Koranic	= 1, if the economic head went to traditional school
	= 0, if not.
school 1–5	= 1, if the economic head went to modern school for 1–5 years
	= 0, if not.
school 6	= 1, if the economic head went to modern school for 6 years or more
	= 0, if not.
none	= 1, if the economic head did not attend school
	= 0, if not.
March	= 1, if the interview occurred in February, March or April
	= 0, if not.
June	= 1, if the interview occurred in May, June or July
	= 0, if not.
September	= 1, if the interview occurred in August, September or October
	= 0, if not.
December	= 1, if the interview occurred in November, December or January
	= 0, if not.
single	= 1, if the economic head is single
	= 0, if not.
married	= 1, if the economic head is married
	= 0, if not.
divorced	= 1, if the economic head is divorced
	= 0, if not.
widow(er)	= 1, if the economic head is widowed
	= 0, if not.
female	= 1, if the economic head is female
	= 0, if not.
Moor	= 1, if the head is from that ethnic group
	= 0, if not.
young	proportion of household members aged less than 15 years
elderly	proportion of household members aged more than 64 years
unemployed	= 1, if the household is classified as 'unemployed'
	= 0, if not.
non-active	= 1, if the household is classified as 'non-active'
	= 0, if not.

Definition of variables

public emp.	= 1, if the household is classified as 'public sector employee' = 0, if not.
private emp.	= 1, if the household is classified as 'private sector employee' = 0, if not.
indep.-bus.	= 1, if the household is classified as 'independent – nonfarm' = 0, if not.
indep.-agric.	= 1, if the household is classified as 'independent – farm' = 0, if not.
transfer	= 1, if the household received private remittances = 0, if not.
saving	= 1, if the household possesses formal sector savings = 0, if not.
loan	= 1, if the household has an outstanding loan = 0, if not.
government	= 1, if the head works for the government = 0, if not.
state	= 1, if the head works for a state firm = 0, if not.
society	= 1, if the head works for a private firm = 0, if not.
individual	= 1, if the head works for a private individual = 0, if not.
formal	= 1, if the head works in the formal sector = 0, if not.
herder	= 1, if the household keeps animals but does not cultivate = 0, if not.
both	= 1, if the household keeps animals and cultivates = 0, if not.
cultivator	= 1, if the household cultivates but does not keep animals = 0, if not.
owner	= 1, if the farming household owns its land = 0, if not.
fertilizer	= 1, if the farmer uses fertilizer = 0, if not.
insecticide	= 1, if the farmer uses insecticide = 0, if not.
irrigation	= 1, if the farmer incurred irrigation expenses = 0, if not.
dieri	= 1, if the household cultivates as 'dieri' (rain-fed cultivation) = 0, if not.
consult	= 1, if the farmer consulted an extension agent = 0, if not.

continued

Definition of variables

collective	= 1, if the farmer cultivates land collectively
	= 0, if not.
commercial	= 1, if the farmer sells some output on the market
	= 0, if not.
hired-labour	= 1, if the farmer hired off-farm labour
	= 0, if not.
area	= land area, in square meters
area-river	= land area, in square meters, in region 'rural-river'
area-east	= land area, in square meters, in region 'rural-east'
area-centre	= land area, in square meters, in region 'rural-centre'
no. month	number of months for which the business was operational in last year.
contract	= 1, if the employees of the enterprise have signed contracts
	= 0, if not.
fixed	= 1, if the enterprise occupies a permanent location
	= 0, if not.
commerce	= 1, if the enterprise is in the commerce sector
	= 0, if not.
service	= 1, if the enterprise is in the service sector
	= 0, if not.
industry	= 1, if the enterprise is in the industrial sector
	= 0, if not.
other	= 1, if the enterprise is in another sector
	= 0, if not.
construction	= 1, if the enterprise is in the construction sector
	= 0, if not.
labour	= 1, if the enterprise employs non-household labour
	= 0, if not.

Notes

1. A wide range of alternative welfare measures may be considered, such as the share of total expenditure devoted to food (based on the assumption that Engel's Law holds), measures of basic needs fulfilment (which by their nature only capture one dimension of welfare) and anthropometric measures for young children. In fact, evidence from other countries (Glewwe and van der Gaag, 1988; Coulombe, McKay and Pyatt, 1992 *inter alia*) suggests that these alternative measures often give a conflicting pattern. The money metric measure is preferred here as it is more comprehensive and generally less reliant on untested assumptions than the alternatives.
2. Haddad and Kanbur (1990) discuss the issue of intra-household inequality with reference to a household survey data set for the Philippines. They find that, while ignoring intra-household inequality may lead to biases in

estimates of poverty and inequality indices, the observed *pattern* of poverty and inequality is not greatly affected.

3. In fact, the estimate of average household expenditure, when aggregated to the national level, is broadly consistent with the estimate of private consumption expenditure in the national accounts. In contrast, the estimate of average household income is much lower. This supports our choice of expenditure rather than income and allows us to have reasonable confidence in the accuracy of the expenditure data.

4. The household head is defined here on economic criteria, that is, as the most economically active household member.

5. A similar methodology has been applied by Glewwe (1991) in the case of Côte d'Ivoire and Kyereme and Thorbecke (1991) in the case of Ghana, although the latter authors used a welfare measure based on food expenditure only.

6. The value of home produced food in rural areas as recorded in the survey accounts for only 10 per cent of purchased food in rural areas. This is believed to underestimate the importance of home produced food and thus will lead to an exaggeration of the rural–urban living standards differential.

7. Note that education level is also likely to affect living-standards by influencing the type of economic activity to which individuals have access and hence the socio-economic group to which they belong.

8. The level of education of the non-working households, especially those which are non-poor, partly reflects the presence of a relatively large number of students among the non-active households, who by definition have relatively high levels of education (McKay, Coulombe and Houeïbib 1993).

References

Altimir, O. (1982), 'The Extent of Poverty in Latin America', World Bank Staff Working Paper No. 522, World Bank, Washington DC.

Anand, S. (1983), *Inequality and Poverty in Malaysia: Measurement and Decomposition*, New York: Oxford University Press for the World Bank.

Boateng, E.O., Ewusi, K., Kanbur, R. and McKay, A. (1992), 'A Poverty Profile of Ghana, 1987–88,' *Journal of African Economies*, Vol. 1, No. 1, pp. 25–58.

Coulombe, H., McKay, A. and Pyatt, G. (1992) 'Measuring Changes in Household Welfare Over Time: Theory and Application to Côte d'Ivoire, 1985–88', mimeo, CREDIT, University of Nottingham and DERC, University of Warwick.

Deaton, A. (1980), 'The Measurement of Welfare: Theory and Practical Guidelines', Living Standards Measurement Study Working Paper No. 7, World Bank, Washington DC.

Deaton, A. and Muellbauer, J. (1980), *Economics and Consumer Behaviour*, Cambridge: Cambridge University Press.

Deaton, A. and Muellbauer J. (1986), 'On Measuring Child Costs: With

Applications to Poor Countries', *Journal of Political Economy*, Vol. 94, No. 4, pp. 720–744.

Foster, J., Greer, J. and Thorbecke, E. (1984): 'A Class of Decomposable Poverty Measures', *Econometrica*, Vol. 52, No. 3, pp. 761–766.

Glewwe, P. and van der Gaag, J. (1988), 'Confronting Poverty in Developing Countries: Definitions, Information and Policies', Living Standards Measurement Study Working Paper No. 48, World Bank, Washington D.C.

Glewwe, P. (1991), 'Investigating the Determinants of Household Welfare in Côte d'Ivoire', *Journal of Development Economics*, Vol. 35, pp. 307–337.

Grootaert, C. (1986), 'Measuring and Analysing Levels of Living in Developing Countries: An Annotated Questionnaire', Living Standards Measurement Study Working Paper No. 26, World Bank, Washington DC.

Haddad, L. and R. Kanbur (1990), 'How Serious is the Neglect of Intra-household Inequality?', *Economic Journal*, Vol. 100, No. 402, pp. 866–881.

Johnson, M., McKay, A.D. and Round, J.I. (1990), 'Income and Expenditure in a System of Household Accounts: Concepts and Estimation', Social Dimensions of Adjustment Working Paper No. 10, World Bank, Washington DC.

Kanbur, R. (1990), 'Poverty and the Social Dimensions of Adjustment in Côte d'Ivoire', Social Dimensions of Adjustment Working Paper No. 2, World Bank, Washington DC.

Knight, J.B. and Sabot, R. (1990), *Education, Productivity and Inequality: the East African Natural Experiment*, World Bank and Oxford University Press.

Kyereme, S.S. and E. Thorbecke (1991), 'Factors Affecting Food Poverty in Ghana', *Journal of Development Studies*, Vol. 28, No. 1, pp. 39–52.

Lockheed, M., Jamison, D. and Lau, L. (1980), 'Farmer Education and Farm Efficiency: A Survey', *Economic Development and Cultural Change*, Vol. 29, pp. 37–76.

Maddala, G.S. (1983), *Limited-Dependent and Qualitative Variables in Econometrics*, Cambridge: Cambidge University Press.

McKay, A. and Cheikh Abdallahi Ould Houeïbib (1992), 'Profil de pauvreté en Mauritanie: partie descriptive', mimeo, Ministère du Plan, Nouakchott, Mauritania.

McKay, A., Coulombe, H. and Cheikh Abdallahi Ould Houeïbib (1993), 'Profil de pauvreté en Mauritanie: Deuxième partie', mimeo, Ministère du Plan, Nouakchott, Mauritania.

Orshansky, M. (1965), 'Counting the Poor: Another Look at the Poverty Profile', *Social Security Bulletin*, Vol. 28, pp. 3–29.

Scott, C. and B. Amenuvegbe (1989), 'Sample Design for the Living Standards Surveys in Ghana and Mauritania', Living Standards Measurement Study Working Paper No. 49, World Bank, Washington DC.

World Bank (1990), *World Development Report 1990*, Washington DC: World Bank.

4 Household Resource Allocation in the Côte d'Ivoire: Inferences from Expenditure Data[1]

Lawrence Haddad and John Hoddinott

4.1 INTRODUCTION

The ultimate goal of rural development policies is to raise the living standards of individuals. Their success in this regard is a function of their design and implementation, issues discussed in the Introduction to this volume. But the technical aspects of policy intervention are not the sole determinants of success. The vast majority of individuals in developing countries reside in multi-member households and the efficacy of policies targeted towards individuals will partly depend on how the household, acting as an intermediary between policies and individuals, (re)allocates resources in response to it.

For example, suppose there is concern regarding the well-being of young girls in a particular rural area; specifically, there is a perception that they do not get enough food to eat. A possible policy response is the implementation of a school meals programme. However, the success of this intervention cannot be ascertained in the absence of information on how households allocate food amongst their members. Households might respond to this programme by reducing the amount of food girls receive at home (and increasing the amount of food consumed by other household members). Such an action frustrates, at least partly, the goals of the policy intervention. This aspect of household behaviour has received a great deal of attention in the Asian context (Harriss, 1990). Much of this work has been motivated by concern regarding systematic discrimination against females in parts of the Indian sub-continent. The consequences of this 'gender bias' have been dramatic, being responsible for the loss of 60–100 million women (Sen, 1990, Coale, 1991). However, this issue is comparatively understudied in an African context.

The purpose of this chapter is twofold. First, we examine a methodology that yields insights into the intra-household allocation of resources. This approach, termed 'outlay equivalents', is inferential rather than direct. Instead of considering the allocation of food or other goods, we will make inferences based on the pattern of expenditures on 'adult goods'. Since additional children have the effect of reducing the income available to spend on such goods, examining whether male or female children, or children who are offspring of the head or foster children, have differential impacts on the reduction in expenditures on such goods, will give some indication of the presence and extent of bias in the allocation of household resources. At first glance, this might seem somewhat roundabout. However, as we discuss below, this approach has two attractions – it gets around the problem of the fungibility of household resources and its data requirements are minimal. Our second goal in this chapter is to look for the presence and extent of gender bias in an African setting, by drawing on data from the Côte d'Ivoire.

The chapter begins with a brief review of the theory of the intra-household allocation of resources, followed by a brief review of existing evidence. The method for examining bias, termed 'outlay equivalent analysis', is discussed in detail in Section 4.3. Results are presented and interpreted in light of existing theory and circumstances unique to the Ivorian case in Section 4.4. Concluding comments are found in Section 4.5.

4.2 HOUSEHOLD RESOURCE ALLOCATION: THEORY AND EVIDENCE

Theory of Household Resource Allocation

Before discussing the concept of outlay equivalents, it is helpful to examine why households, or individuals within the household, consciously favour some children over others. A useful introduction to this is the general preference model, first developed by Behrman, Pollak and Taubman (1982). They assume that parents' decisions regarding the allocation of household resources are guided by two concerns. On the one hand, they may be interested in ensuring that all children are equally well-off. Alternatively, they may have preferences for particular children; for example boys over girls, first born over last born, their own children over those whom they are raising as foster children. This aspect shall be termed 'equity' concerns, though of course it is entirely possible that parents prefer unequal outcomes amongst their offspring. Secondly, parents are assumed to be aware of their children's prospects, such as their future earnings. Parents are also interested in maximising the return on their investment in children. This is a particularly plausible assumption in a developing country context where they may rely on their offspring for support in the future. This is termed 'efficiency' concerns.

Two cases are readily apparent. Suppose parents care only about equity and have no concerns regarding efficiency. These preferences imply that they will seek to equalise their children's future earnings. Note that this does not imply that all children will be treated equally. Consider the case of parents who want their daughter and son to receive equal earnings. Suppose the daughter will face discrimination in the labour market, specifically her wages will be less than that of her comparably qualified brother doing the same work. Here, parents will devote more resources to their daughter (for example, they provide her with more education) in order to equalise future earnings. Put another way, parents compensate the child with the poorer initial endowment (in the sense that the existence of discrimination in the labour market puts the female at a disadvantage) through higher investment. Conversely, where parents seek to maximise the total future earnings of their offspring, they invest relatively more in those children with the best future prospects. In the example considered here, parents would invest more in their son than in their daughter. That is, parents 're-inforce' existing inequalities in child endowments. Clearly, it is possible to imagine intermediate cases where both equity and efficiency concerns play a role. These are termed equity-efficiency trade-offs.

Note that all three approaches assume that parents are agreed on the degree of (in)equality they wish to see in their children. This need not be so (the existing literature is surveyed in Haddad and Hoddinott, 1991). Folbre (1986) has argued that women are less likely to discriminate against daughters because their labour can be used for domestic tasks that are women's responsibility. Consequently, differences in intra-household allocations (as indicated by anthropometric status[2] or food allocation) reflect the low bargaining power of women within the household rather than parental preferences for children of a particular gender. This is an important qualification that we return to at the end of Section 4.4.

Evidence on Household Allocation

Much of the existing empirical evidence of household resource allocation comes from south Asia. It indicates that girls receive fewer household resources than boys, as reflected in measures of anthropometric status, food allocation and mortality. As Harriss (1990) provides thorough reviews of the empirical literature in this area, discussion is restricted to three studies that illustrate the theoretical approaches noted above.

An example of the 'equity approach' is provided by Behrman (1988). He examines whether parents in parts of semi-arid India have preferences for boys over girls by looking at the intra-household allocation of nutrients (specifically calories and vitamins). In Behrman's model, parents utility depends on the health of their children, as captured by anthropometric measurements weighted according to their preferences for particular children. This is maximised subject to both an income constraint and a constraint reflecting the production of child well-being. The latter constraint includes purchased inputs such as nutrients and endowments such as the child's genetic make-up. Behrman finds that during the surplus (post-harvest) season, nutrients are distributed in such a way that less well-endowed children are favoured. That is, parents' behaviour can be described as compensatory (Behrman, 1988, p. 48). By contrast, during the lean (pre-harvest) season, when food supplies are relatively limited, parents value improvements in the health of male children more than they do an equal improvement in female child health. That is, parents do not prefer equality amongst their children. Rather, they are biased towards male offspring.

Rosenzweig and Schultz (1982) provide an example of the efficiency approach. They develop a model in which parents derive utility from the consumption of goods and the number of surviving children. The latter are assumed to have both direct consumption benefits as well as providing pecuniary contributions, such as labour and remittances, to their parents. Parents, through the allocation of resources, can influence the survival of children. Accordingly, Rosenzweig and Schultz argue that an increase in the potential contribution of girls to their parents leads to an increase in the likelihood of their survival. Using data from rural India, they find that areas with higher female labour force participation (a proxy for contributions to parents) have higher rates of female survival relative to male survival.

The equity-efficiency trade-off is illustrated by a study of Bangladeshi households by Pitt, Rosenzweig and Hassan (1990). In their model, households may desire a reasonably equitable distribution of household resources. However, they recognise that skewing resources towards particular members, who face better prospects, may be necessary to raise productivity (an efficiency wage argument). In well-off households, this does not present a problem as they have sufficient resources to provide enough food for all individuals to meet their calorific requirements. However, households below this point face a trade-off between an equitable distribution of resources and providing additional resources to those members who are best placed to generate additional income. Pitt, Rosenzweig and Hassan find that Bangladeshi households tend to skew calories towards those members engaged in more energy intensive activities, though some attempt is also made to equalise intake across individuals.

Discussion of these issues in the sub-Saharan African context has been more limited and most studies tend to be less strongly grounded in the theoretical models discussed above. Attention has focused on gender differences in anthropometric status. Existing studies suggest that there is little evidence of discrimination in the allocation of household resources as measured in this way:

> The main finding is that females, whatever their age, are not at a disadvantage *vis-a-vis* males in anthropometric status. This may not be true in each and every part of the continent, but it is in the great majority of the Sub-Saharan African countries. (Svedberg, 1990, p. 482).

Statistical and econometric evidence, broadly speaking, bears this out. Results from Kenya (Kennedy and Cogill, 1987), Ghana (Haddad, 1990) and Côte d'Ivoire (Strauss, 1990, Haddad and Hoddinott, 1991) do not indicate any statistically significant differences in anthropometric status between boys and girls. Indeed, Sahn (1990) and von Braun (1988) suggest that in urban Côte d'Ivoire and rural Gambia respectively, boys are worse off in terms of height-for-age. The relationship between child health and relationship to the household head is also of interest, especially in west Africa where it is not uncommon for children to be living outside the natal home. Strauss and Mehra (1989) suggest that these children are slightly healthier than offspring of the household head, a point returned to in Section 4.4.

4.3 OUTLAY EQUIVALENT ANALYSIS OF EXPENDITURE ON ADULT GOODS: THEORY

The analysis of intra-household resource allocation in sub-Saharan Africa has been hampered by the absence of high quality data. Consider again the issue of food allocation. An obvious source of data, household expenditure surveys, are, on closer examination, not well suited to examining this issue because they report household, not individual consumption. Direct measurement of food intake – for example, by recording the quantity consumed by each person throughout the day – is possible but extremely difficult. Firstly, it requires highly skilled enumerators. Secondly, to be accurate, these surveys must account for plate wastage, consumption of leftovers, snacks and meals consumed outside the home. Thirdly, they must be carried out continuously, or at least frequently, over a reasonably long period of time. Random fluctuations in individual food intake make information obtained from a 'one-shot' survey difficult to interpret. Finally, and perhaps most importantly, such an approach assumes the absence of reflexivity – the possibility that individuals change their behaviour when being observed.

Given such problems, it would be useful if a methodology was available that permitted examination of intra-household resource allocation without requiring specialised data collection efforts. This section introduces such an approach, Deaton's outlay equivalent approach (Deaton, 1989; Deaton, Ruiz-Castillo and Thomas, 1989; Subramanian and Deaton, 1990). Its data requirements are comparatively simple. Any survey containing reasonably disaggregated expenditure data and information on household composition can be used.

> The basic idea [behind the outlay equivalent approach] is to use expenditure on some 'adult' good or goods, known not to be consumed by children, as an indicator of the extent to which parents give up their own consumption to provide the resources required by the child. (Subramanian and Deaton, 1990, p. 9).

Consider two types of goods consumed by a household: food and alcohol. What effect would an additional child have on that household's demand for those goods? *A priori*, the effect on the consumption of food is difficult to ascertain. The cost of raising an extra child could reduce food spent on adults, but in a household survey this might not be observed because of food's substitutability among household members. However, the presence of an additional child reduces the resources available for other goods. Consequently, consumption of goods such as alcohol might well fall. This reduction is analogous to an income effect, that is, the additional child effectively causes the household's budget line to shift inwards. If the presence of an additional male child produces a greater reduction in the budget share of the adult good than does an additional girl, then this provides some evidence of discrimination within the household.

Outlay equivalents require the identification of goods that can be plausibly taken to be consumed only by adults. As Gronau (1988) stresses, only for adult goods can it be assumed that children act as if to shift the household budget constraint to the left. Further, it is implicitly assumed that parental preferences are exogenous. A reduction in the consumption of an adult good is due to the income effect of an additional child, not a 'loss of taste' for, say, eating out or going to the cinema (Gronau, 1988). Consequently, the first step in this analysis is to determine whether particular commodities are adult goods.

The test for this is based on the concept of 'demographic separability' (Deaton, Ruiz-Castillo and Thomas, 1989). If children only generate income effects on the purchase of adult goods, the disposition of total expenditure on adult goods amongst those goods must be independent of child characteristics. Put another way, it is assumed that children reduce the amount available to spend on adult goods (the income effect). However, within the budget for adult goods, they should have no effect on the composition of demand for these goods. By contrast, if an additional child re-allocates demand away from alcohol and towards cigarettes, then the child is having some effect on the demand for adult goods beyond the income effect. Also, the number of adults should affect the consumption of adult goods (if this was not the case, these would not be adult goods). These assumptions can be taken as given, or they can be tested. Deaton (1989) suggests the following, three step approach. First, specify an adult good expenditure function. To be consistent with our work throughout this chapter, and with Deaton's original analysis, we use a linear expenditure function taking the following form:

$$expAG_j = \tau_1 + \tau_2 expAG + \sum_{a=1}^{A} \tau_a N_a + \sum_{c=1}^{C} \tau_c N_c + \sum_{s=1}^{S} \tau_s z_s + e_j \qquad (4.1)$$

where:
$expAG_j$ household expenditure on the jth adult good;
$expAG$ total household expenditures on all adult goods;

N_a number of adults (by age and gender) in the household, $(a = 1, 2, \ldots, A)$;

N_c number of children (by age, gender and relationship to head) in the household $(c = 1, 2, \ldots, C)$;

z_s a vector of dummy variables for household location $(s = 1, 2, \ldots, S)$;

e_j is the error term in the jth equation; and

τ's   are parameters to be estimated.

The next step is to estimate, using regression analysis, restricted $(\tau_a = 0 \text{ or } \tau_c = 0)$ and unrestricted $(\tau_a \neq 0 \text{ and } \tau_c \neq 0)$ versions of (4.1). Having done so, we construct two F-tests. A well defined adult good is one where: (a) the F-test does not reject the null hypothesis that the estimated coefficients for children (τ_c) are jointly zero; and (b) does not accept the null hypothesis that the estimated coefficients for adults (τ_a) are jointly zero.

Having found plausible adult goods, we now turn to measuring the income effects of additional male and female children. It is desirable to do so using a unit-free measure, facilitating, for example, comparison across countries. Following Deaton, we measure this via an outlay equivalent. An outlay equivalent, or pi-ratio (π_{jr}), equal to –0.30 can be given the following interpretation: an extra individual in the rth household demographic group has the same effect on the household's expenditure on adult good j as would a reduction of 30 per cent in household per capita total expenditure. The general formula is given by the following:

$$\pi_{jr} = \left[\frac{\partial exp_j / \partial n_r}{\partial exp_j / \partial texp} \right] \frac{n}{texp} \qquad (4.2)$$

where:

exp_j household expenditure on the jth adult good;

nr the number of individuals in the rth household demographic group;

$texp$ total household expenditure; and

n household size.

Equation (4.2) requires an estimate of the change in total expenditure on the jth adult good generated by an additional household member $(\partial exp_j / \partial n_r)$ and the change in expenditure on the jth adult good generated by a change in total per capita expenditure $(\partial exp_j / \partial texp)$. Note that equation (4.1) cannot be used to obtain this information.

Equation (4.1) indicates whether children affect the allocation of expenditures *amongst* adult goods, given total expenditures on these commodities. By contrast, the relevant datum for our purposes is the effect of children on individual adult goods, given total expenditures on *all* commodities purchased by the household (Deaton, 1989). This requires a slightly different expenditure equation. Remaining consistent with Deaton's work, we use a Working-Leser expenditure function. This has a number of desirable theoretical properties, in particular, it satisfies the constraint that, when applied to all goods, the predicted budget shares sum to unity. Here, the dependent variable is the budget share of each good (the total amount spent on that good divided by the total amount of household expenditures). This is a function of the logarithm of total per capita expenditures, the logarithm of household size and the proportions of different demographic groups (for example, sons of the head aged less than six). In addition, recognising that expenditures may vary by location and identity of income earner within the household, we include locational dummy variables and the proportion of household income accruing as cash to spouses of the head. Accordingly, our expenditure function is:

$$w_j = \alpha + \beta_1 lpcexp + \beta_2 lsiz + \sum_{r=1}^{R-1} \psi_r dem_r + \sum_{s=1}^{S} \theta_s z_s + \beta_3 PFINC \qquad (4.3)$$

where:

w_j is the budget share of the jth good ($exp_j/texp$);
$lpcexp$ is the log of total per capita cash expenditures;
$lsiz$ is the log of total household size;
dem_r proportion of demographic group r in the household (n_r/n);
z_s is a vector of s dummy variables indicating household location;
$PFINC$ proportion of household income accruing as cash to spouses of head;
α, β_1, β_2, β_3, ψ_r, and θ_s are parameters to be estimated.

By partially differentiating (4.3) with respect to total expenditures and each demographic group, we can derive the outlay equivalent ratios. To obtain these for the Working-Leser expenditure, note that equation (4.3) can be re-written as:

$$exp_j = texp \left\{ \alpha + \beta_1 lpcexp + \beta_2 lsiz + \sum_{r=1}^{R-1} \psi_r dem_r + \sum_{s=1}^{S} \theta_s z_s + \beta_3 PFINC \right\}$$

which also equals,

$$exp_j = texp\{\alpha + \beta_1[\log(texp) - \log(n_1 + n_2 + \ldots + n_r)] +$$

$$\beta_2\log(n_1 + n_2 + \ldots + n_r) + \sum_{r=1}^{R-1}\psi_r(n_r \, / \, n) + \sum_{r=1}^{S}\theta_s z_s + \beta_3 PFINC\}$$

Partial differentiation yields:

$$\frac{\partial exp_j}{\partial n_r} = \frac{exp_j}{texp} + \beta_1$$

$$= w_j + \beta_j$$

$$\frac{\partial exp_j}{\partial texp} = \frac{texp}{n}\left[-\beta_1 + \beta_2 + \psi_r - \sum_{r=1}^{R-1}\psi_r \, (nr \, / \, n)\right]$$

Hence, our outlay equivalent for the jth good and r^{th} demographic group is:

$$\pi_{jr} = \frac{-\beta_1 + \beta_2 + \psi_r - \sum_{r=1}^{R-1}\psi_r dem_r}{\beta_1 + w_j} \tag{4.4}$$

The βs and ψs are parameters obtainable from estimating (4.3). The values for dem_r and w_j can be taken from their sample means.

4.4　OUTLAY EQUIVALENT ANALYSIS OF EXPENDITURE ON ADULT GOODS: EVIDENCE FROM THE CÔTE D'IVOIRE

The analysis here follows the methodology discussed in Section 4.3. The first step is a test of the adequacy of the hypothesised adult goods. Attention is then turned to the possibility of gender differences in household resource allocation. Deaton (1989), using data from the 1985–86 Côte d'Ivoire Living Standards Surveys (CILSS), found little evidence to support the hypothesis that boys are treated differently compared to girls with respect to the amount of adult goods expenditure foregone by the household. Here, his analysis is extended by refining the household demographic groups into offspring of household head and non-offspring children (who tend to be adopted or are residing with the family for school purposes). Of primary interest is whether a child's gender or relationship to head of household affects the magnitude of the decline in the expenditure on adult goods.

Ivorian Household Expenditure Data

The data used to estimate this model are taken from the 1986–87 round of the CILSS. There are 1600 households in the survey, though it was necessary to drop 93 for whom insufficient data were available. Survey methodology and implementation are discussed in Ainsworth and Munoz (1986). Candidates for adult goods in the Côte d'Ivoire include adult clothes (shirts and trousers), cigarettes, alcohol, adult shoes, adult fabric, and food purchased outside the home. Their mean budget shares with standard deviations are presented in Table 4.1.

The right hand side of equation (4.3) requires the construction of four types of variables: expenditures, location, demographic composition and women's share of income. Summing all expenditures, dividing by household size and taking the logarithm of the resultant quotient yields the variable *lpcexp*, the log of total expenditures per capita. Location variables indicate whether the household lives in Abidjan or, if in a rural area, the principal ethnic group. The demographic variables are straightforward to construct. The household roster was used to sum the total number of household members, the log of which is given by *lsiz*. Individuals were divided into ten demographic categories based on age, sex and relationship to the household head (own offspring and foster children). The number in each was divided by household size to give a proportion. The proportion of household cash income accruing as cash to wives of the head, or widows where the male head is deceased, is included as *PFINC*. Its computation embodies a number of strong assumptions that are detailed in Haddad and Hoddinott (1991). A summary of the right hand side variables and their means and standard deviations is in Table 4.2.

Empirical Results

The first step is to test the adequacy of the candidate adult goods. As outlined in Section 4.3, the expenditure on each adult good is regressed on total expenditure for all adult goods, the female income share variable, the number of people (not ratios) in each of the demographic groups, and the location dummies. The purpose of this is to test parameter restrictions, hence, only these are reported below.[3] Two *F*-tests are constructed and the results of these are reported in

Table 4.1 *Dependent variables*

Variable	Description (measured as share of total budget)	Mean	Standard deviation
padltexp	expenditures on all adult goods	0.126	0.092
paclothe	expenditures on adult clothes	0.011	0.014
pafabric	expenditures on fabric for adult clothes	0.041	0.033
pashoes	expenditures on adult shoes	0.011	0.013
palc	expenditures on alcohol	0.017	0.034
pcig	expenditures on cigarettes	0.016	0.029
pfoodout	meals consumed outside the home	0.029	0.065

Table 4.2 *Explanatory variables*

Variable	Description	Mean	Standard deviation
lpcexp	log of per capita expenditures	11.92	0.76
lsiz	log of household size	1.90	0.69
PFINC	proportion of household income accruing as cash to spouses of the head	0.20	0.29
dem1	proportion of males aged over 15	0.28	0.21
dem2	proportion of females aged over 15	0.28	0.16
dem3	proportion of male own-offspring aged 6 to 15	0.10	0.12
dem4	proportion of female own-offspring aged 6 to 15	0.08	0.11
dem5	proportion of male own-offspring aged below 6	0.07	0.10
dem6	proportion of female own-offspring aged below 6	0.07	0.11
dem7	proportion of male fostered aged 6 to 15	0.04	0.08
dem8	proportion of female fostered aged 6 to 15	0.04	0.09
dem9	proportion of male fostered aged below 6	0.03	0.06
dem10	proportion of female fostered aged below 6	0.02	0.06
dabidj	=1 if household located in Abidjan	0.19	0.39
dbet	=1 if household located in Bete area	0.15	0.36
dbao	=1 if household located in Baoule area	0.25	0.43
dguo	=1 if household located in Guoro area	0.11	0.32
dsen	=1 if household located in Senoufo area	0.07	0.26

Table 4.3   *F-tests for adult goods*

Adult good	H_0: τ_c=0; H_1: $\tau_c \neq 0$ F-test	H_0: τ_a=0; H_1: $\tau_c \neq 0$ F-test
adult clothes	1.1985	0.5509
adult fabric	5.8768**	47.8797**
adult shoes	0.7577	4.0397**
alcohol	1.4840	0.2569
cigarettes	0.9494	2.9723**
meals out	0.5623	14.1110**

** significant at the 5% level (except cigarettes – significant at the 5.2% level).

Table 4.3. In the first column, the null hypothesis is that $\tau_c = 0$, i.e. the number of children does not affect expenditure on the good in question. This is rejected only in the case of adult fabric, i.e. we can say that the number of children has a significant effect on expenditures on this good, suggesting that it may not be an adult good. In the second column the null hypothesis is that $\tau_a = 0$, i.e. the number of adults does not affect expenditure. This is rejected in four cases. The results offer strong support for three goods – adult shoes, cigarettes and meals out – being especially plausible choices as adult goods.

The next step is to estimate our version of the Working-Leser expenditure function for the three strongest candidates as adult goods and the composite good (total expenditure on hypothesised adult goods).[4] Before discussing the results, several estimation issues are worth noting. It is necessary to drop at least one of the household composition variables in order to estimate the budget shares. In Table 4.4, adult females (*dem2*) has been dropped. Secondly, because *lpcexp* and *PFINC* may not be exogenous, two stage least squares has been used. Finally, Breusch-Pagan tests rejected the null hypothesis of homoscedastic errors in all budget share equations. Consequently, all equations were estimated using the generalised least squares estimation procedure proposed by White (1980). A full discussion of these results is beyond the scope of this Chapter (Haddad and Hoddinott, 1991, provide a detailed commentary). However, note that the coefficients on *PFINC* (the proportion of household income accruing as cash to spouses of the head) are negative and significant for three of the four adult goods examined here. This finding will be returned to later.

The next step is to calculate the outlay equivalents using the estimated parameters of equation (4.3) – some of which are reported in

Table 4.4   *Two-stage least squares budget share regressions for candidate adult goods (N=1507)*

	Padltexp	Pashoes	Pcig	Pfoodout
Lpcexp	−0.0101	0.0015	−0.008	−0.001
	(1.51)	(.176)*	(3.94)**	(0.12)
Lsiz	−0.0221	0.0005	−0.007	−0.015
	(3.65)**	(0.69)	(3.54)**	(3.23)**
PFINC	−0.0549	−0.0045	−0.011	−0.012
	(3.93)**	(2.31)**	(2.32)**	(1.34)
Deml	0.1066	0.0034	0.013	0.095
	(4.20)**	(0.95)	(1.62)	(4.70)**
Dem3	−0.0015	−0.0040	−0.012	0.035
	(0.07)	(1.17)	(1.85)*	(2.23)**
Dem4	0.0116	−0.0059	−0.005	0.051
	(0.48)	(1.52)	(0.64)	(3.15)**
Dem5	0.0945	0.0013	0.004	0.085
	(3.52)**	(0.36)	(0.43)	(4.36)**
Dem6	0.0405	0.0021	−0.007	0.060
	(1.55)	(0.55)	(0.82)	(3.52)**
Dem7	0.0404	−0.0025	−0.009	0.060
	(1.28)	(0.66)	(0.93)	(2.61)**
Dem8	0.0249	−0.0041	−0.014	0.063
	(0.71)	(0.98)	(1.76)*	(2.23)**
Dem9	0.1262	0.0104	−0.008	0.080
	(2.97)**	(1.82)*	(0.61)	(3.01)**
Dem10	0.1509	0.0144	0.019	0.076
	(3.47)**	(1.60)	(1.45)	(3.03)**
Location[a]	—	Dbao	—	Dabidj; Dsen
Intercept	0.2602	−0.0064	0.131	0.013
	(2.81)**	(0.60)	(4.70)**	(0.19)
Adj R^2	0.082	0.012	0.06	0.13

t statistics in parentheses: ** significant at the 5% level; * significant at the
10% level.
[a]   All location dummies were included, only the significant ones are indicated.

Table 4.4 – and the formula given by equation (4.4). The four (three adult goods plus the composite good, *padltexp*) by ten (demographic groups) matrix of outlay equivalents and their standard errors (*se*) are in Table 4.5. (Deaton, Ruiz-Castillo and Thomas, 1989, explain how to construct the standard errors for the outlay equivalents). If the selection of adult goods and their measurement is accurate, all 12 coefficients on the *dem3 – dem6* variables (for the three adult goods) for boys and girls who are offspring of the head of household should

Table 4.5 Outlay equivalents for 6 candidate adult goods and 10 demographic groups

	dem1 males 16 & over	dem2 females 16 & over	dem3 own sons 6–15	dem4 own daughters 6–15	dem5 own sons 0–5	dem6 own daughters 0–5	dem7 foster males 6–15	dem8 foster females 6–15	dem9 foster males 0–5	dem10 foster females 0–5
all adult goods										
π	0.3815	−0.5102	−0.5554	−0.4599	0.2707	−0.1259	−0.1168	−0.3152	0.4901	0.6253
se	0.1283	0.1036	0.1414	0.1553	0.1763	0.1687	0.2254	0.2146	0.2995	0.3368
adult shoes										
π	0.3650	−0.0047	−0.4561	−0.6562	−0.0973	−0.0057	−0.3434	−0.5712	0.5623	0.9385
se	0.1922	0.1658	0.2130	0.2342	0.2619	0.2547	0.3373	0.2113	0.4510	0.5091
cigarettes										
π	1.3793	0.0421	−1.331	−0.6668	0.4530	−0.2870	−0.6433	−1.374	−0.8712	1.8134
se	0.6903	0.4620	0.6076	0.6472	0.7402	0.6991	0.9308	0.9006	1.2573	1.4463
food outside home										
π	0.6805	−1.992	−1.004	−0.6053	0.6230	−0.1009	−0.1513	−0.1026	0.2672	0.1891
se	0.3567	0.3238	0.3675	0.4009	0.4650	0.4352	0.5802	0.5571	0.7698	0.8655

be negative. From Table 4.5 we can see that 10 of the 12 outlay equivalents are negative as expected, although only six are statistically significant.[5] For the children in the 6–15 age group who are not offspring
of the household head, all six coefficients are negative. This is in stark
contrast to foster children under 6 years old for whom only one of the
coefficients is negative.

The evidence in Table 4.5 can be interpreted by recalling the mean-
ing of outlay equivalents. An additional daughter aged between six
and 15 has the effect of reducing consumption on all adult goods
equivalent to a 45.99 per cent reduction in per capita expenditure. By
contrast, a daughter aged 0 to 5 reduces consumption on all adult
goods by an amount equivalent to a 12.59 per cent reduction in per
capita expenditure. This is an entirely plausible result. Children become more expensive as they get older and this is reflected in a larger
outlay equivalent for older daughters. An additional son aged between
6 and 15 has an effect on expenditure on cigarettes equivalent to a
133 per cent reduction in per capita household expenditure, and the
coefficient is significant. In contrast, an additional girl in the same
age range has an effect on expenditure on cigarettes equivalent to a
67 per cent reduction in per capita household expenditure, but the
coefficient is insignificant. Despite this example, the overall evidence
does not suggest discrimination against females. The evidence does,
however, suggest that own children are favoured over foster children.

To determine whether the differences in outlay ratios are statistically significant, we construct a series of F-tests based on the values
of π_{jr} and the computed standard errors. Table 4.6 presents these
across different gender and 'relationship to household head' groups
for the three adult goods and the composite adult good. In the upper part of the table the null hypothesis is that, for given age and
'relationship to head' groups, the estimated outlay equivalent is the
same irrespective of gender. The F-statistics are small and in no
case can the null hypothesis of gender equality be rejected. The lower
part of Table 4.6 tests the null hypothesis that, for given age and
gender groups, the estimated outlay equivalent is the same irrespective of 'relationship to head'. The null is rejected in only three cases.
For example, the F-test suggests that an additional own daughter
under the age of six leads to a reduction in expenditure on adult
shoes to a greater extent than does an additional foster daughter of
the same age.

Table 4.6   *F-tests across gender and relationship to head of household*

	male vs female 6–15, own child F-test	male vs female <6, own child F-test	male vs female 6–15, fostered F-test	male vs female <6, fostered F-test
all adult exp	0.1671	2.3954	0.3442	0.0803
adult shoes	0.3244	0.0564	0.2007	0.2751
cigarettes	0.4681	0.4830	0.2703	1.8353
meals out	0.4397	1.2016	0.0031	0.0040
Rejections (at 10% level)	0	0	0	0

	own vs foster male, 6–15 F-test	own vs foster female, 6–15 F-test	own vs foster male, <6 F-test	own vs foster female, <6 F-test
all adult exp	2.7906	0.3059	0.4212	4.1345
adult shoes	0.0814	0.0467	1.6835	2.8887
cigarettes	0.3973	0.4232	0.8887	1.8725
meals out	1.5900	0.5559	0.1679	0.0928
Rejections (at 10% level)	1	0	0	2

Discussion of Results

Despite the imprecision and subsequent lack of statistical significance of any differences across estimates, the relative magnitudes of π_{jr} across gender and relationship to household head reveal three features of interest. Comparing sons and daughters in the 6–15 age group, in two of the three adult goods the negative income effect of a boy is larger than that for a girl, and the weighted figure for all adult goods shows girls have a marginally smaller (but not significantly so) effect. For sons and daughters in the 0–6 range, the negative income effect of the girl is smaller for the three adult goods, but for the composite good (which includes all six hypothesised adult goods) the coefficient on daughters is negative whereas that for sons is positive (but the difference is not significant). However, for the sample as a whole, there is little evidence to reject the hypothesis that boys and girls are treated equally with respect to the amount of adult good expenditure foregone by the household.

These results, which are consistent with the anthropometric evidence discussed earlier, differ dramatically from the evidence from south Asia. A number of authors, including Boserup (1970) and Svedberg (1990), suggest that the absence of discrimination flows from the nature of agricultural production. In many parts of sub-Saharan Africa, including much of Côte d'Ivoire, agriculture is not mechanised, nor is substantial use made of animal traction. These features increase the value of labour, and this is reflected in the practice of bridewealth. In Côte d'Ivoire, as in much of Africa, on marrying a daughter the parents of the bride receive payment (typically in livestock or cash) as compensation for the loss of a valuable worker. This contrasts with the practice in much of India where dowry is the norm (parents of the bride transfer assets to the groom's family on marriage). The prospect of bridewealth payments discourages parents from discriminating against daughters. In the context of the general preference model discussed in Section 4.2, this is an efficiency rationale.

The contrast between own and foster children is more marked. Indeed, one surprising result of Table 4.5 is the positive outlay equivalents for foster children aged less than six. A greater quantity of adult goods are sacrificed for own children in nine of the 12 (three adult goods) possible age-gender-relationship to head comparisons. This also holds true for the composite adult good. Two features account for these results.

The practice of child fosterage is widespread in Côte d'Ivoire. Children are sent to live with other relatives for a number of reasons. These include: child labour – providing assistance with household tasks; attending school; child care – for example, in cases where both parents are engaged in urban wage employment; and consumption smoothing – as a response to a sudden fall in income (Ainsworth, 1991). Parents who foster children out often send money or goods to provide for their upkeep. Indeed, there can be cases where relatives compete for foster children.

> Parents know that one of the main reasons why grannies lobby for children is that they will soon begin asking the children's parents for things they would ask for anyway – food, clothes, and money – but would ordinarily have little leverage to demand. (Bledsoe and Isiugo-Abanihe, cited in Ainsworth, 1991).

Such children are effectively coming with an income that offsets their costs as measured by their effect on the consumption of adult goods. Own children, who come 'unsubsidised', consequently have a larger negative impact on the consumption of adult goods. Secondly, healthier children may be selected to be fostered in and out of households; Strauss and Mehra (1989) report that foster children in the Côte d'Ivoire have a lower incidence of stunting than children of the household head. Recall from Section 4.2 that, if parents prefer equity amongst children, they compensate the more poorly endowed. In the Ivorian case, this would require a greater sacrifice of adult goods in the presence of own children, precisely the result found in Tables 4.5 and 4.6.

Some caution is needed in accepting this interpretation. While the differences between own and fostered children are certainly more marked than the boy–girl comparison, only in the case of own versus foster children aged 0–6 are the differences statistically significant. One possible reason why the difference is so marked in this case is that parents, while entitled to brideprice payments for their own daughters are less likely to receive them for foster girls. This reduces their incentive to invest in such children (reflected here by a reduction in consumption of adult goods). Put another way, efficiency concerns also motivate allocations of household resources, here to the detriment of foster girls below the age of six.

A final comment relates to an idea mooted in Section 4.2. Is it possible to incorporate bargaining into the analysis of outlay equivalents? Recall that in Table 4.4, the coefficient on *PFINC* (women's share of household cash income) is negative. Haddad and Hoddinott (1991) argue that this could be a manifestation of bargaining within the household. Adult men and women have different preferences which they enforce through control of income. Specifically, men derive greater utility from the consumption of alcohol, cigarettes and other adult goods. As their share of household income falls (i.e. *PFINC* rises), the consumption of these commodities is reduced. Since these goods are those used to construct the outlay equivalents, the analysis here may be capturing adult male, rather than parental, preferences. Suppose it were possible to identify a female adult good and calculate outlay equivalents for it. If these differed systematically from those derived from adult male goods (for example, adult males discriminate in favour of boys whereas adult females discriminate against boys), this would suggest that male and female preferences differ. Unfortunately, the Ivorian data do not permit such a test, but it remains an idea that would be worth developing in the future.

4.5 CONCLUSION

We began this chapter by arguing that the successful implementation of rural development policies requires an understanding of the manner in which households allocate resources amongst members. Yet, the data requirements for this can be formidable. Certainly, there is no data available that would permit a direct examination of this issue in the Côte d'Ivoire. However, it is possible to draw some inferences about intra-household resource allocation by examining household expenditures on adult goods using Deaton's outlay equivalent method. Doing so here does not reveal any evidence of discrimination against girls in the Côte d'Ivoire. There is some indication of bias against fostered girls under the age of six. Using both theory and evidence from other studies, we suggest that these results may reflect equity and efficiency concerns and the tendency of foster children to be 'subsidised' which mitigates any income effect.

Notes

1. We would like to thank, without implicating in the final product, Paul Collier, Angus Deaton and Duncan Thomas for their comments on this work and Daniel Driscoll for programming assistance. We would also like to thank the Women in Development Division, the World Bank, who funded this study, but stress that we are responsible for the views expressed here and any errors that remain.
2. Anthropometric measures are indicators of child growth. Studies conducted in different parts of the world indicate that well nourished, healthy children tend to grow at the same rate everywhere. Consequently, the growth of a child, in terms of height or weight, can be compared to a reference population of healthy children. The two most common measures are age-for-height, which captures long-term growth, and weight for height, which is an indicator of short-term health status.
3. A full set of results for this section is available from the authors.
4. The analysis has been conducted for the six adult goods listed in Table 4.3, plus total expenditure on all adult goods. Further details can be found in Haddad and Hoddinott (1991).
5. Statistical significance is tested here by dividing the outlay equivalent by its standard error and comparing the results with percentiles of the Students' t distribution.

References

Ainsworth, M. (1991) 'Economic Aspects of Child Fostering in Côte d'Ivoire', mimeo, World Bank.

Ainsworth, M. and Munoz, J. (1986), 'The Côte d'Ivoire Living Standards Survey: Design and Implementation', Living Standards Measurement Study Working Paper No. 26, Washington DC.: The World Bank.

Behrman, J. (1988), 'Intra-household Allocation of Nutrients in Rural India: Are Boys Favoured? Do Parents Exhibit Inequality Aversion?', *Oxford Economic Papers*, 40, 32–54.

Behrman, J., Pollak, R. and Taubman, P. (1982), 'Parental Preferences and Provision for Progeny', *Journal of Political Economy*, 90, 52–75.

Boserup, E. (1970) *Woman's Role in Economic Development*, Gower, Wiltshire.

von Braun, J. (1988), 'Effects of Technological Change in Agriculture on Food Consumption and Nutrition: Rice in a West African Setting', *World Development*, 16, 1083–1098.

Coale, A.J. (1991), 'Excess Female Mortality and the Balance of the Sexes in the Population: An Estimate of the Number of "Missing Females"', *Population and Development Review*, 17, 517–524.

Deaton, A. (1989), 'Looking for boy-girl Discrimination in Household Expenditure Data', *World Bank Economic Review*, 3, 3–15.

Deaton, A., Ruiz-Castillo, J. and Thomas, D. (1989), 'The Influence of Household Composition on Household Expenditure Patterns', *Journal of Political Economy*, 97, 179–200.

Folbre, N. (1986), 'Hearts and Spades: Paradigms of Household Economics', *World Development*, 14, 245–255.

Gronau, R. (1988), 'Consumption Technology and the Intra-family Distribution of Resources: Adult Equivalence Scales Reexamined', *Journal of Political Economy*, 96, 1119–1143.

Haddad, L. (1990), 'Gender and Poverty in Ghana: A Descriptive Analysis' Social Dimensions of Adjustment in Sub-Saharan Africa Working Paper, Washington, World Bank.

Haddad, L. and Hoddinott, J. (1991), 'Gender Aspects of Household Expenditures and Resource Allocation in the Cote d'Ivoire', mimeo, University of Oxford.

Harriss, B. (1990), 'The Intra-family Distribution of Hunger in South Asia' in *The Political Economy of Hunger*, Volume I edited by J. Dreze and A. Sen, Oxford: Clarendon Press.

Kennedy, E. and Cogill, B. (1987), 'Income and Nutritional Effects of the Commercialization of Agriculture in Southwestern Kenya' International Food Policy Research Institute Research Report No. 63, Washington DC.

Pitt, M., Rosenzweig, M. and Hassan, Md. (1990), 'Productivity, Health and Inequality in the Intra-household Distribution of Food in Low-Income Households', *American Economic Review*, 80, 1139–1156.

Rosenzweig, M. and Schultz, T.P. (1982), 'Market Opportunities, Genetic Endowments and Intra-family Resource Distribution', *American Economic Review*, 72, 803–815.

Sahn, D. (1990), 'Malnutrition in Côte d'Ivoire', Social Dimensions of Adjustment in Sub-Saharan Africa Working Paper no. 4, Washington DC, World Bank.

Sen, A. (1990), 'More than 100 million women are missing', *New York Times Review of Books*, 20 (December), 61–66.

Strauss, J. (1990), 'Households, Communities and Pre-school Children's Nutrition Outcomes: Evidence from Rural Côte d'Ivoire' *Economic Development and Cultural Change*, 38, 231–262.

Strauss, J. and Mehra, K. (1989), 'Child Anthropometry in Côte d'Ivoire: Estimates from Two Surveys, 1985 and 1986' Living Standards Measurement Study Working Paper No. 51, Washington DC, World Bank.

Subramanian, S. and Deaton, A. (1990), 'Gender Effects in Indian Consumption Patterns' Research Program in Development Studies Discussion Paper No. 147, Woodrow Wilson School, Princeton University.

Svedberg, P. (1990) 'Undernutrition in Sub-Saharan Africa: Is There a Gender Bias?' *Journal of Development Studies*, 26, 469–486.

White, H. (1980), 'A Heteroskedasticity-Consistent Matrix and a Direct test for Heteroskedasticity' *Econometrica*, 48, 721–746.

5 Is China Egalitarian?

J.B. Knight[1]

5.1 INTRODUCTION

Concern for equality is a phenomenon that runs deep in Chinese cul-
ture, and it is not just to be found under China's communist government of the past forty years. Confucius, writing in 500 BC, put it as
follows: 'What worries those who have the state and family under
their charge is not the scantiness of wealth but its inequality of distribution – not poverty but disquietude. Under equal distribution there
will be no feeling of poverty' (quoted in Hu Jichuang, 1988). Since
the communists came to power in 1949 the Chinese government has
adopted objectives that are extremely egalitarian by comparison with
other developing countries. Moreover, the high degree of central planning
gave the state great powers to pursue these objectives: it had redistributive
instruments not available in a mixed economy. The 'three great inequalities', as they have been called – inter-regional, rural-urban and
intra-work unit – have been consistently addressed by policy-makers.
There are at least four interesting questions:

(i)   Does a socialist strategy of development result in an egalitarian
      society?
(ii) How does the distribution of income in China compare with that
      in other developing countries which have relied more on market
      forces?
(iii) In the Chinese experience, are there trade-offs apparent between
      efficiency and equality, and between growth and equality?
(iv) How is the distribution of income changing as a result of the
      economic reforms that began in 1978?

China is an important economy for at least two reasons. It contains a
quarter of the world's population and a still higher proportion of its
poor people. China began a process of introducing basic economic reforms
earlier and more successfully than other communist countries. It de-
serves the attention of economists. Good data are increasingly available but the need for investment in country-specific skills remains

considerable. Up to now it has not been possible systematically to address distributional questions, such as those posed above, because the statistical information available has been inadequate. However, in 1988 a major research project was launched to begin to improve knowledge about the distribution of income in China. It is an international, collaborative project, involving the Institute of Economics of the Chinese Academy of Social Sciences in Beijing and various foreign scholars including the author. Its major findings will be published in Griffin and Zhao (1994).

The project is based on a 1988 national survey of households in China, covering both rural and urban areas. The survey contained some 10,000 rural households with 51,000 individual members in 28 provinces, and 9000 urban households with 32,000 members in ten provinces. Exhaustive information was obtained, not only on income but also on a great many explanatory variables. A special effort was made to measure various forms of income that seem to be inadequately covered in the official estimates of income made by the State Statistical Bureau (SSB). These include the elements of income-in-kind and subsidies that appear to be important in socialist economies such as China. The project is a large one which attempts to answer many questions. I shall try to convey here the flavour of the research by presenting a few of the interesting results, drawing on a number of research papers written by colleagues or myself.

Section 5.2 addresses the first two of the four questions posed above, comparing China with some other developing countries and providing detail on the rural–urban divide, the most prevalent form of inequality present in China. Sections 5.3 and 5.4 probe the factors behind inequality in China, considering urban wages and education respectively. Section 5.5 addresses the fourth question, regarding the effects of recent market-oriented reforms on inequality, and also provides some answers to the third. The conclusion in Section 5.6 discusses the evidence for answering the basic question posed in the title of this chapter.

5.2   THE RURAL–URBAN DIVIDE

In many developing countries there is a difference in the mean incomes of rural and urban dwellers. The explanation for this phenomenon that is normally put forward is in terms of the disproportionate political power of urban people, giving rise to 'urban bias' in policies. This section explores whether such a difference exists in China and, if so, how it can be explained.

It is clear that egalitarian China has not managed to equalise urban and rural income levels. Even the official SSB estimates give a ratio of 2.2 to 1 in favour of the urban areas in 1988. Moreover, our survey shows this to be an underestimate. Both rural and urban incomes are underestimated, but urban income more so. This is mainly due to subsidies and income-in-kind, the most important element being the housing subsidy received by urban workers from their employers. The estimate of the urban–rural income ratio obtained from the 1988 survey is no less than 2.6 to 1 (Khan et al., 1994). This is a relatively high figure by comparison with most Asian countries. For instance, national sample surveys yield ratios of 1.6 in Taiwan in 1990, 1.7 in Malaysia in 1987, 1.9 in India in 1975/76 and 2.0 in Thailand in 1988 (official statistical yearbooks).

The other remarkable fact is that the ratio in China is made worse by government fiscal intervention. The average rural household is found to make a net payment of four per cent of its income to the government. By contrast, 40 per cent of the average urban household income represents net subsidies. Some qualification is in order. First, there are difficult problems of valuation in the absence of markets; for example, the value of the housing subsidy depends on what rents would be in a free market. Second, with state ownership there is a fine line between subsidies and wages; for example, housing subsidies, often provided by state enterprises, are treated as a state subsidy but might equally be considered as part of the wage. In the absence of public intermediation, the urban–rural income ratio would be 1.5 to 1.

How is the urban–rural income gap to be understood? A market explanation springs to mind. For a long time migration in China was strictly controlled and restricted, and only in recent years have the controls partly broken down. If urban wages were competitively determined, the supply restrictions would keep the urban wage above the rural supply price. However, urban wages are in practice centrally controlled according to a national pay system. The answer to this question normally elicited from Chinese economists is in terms of the state's policy of rapid urban industrialisation. The famous price-scissors debate in the Soviet Union in the 1920s is recalled: the state has held down agriculture's terms of trade with industry in order to finance industrialisation. However, this does not seem to be a sound justification because the object of holding down the price of food is to permit lower wages in order to generate industrial profits. It is possible that the explanation is to be found in terms of the potential political power of urban people, or in efficiency wage considerations, or in govern-

Table 5.1   *Income inequality in China and other Asian countries:*
Gini coefficients

Country	Year	Urban	Rural	Total
China	1988	0.23	0.34	0.38
China	1978	0.19	0.24	
Bangladesh	1985/86	0.37	0.36	0.37
India	1967/68	0.44	0.41	
Philippines	1985	0.43	0.37	0.43
Thailand	1975/76		0.39	0.47
Taiwan	1978	0.28	0.29	0.29

Sources: Sinha et al. (1979, p. 69) for India; Zhao (1994, p. 119) for China
in 1978; otherwise Khan et al. (1994, Table 1.4).

ment leaders' view of the urban sector as a symbol of China's progress
and modernity. In favour of the first of these three explanations is
the way in which the government increased urban consumer grain subsidies in the 1980s as a response to the rise in producer prices of
grains. But it remains an unsolved puzzle.

Estimates of the extent of inequality in income per capita among
households show that inequality is higher in rural than in urban areas
(Table 5.1). This is the opposite to India (also shown in the table).
The Gini coefficient is 0.23 in urban China, low by comparison with
almost all countries. The Gini coefficient in rural areas is 0.34. However, the smaller the unit of area, the lower is rural inequality: the
relatively high Gini is not so much due to inequality among people
living together in a community as it is to the spatial variations in
income levels in such a large country (Knight and Song, 1993). There
is a problem of provincial income inequality which is ameliorated by
central government redistribution of funds from rich to poor provinces (Knight and Song, 1993) but exacerbated by restrictions on the
migration of labour, making it difficult for people to attempt to mi-
grate out of their poverty. Most interesting is the value of the Gini
coefficient when the urban and rural samples are combined (0.38).
The value at the national level is higher than either of its component
values because the rural-urban income gap contributes to overall income inequality. The overall Gini is low by comparison with many
less developed countries but nevertheless higher than in 'capitalist China'
(Taiwan, also listed in Table 5.1).

5.3 URBAN WAGES

The Chinese government has considerable power to pursue egalitarian policies with respect to urban wages. There is no effective urban labour market. The state remains the dominant employer, it lays down a national wage structure and it allocates workers to jobs, affording very little opportunity for workers to move jobs either between enterprises or between places. In the absence of market forces it is questionable whether the Chinese wage structure will resemble the productivity-related and human capital-related wage structures of market economies.

Analysing our sample of 18,000 urban employees (Knight and Song, 1994) we found the familiar inverted U-shaped relationship between earnings and age, no less than in economies characterised by more competitive labour markets. The reason for stressing seniority could well be cultural and bureaucratic rather than economic, but it has the effect of rewarding post-school human capital acquisition. Earnings are also positively related to education in urban China, but the relationship is much weaker than in most other countries. Education is better rewarded outside the state sector, where market pressures are likely to be stronger. Occupational wage differences also exist but are relatively small. It seems that government concern for equality has overriden efficiency considerations in the formulation of wage policy. It is questionable whether skills are compensated sufficiently to provide workers with the incentive to acquire skills, or for employers to economise on the use of skilled labour.

Type of ownership (of business enterprises) proved to have an important effect on pay. The collective sector paid less than the state sector, whereas the small private sector paid more than the state if there was foreign participation, but less otherwise. This suggests that a market-determined wage level would probably be lower than the state-imposed level. The national wage system ensures that the range of basic wages among provinces is very small. There are also non-basic sources of wage income, comprising bonuses, payments-in-kind, subsidies, etc. Although non-basic sources of wage income do vary regionally, the variation in total wage income is less than it would be if labour markets were competitive. The Gini coefficient for basic wages is a very low 0.20 and for non-basic wages is 0.34.

We have, therefore, a picture of an unreformed urban labour market. The institutional arrangements offer the majority of urban workers great security, provide scope for firm-specific skill formation, and enable the state to pursue egalitarian objectives. Against these advantages, the arrangements involve allocative inefficiency, they are insensitive to preferences, are inflexible in response to change, and provide limited economic incentives for individual performance. If the government decides to create an urban labour market, it needs not only to decentralise wage and employment decisions to enterprises but also to centralise the provision of social welfare, pensions and housing from enterprises.

5.4 ACCESS TO EDUCATION

The 1988 survey provides information on the educational level attained by each individual and on many of the characteristics which might explain why some people are better educated than others. It was therefore possible to estimate 'educational attainment functions' for rural and urban China (Knight and Li, 1994). Age is a crucial determinant of educational attainment. The general expansion of education since 1949, the convulsions of the Cultural Revolution, and the subsequent reactions to it are all faithfully reflected in the age group variables. Women are at an educational disadvantage but this has been gradually eroded over forty years, and the difference is negligible for urban-dwellers under 30. The greater educational disadvantage of rural women has a plausible economic explanation, in terms of their opportunity cost and future allegiance: girls are more often expected to do household work and they become part of their husbands' families.

Spatial considerations are also major determinants of educational attainment. After age, the most important factor influencing a person's education is whether he or she was born in a rural or an urban area. The average difference in the length of education of rural and urban people is five years, and it has not diminished over the decades. The reasons are to be found in the separate administrative and funding arrangements for rural and urban education, but also in terms of opportunity costs. Provincial differences are greater in the rural than in the urban areas. The rural educational attainment function of a province is strongly positively related to rural income per capita, reflecting the decentralised funding of rural public expenditures. There is no corresponding urban relationship.

As in many countries, family background was found to play a powerful role in educational access. Even in a system of educational rationing based on meritocratic criteria, educated parents can improve the educational opportunities of their children, for instance through their adoption of attitudes and acquisition of human capital in the home. We found that the educational attainment of parents does indeed assist the education of their children, and that there are often increasing marginal returns to parental education. Female education is more discretionary and thus more sensitive to the education of parents than male. The phenomenon of 'assortative mating' – the tendency for the educated to marry among themselves – in China, as elsewhere, strengthens the transmission of inequality from one generation to another.

The expansion of mass education since 1949 is greatly to be applauded. What government has not solved is the problem of unequal opportunities at the higher levels. The 'virtuocratic' selection procedures (based on social and political criteria) adopted during the Cultural Revolution created incentive inefficiency in the schools and allocative inefficiency in the economy. But the 'meritocratic' (academically based) selection procedures now in place put the children of rural-dwellers, the poor and the uneducated at an educational disadvantage.

5.5 HAVE THE ECONOMIC REFORMS INCREASED INEQUALITY?

On the face of it, there does not appear to have been a significant trade-off between growth and equality objectives. China has achieved an impressive growth rate. Assisted by a very high share of investment in national income, growth of recorded national income per capita averaged 4.7 per cent per annum between 1952 and 1985. There is more reason to believe that the planned economy suffered a trade-off between static efficiency and equality objectives; that is, between the level and the distribution of current income. Economic agents operating within the centrally planned economy have lacked incentives for efficiency. For instance, under the communes of the 1960s and 1970s, the workpoint system required peasants to be in the fields but not necessarily to work well. The urban state enterprises have been characterised by soft budgets, low efficiency and overmanning. The efficiency with which resources were allocated under central planning has been questioned. It was concern about low efficiency that propelled China into the economic reforms after the end of the Cultural Revolution.

It is difficult to measure the effect of the economic reforms on income inequality. There is a lack of consistent time series evidence.

An SSB estimate of the Gini coefficient in urban China in 1978 was 0.19 whereas our estimate for 1988 was 0.23 (Table 5.1). The same source estimated a rural Gini coefficient of 0.24 in 1978; we obtained 0.34 in 1988. It is likely therefore, that income inequality has risen in both urban and rural areas.

Consider the main policy changes. The reforms began in the rural areas in 1978, with a grass-roots disbanding of the communes and the restoration of household farm production. This produced remarkable output gains in the period 1978–85. Although land was distributed (on a leasehold basis) very equally according to the number of household members, we would expect some increase in inequality according to the effort and efficiency of household producers. The other agricultural reform was the raising of official food producer prices and the introduction of market prices for food production above quota. These changes narrowed the urban-rural income gap. Another rural reform involved encouraging the rapid growth of rural industries. Agricultural and industrial prosperity seemed to go hand-in-hand: growth of one contributed to growth of the other. A growing spatial inequality resulted from this process of cumulative causation. Supporting evidence is to be found in the data on mean rural income per capita by province. Its coefficient of variation among 26 provinces rose from 28 per cent in 1980 to 38 per cent in 1988 (Knight and Song, 1993).

In various ways the village is the most important unit in rural China. Almost all revenue for village investment and welfare must come from the village itself, in the forms of taxes on village people and production, the rent of land or factories, and the profits of village collective enterprises. In the past the main source of income differences among villages was the quantity and quality of agricultural land available to each village. The development of rural industry produced a new source of income stratification among villages. Some were more successful than others in establishing industry, and others could not industrialise at all. Some were launched into virtuous circles of economic growth while others were trapped in vicious cycles. For instance, a process of learning-by-doing can improve the quality and initiative of managers; training-on-the job can raise the quality of workers and village success can improve their attitudes and aspirations; additional village revenues can improve welfare services such as education and health, with subsequent effects on labour quality, and can raise investment in infrastructure such as irrigation, communications and transport. Village success is not fully shared with in-migrant workers, the labour market being segmented between 'insiders' and 'outsiders'. The development of one village is not necessarily at the expense of another, but it has the effect of increasing spatial inequality.

It is arguable that spatial inequality is less important than other forms of inequality: inequality among people who have little or no contact with each other is less a cause for concern than inequality amongst interacting people. Such a value judgement might be defensible if one's concern about inequality stemmed from peoples' perceptions of relative deprivation. (It appealed to Confucius, and it was recognised but rejected by Marx). The more important issue would then be the extent of poverty, as measured by absolute levels of income, in different communities. The growing inequality that can be observed among provinces in the 1980s might be defended in those terms. In 1980 no fewer than 17 of the 29 provinces had a mean income of less than 200 yuan per annum. At constant prices, in 1988 not one province fell short of this figure. Insofar as greater spatial inequality was a consequence of the policy reforms that brought rapidly increasing rural incomes, it might have been a price worth paying.

The urban reforms began in 1984. On pricing, they took the form of a dual price system, there being controlled prices applying to quota production and market prices applying to above-quota production of the same commodity. This reform might be justifiable as a step on the road from a centrally planned to a market economy but it had the side-effect of generating economic rents: rent-seekers attempted to secure goods at the controlled prices and to sell at the higher market prices. Rent-seeking activities, often by powerful people, will have increased income inequality but in ways that are likely to be concealed from household income surveys.

The other major reform was the decentralisation of some decision-taking from the planners to enterprise managers. Enterprises no longer had to transfer all their profits to government. Enterprises, especially profitable ones, were now better able to supplement the basic wages of their workers. However, these bonuses were distributed fairly equally among workers in order to minimise discontent. It seems that the enterprise reforms served more to increase wage segmentation among enterprises than to create individual incentives for workers.

With the disbanding of the communes, controls on migration to the cities weakened and there might now be a so-called 'floating population' of 27 million people in urban China (People's Republic of China, 1991, pp. 484 and 676). However, there was little evidence of urban poverty in the 1988 survey. China is quite different from many developing countries in this respect, and that is one reason why the extent of income inequality in urban China remains remarkably low. What the urban reforms after 1984 did do, however, was to raise non-basic wages rapidly, once more widening the urban–rural income gap. By 1990, the 1978 urban–rural income differential had been restored (Zhao, 1994).

It has been argued that two Chinese economies are now observable, the planned economy and the economy outside the plan (Zhao, 1994). It is the economy outside the plan that is growing in relative size. Moreover, it is in this market economy that inequality among individuals is high. Thus, for instance, the Gini coefficient among workers in the small urban private sector is 0.49, and the Gini coefficient among workers in rural (township, village and private) enterprises is 0.46. As the market economy grows in importance and the planned economy declines, so we can expect income inequality to grow further.

5.6 CONCLUSION

The 1988 household income survey has provided persuasive evidence that the analysis of surveys in China can be a very fruitful research method, despite the weakness of market forces. We found many powerful regularities which were amenable to economic explanation. Although the econometric analysis of survey data may be a necessary condition for the advancement of knowledge on income and its distribution in China, it is not a sufficient condition. The 'bottom line' is the formulation of hypotheses and the interpretation of results. Especially in an economy as divorced from the free play of market forces as China still is, this requires a thorough knowledge of institutions, interventions and political economy.

Is China egalitarian? Certainly its overall Gini coefficient is low by comparison with many developing countries. Moreover, various policy interventions have been egalitarian both in intent and in effect. Notable among these are the distribution of land to peasants and the basic pay structure of urban workers. The national pay system and restrictions on rural–urban migration severely limit inequality in the distribution of urban income. The important spatial element in rural income inequality is not readily amenable to policy and involves a trade-off between efficiency and equity. However, the heavy reliance on self-help at the rural grass-roots level implies that some villages, and larger communities, fail to launch themselves on the cumulative growth paths that others have achieved. The inequality observed in educational access partly reflects a trade-off between efficiency and equality (meritocratic promotion criteria) and partly unequal opportunities (the stress on financial self-reliance). The most glaring inequality, high even by international standards, is that between rural and urban areas. This gap would nevertheless be amenable to state pricing and spending policies should its narrowing be favoured by the government. As planning withers and markets grow in importance, so income inequality can be expected to increase. The shortest answer to the question posed in the title, then, is: in many of its objectives and some of its outcomes, extremely; in most other dimensions, not particularly; in one dimension (the rural-urban gap) not even relatively.

Notes

1. The author is grateful to Lina Song for advice and comment, and to the Leverhulme Trust for financial support of the research on which the chapter is based.

References

Griffin, Keith and Zhao Renwei (eds) (1994), *The Distribution of Income in China*, London: Macmillan (forthcoming).

Hu Jichuang (1988), *A Concise History of Chinese Economic Thought*, Beijing: Foreign Languages Press.

Khan, Azizur Rahman, Griffin, K., Riskin, C. and Zhao Renwei (1994), 'Household Income and its Distribution', in Keith Griffin and Zhao Renwei (1994).

Knight, John and Lina Song (1993), 'The Spatial Contribution to Income Inequality in Rural China', *Cambridge Journal of Economics*, (forthcoming).

Knight, John and Lina Song (1994), 'Why Urban Wages Differ in China', in Keith Griffin and Zhao Renwei (1994).

Knight, John and Li Shi (1994), 'The Determinants of Educational Attainment', in Keith Griffin and Zhao Renwei (1994).

People's Republic of China (1991), *Ten Per Cent Sample Tabulation on the 1990 Population Census of the People's Republic of China*, Beijing: State Statistical Bureau, Population Census Office (in Chinese).

Sinha, R., Pearson, P., Kadekodi, G. and Gregory, M. (1979), *Income Distribution, Growth and Basic Needs in India*, London: Croom Helm.

Zhao Renwei (1994), 'Three Features of the Distribution of Income During the Transition to Reform', in Keith Griffin and Zhao Renwei (1994).

6 Government Failures and NGO Successes: Credit, Banking and the Poor in Rural Bangladesh, 1970–90

J. Allister McGregor

6.1 INTRODUCTION

At the beginning of the 1990s the banking system in Bangladesh was described as 'in distress' (Watanagase 1990). High levels of overdue payments and defaults, especially on rural credit, had undermined the loan portfolio of most of the country's major banks to the extent that they were completely dependent upon government refinancing and on government guarantees of their viability. Given the importance placed upon the role of the banking system, or financial markets, in the development process by a diverse range of theorists, this bodes ill for the development prospects of the country as we move towards the end of the century.

Yet, during the period in which rural lending was getting the formal banking system into ever deeper trouble, a number of non-governmental organisations (NGOs) in Bangladesh were evolving successful savings and credit programmes for the rural poor. The high credit repayment rates which have been recorded by many of the NGOs, ranging up to 98 per cent for the Grameen Bank (Hossain 1988), compare extremely favourably with the low repayment performance of the banks. Equally, the effective targeting strategies of the NGOs have ensured that, unlike government programmes, the credit has tended to go to those for whom it was intended. Most of the NGO credit programmes have targeted landless men and women, usually defined as being where the household has an effective landholding of less than half an acre. Apart from the indicator of the repayment rate itself, evaluations of the NGO programmes have tended to confirm that the credit can have a beneficial developmental impact on those households which receive it (Hossain 1988, BRAC 1988, Proshika 1991).

100

While the best-known of these Bangladeshi organisations on the international development scene is the Grameen Bank, it should be emphasised that this has been but one of a number of organisations which has been working effectively with the rural poor in Bangladesh over the past two decades. The Bangladesh Rural Advancement Committee (BRAC), Proshika, the Rangpur and Dinajpur Rural Service (RDRS) and many others, provide evidence alongside the Grameen Bank that the rural poor can save, do repay loans and, generally, can make effective use of appropriate savings and credit institutions.

However, the lessons of these NGO successes have been ignored almost completely in banking policy thinking in Bangladesh. For domestic political reasons government and the civil service in Bangladesh find it extremely difficult to admit to learning anything from the NGOs. With respect to international policy advice, the fact that the international literature on financial markets has been highly theory-driven has meant that the successes of minor institutions, if recognised at all, have been difficult to assimilate (see World Bank 1989, Adams 1988).

This chapter will provide an account of the evolution of the banking system in Bangladesh over the past two decades. It will review the ways in which both the banks and NGOs have responded to changes in banking policy and will consider some of the possible reasons for the failures of the public banking system and the successes of the NGOs with respect to credit and savings. Section 6.2 concentrates on credit policy during the 1970s, Section 6.3 charts the emergence and evolution of NGO involvement in credit and savings activities, and Section 6.4 considers the policy changes during the 1980s. In the final section, 6.5, it will be argued that the policy changes undertaken in Bangladesh over the last ten years have generated a considerable gap between the banks and the rural poor and that this gap can be filled by the NGOs only to a limited extent. A danger in talking of government failures and NGO successes is of slipping into one of the current forms of development studies populism; where NGOs are seen as being good, almost by definition, to be contrasted with bad government. Every effort will be made to avoid such an unconstructive analysis and it is stressed that the overall purpose of the chapter is to assess the implications of the changes in the banking system for the development prospects of Bangladesh, and particularly for its rural poor.

6.2   THE 1970s: CREDIT FOR DEVELOPMENT AND RELUCTANT BANKS

The economic historian Rondo Cameron (1972) points out that there are two primary determinants of the qualitative and quantitative structure of the banking system in any economy. These are the demand for the services of the banks and the policies of the state towards the system. Cameron's edited volume of case-studies, which explore the relationship between the evolution of banking systems and the development of a number of mainly industrialised economies, follows the work of Joseph Schumpeter who 'regarded the banking system as one of the two key agents (the other being entrepreneurs) in the whole process of development' (Cameron, 1972, p. 6).

In this schema the banking system is identified as the main mechanism through which scarce capital resources are gathered up, multiplied through circulation, and are channelled to their most productive and entrepreneurial uses in the economy. In terms of the evolution of nation state economies, banks facilitate the dynamic of the development process. They are seen as crucial intermediary institutions in providing the necessary non-parochial link between savers and borrowers. Given concerns elsewhere in development economics about the adverse effects of local power structures on the development process (see Bhaduri, 1983; Basu, 1983; and Bardhan, 1989), this role is no less significant for developing countries now than it was for the industrialising countries of the nineteenth and early twentieth centuries.

While it is difficult to assess the relative influence of the demand for services on the banking system in developing countries such as Bangladesh, there can be little doubt about the inuence of the large degree of government involvement. The emphasis in post-war development theories upon capital and savings helped to pin-point the banking system as a key area of public development intervention. Something of the particular attitude of post-war development thinkers towards the banking systems of developing countries is caught in a quote from a small book of the era, '... the pressure of poverty in them is so intense that the need for specialised agencies for the finance of investment cannot be left safely to the processes of slow evolution' (Nevin, 1963, p. 73).

Although Bangladesh started late in the management of its own economic affairs it nevertheless quickly embarked on the development adventure. In 1972, as a keystone of its socialist economic strategy, the government of the newly independent People's Republic of Bangladesh brought the banking sector completely into public ownership. The main action with respect to rural banking was the nationalisation of the six private commercial banks which had been operating in East Pakistan. It was a matter of concern to the new government that prior to independence these banks had been little concerned with development finance and had only limited involvement in rural areas. Six Nationalised Commercial Banks (NCBs) were established in 1972 and, along with the Bangladesh Krishi Bank (BKB, an agricultural development bank) and two co-operative systems, were the major organisations involved with banking in rural areas. All of these organisations operated under the guidance and supervision of the central Bangladesh Bank.

There have been a number of minor changes in the organisational make-up of the system. As part of the liberalisation policies embarked upon in the mid 1980s, the two smallest NCBs were returned to private ownership in 1985 and adopted a narrower approach to their operations; being free of Bangladesh Bank pressure, they withdrew substantially from the rural sector. The two tier co-operative system had arisen out of the experiments carried out by the Academy for Rural Development in Comilla during the 1960s. This system, launched first on a nationwide basis as the Integrated Rural Development Programme and then renamed as the Bangladesh Rural Development Board, represented one of the mainstays of the government's approach to rural development during the 1970s. Despite its earlier successes, the Comilla model, when expanded nationwide, proved to be a less reliable vehicle for rural development than had been hoped. Organisational problems and management weaknesses ensured that by the mid 1980s the co-operative system's financial operations were in an even more calamitous state than those of the banks.

Credit has occupied a central role in the Bangladesh government's rural development strategies and its approach in the 1970s was highly interventionist in character. Development credit provision, and the conditions and procedures for its disbursement, were closely directed and controlled by the Bangladesh Bank. In accordance with the consensus of the time, credit for rural development was subsidised, although the extent of the subsidy varied considerably. Nevertheless, a minimum level of subsidy was assured by what was effectively an interest rate ceiling, set at 12 per cent for most of the 1970s. Estimates of inflation during these periods suggest that the real rates of interest imposed by this ceiling were either very low or negative; between 1976 and 1982 the real interest rate ranged between 9 and -4 per cent (Watanagase, p. 14a).

To illustrate government policy during this time we can consider one of the main development credit initiatives of the period. At the peak of the government's enthusiasm for credit as a means of stimulating agricultural modernisation, the 'Taka 100 Crore Special Agricultural Credit Programme' (SACP) was launched.[1] The SACP operated through the NCBs and BKB between 1977 and 1984, alongside what was referred to as the Normal Programme, through which credit on a commercially assessed basis was also available. The broad aim of the SACP was to expand the availability of credit in rural areas. This was to be achieved not only by increasing the quantity of funds specially earmarked and allocated for agricultural purposes, but by forcing the NCBs to become more involved in rural banking. It was also the stated intention of the programme that credit should be made more accessible for small farmers and landless share-croppers by simplifying application procedures and easing collateral requirements.

The SACP did have some major effects upon the rural credit scene in Bangladesh. Over the period it considerably increased the amount of credit moving around the countryside, regardless of how well it was targeted and whether or not it was going to be repaid. It also increased the numbers of bank branches in rural areas; between 1976 and 1984 the number of rural bank branches increased from around 900 to 3,200. As a development credit programme, however, the SACP was spectacularly unsuccessful: credit went to larger farmers rather than the targeted small and marginal farmers; the loans tended to be tied to political patronage; and the recovery of funds lent was very poor. One arguably optimistic observer calculated that 56 per cent of the amount disbursed under the SACP could not be recovered (Ahmad 1983).

Fieldwork by the author in the mid 1980s in Tangail district, with local bank workers and with SACP loan-holders, revealed that despite the policy statements, the banks at the branch level did not relax their collateral requirements. Loan applicants were required to lodge land papers of a minimum of two acres as collateral for their agricultural loans under the SACP (McGregor, 1991). This seriously thwarted the primary goal of the programme, since these collateral conditions excluded not only the landless share-croppers, but also, given the landholding distribution in Bangladesh, the majority of the country's small farmers. If a share-cropper wanted to take a loan under the SACP, the banks required that the loan be guaranteed by the landowner whose land he was cultivating.

More serious problems lay in the lending procedures which the NCBs and the BKB established for the SACP. Interviews with leading officials in the banks reveal that they were highly resentful at being directed into a lending programme of this type. Many senior bank staff felt that the government was presenting them with an insoluble contradiction. On the one hand, they were being instructed to act as a development agency disbursing targeted quantities of credit, yet on the other they were expected to continue to act as bankers, working to internationally accepted principles of prudent banking practice. Moreover, they felt that they were being forced to deal with a client population, the illiterate rural poor, with whom they were not familiar and who were equally unfamiliar with the banks and their procedures.

Demonstrating their general reluctance to be involved in the programme, and perhaps also betraying some inexperience, the banks established lending procedures which abdicated much of the responsibility for the programme. They sought to avoid a direct relationship with the target population by handing over large parts of the application and processing stages of the SACP to locally elected officials. These local political figures acted as 'brokers' between the banks and the target population. The loanee was identified by these intermediaries and his credit eligibility was determined and refereed by them. This brokerage structure of access can be interpreted as having fulfilled a number of functions, at a number of different levels, for the banks.

With respect to the needs of bank workers at branch level, this structure of access undoubtedly helped them avoid conflicts with powerful figures in the rural political economy. The work of Merilee Grindle draws attention to the 'implementability' of economic policies in developing countries (Grindle, 1980; Thomas and Grindle, 1990): the context within which a policy is to be implemented and the types of resistance it is likely to generate, both on the part of the implementors and of the people likely to be affected by it, are crucial factors in determining the 'implementability' of the proposed policy. In these terms, subsidised development credit policies in rural Bangladesh can be seen as facing substantial implementation problems.

As many observers have pointed out, credit is an important feature of the social structure of rural Bangladesh (Jansen, 1986; McGregor, 1989). This importance can be explained by considering the way in which seasonality, poverty and uncertainty interact in rural Bangladesh. The fact that large numbers of the population are affected by the fluctuations in incomes and earning power induced by the seasonality of the agrarian economy, ensures that there is a persistent demand for arrangements which can increase the flexibility of transactions over time. One of the essential features of credit is that it allows consumption or investment, which may be closely related in a household based economy, to be shifted from the future to the present. In the presence of poverty and uncertainty, however, the virtue of such arrangements is further emphasised, since the closer a household gets to a line of absolute subsistence, to the difference between survival and starvation, the greater the importance of access to a credit relationship which permits this kind of flexibility. This then must be considered in relation to the vulnerability of a large proportion of rural households to generalised or specific disasters, whether those are floods, illness and disease, or market slumps. The uncertainty which this vulnerability generates is the final ingredient which makes the credit relationship a vital aspect of economic and social organisation in rural Bangladesh. When disaster strikes, as it can do with alarming regularity, a poor household must be able to turn to someone – a relative, a neighbour, an employer, a trader – to ask for credit, with the expectation that their request will be met. However, in order to ensure that the response is likely to be positive a relationship must already have been built, within which the request for credit is understood as a possibility.

This general observation is already implicit in contemporary development economics, where the centrality of credit to interlinked markets and interlocked contracts is well recognised. The parallel literature in social anthropology on patron-client relations, which deals with essentially the same relationships as the new institutional economics, similarly recognises the importance of credit. Expanding our conception of the credit relationship beyond the economic, to encompass its political and social dimensions, we can regard credit as one of the foundations of the structures of patronage, which connect the resource wealthy to the poor in rural areas of Bangladesh. The wealthy have sufficient resources to meet requests for credit and the poor have a chronic need for it. Under the conditions described above, and considering the ways in which credit is implicated in the reproduction of the very structure of rural society, it is relatively easy to see how control over access to credit can be a source of economic and political power. As such, government programmes which are expected to intervene in rural areas, to offer open access for the poor to credit at cheap rates, can be seen as potentially problematic.

The idea that government credit is intended to break down exploitative relationships between the wealthy and the poor has occasionally been part of the formal rhetoric of development credit programmes in South Asia. However, to expect that rural bank branch managers would be able to confront powerful local figures and to challenge one of the foundations of their power base is unrealistic. An accommodation of interests is a much more pragmatic strategy for poorly supported, and often poorly protected, rural bankers and bureaucrats. The brokerage arrangement for access to loans solves the problem for bankers at branch levels. By handing over the management of access to already powerful figures in the locality it allows them to avoid conflict and goes further, in that additional resources are contributed to the patronage system which underpins the existing distribution of economic and political power. The SACP not only failed to challenge exploitative arrangements in rural areas of Bangladesh, it supported them.

With respect to higher policy levels within the banks, the implementation of the SACP demonstrated to the Bangladesh Bank that there were limits to the effectiveness of their dictates. Despite the increase in the number of bank branches in rural areas, the NCBs showed that they could be highly resistant to being pushed into practices which they perceived as not consistent with good banking principles. Regardless of the bad credit repayment record of those wealthier borrowers who did own collateral, the experience of the SACP gave no grounds to believe that the banks would be willing or able to operate as development institutions for the rural poor.

The failure of the SACP vividly illustrates what can be a chasm between policy statements and implementation in Bangladesh. Not all of the blame for the failure of the programme should be attributed to the banks. Looking at the organisation of the relationship between the banking system and its clients in a range of development credit programmes over the period, one finds that the brokerage structure of access was not uncharacteristic of development credit programmes and projects. Government policy in Bangladesh appears to have encouraged the 'brokerage' model. The rationale behind this was that banks could be assisted in their lending and recovery by relevant, developmentally dedicated organisations or officials. The kinds of 'brokers' that were employed in government sanctioned credit programmes included development project staff; the field-staff of specific government departments or specialised agencies; and even, as in the SACP, local politicians.

However, one only has to cast a glance over such arrangements from a public choice perspective to begin to identify serious problems of conflicting interests and objectives. Regardless of the interest rates which were being charged, this kind of brokerage arrangement has not been successful in Bangladesh. The co-operating agencies or departments tended to be dissatisfied with the performance of the banks, which they claimed were bureaucratic, obstructive and often downright corrupt. The banks, in turn, complained about the quality of the assistance from the mediating agencies. They claimed that the 'brokers' were inefficient, that they too were corrupt, but most importantly that they were much more interested in the disbursement of funds than in assisting the banks in the supervision or recovery of loans. The general problem was one of a confusion of responsibilities and objectives. As Jones (1982, p. 4) points out, in a principal-agent analysis of the problems of public enterprises in developing countries, 'having a plethora of objectives can be equivalent to having no objectives'. Not only did the proliferation of organisations involved in the implementation of development credit projects and programmes generate a number of different objectives, but even within the banks, the conflict between having to disburse credit as a development agency and to act as a bank caused its own internal problems.

In attempting to make the banking system perform a development role during the 1970s, the higher policy-making echelons in Bangladesh, and one suspects in many developing countries, failed to recognise the need for a clear division of responsibilities between the banks and their partners in development projects. Brokerage encouraged patronage, and to the disbursement of loans which were never intended, by either the broker or the receiver, to be repaid. Even where loans were taken in good faith, the confusions over who was responsible for recovery and general market indiscipline resulted in poor repayment performance. Credit programmes in Bangladesh during the 1970s can be regarded as having been organised to fail. Despite this, however, their poor performance represented more evidence for the general case against credit as a form of development intervention.

6.3   EMERGENCE OF THE NON-GOVERNMENTAL ORGANISATIONS

The SACP was also criticised as representing yet another example of the agricultural bias in rural credit policy in Bangladesh. As Professor Mohammad Yunus, the founder and Director of the Grameen Bank, put it, 'Could it be that the term "Agricultural Credit" was invented to cleverly by-pass the big issue: the landless poor and the women?'

(Yunus, 1981, p. 16). Given that more than half of the population of rural Bangladesh is reckoned to be effectively landless, the focus by government on lending only for crop cultivation excluded large sections of the rural population from access to formal credit. A failure to dedicate special funds to non-agricultural rural activities meant that rural artisans, labourers, traders, fishermen, and women in general, were all largely ignored by the banking system. While the activities of these groups represent an important dimension of the rural economy, they also tend to be amongst the poorest in rural communities. This exclusion of the non-agricultural poor, and the perceived obstructive and dysfunctional bureaucratism of the banking system, did much to stimulate the considerable expansion of NGO involvement in credit and savings activities in the late 1970s and early 1980s.

After the liberation war in 1971 a new generation of Bangladeshi NGOs dedicated towards working with the rural poor came into existence. Organisations such as BRAC, Proshika, RDRS, and many others, were founded on the wave of idealism and hope which pervaded Bangladesh after independence. They also drew upon the experiences of a young generation of Bangladeshis who had either been activists of some kind during the independence struggle or who had worked in relief programmes which were a necessary part of its aftermath. Each of the NGOs evolved its own philosophy as to how it would work with the rural poor. These can be roughly characterised as leaning either towards a conscientisation approach, after the work of Paulo Friere, or in the direction of material intervention in the lives of the poor.

The 'conscientising' NGOs argued that the roots of poverty in Bangladesh lay in the fact that the poor were systematically disorganised by the economic, social and political relationships within which they were caught (see BRAC, 1980, 'The Net'). Following this analysis the only long term solution to the problems of poverty in Bangladesh lay in assisting the poor to challenge the relationships which impoverished them. This could be done by increasing the awareness of poor people of these relationships and by helping them to become organised, so that they could use solidarity as a means of escaping their exploitation. The 'materialist intervention' school held that the rural poor needed more than consciousness, they needed material assistance to help them generate the incomes which were necessary to escape from their poverty. Credit was recognised as a key element in this approach, since it would allow the poor to break away from their dependence upon usurers and to invest in their own income and employment generating activities.

During the 1970s, conscientisation and credit appeared to represent two ends of a continuum in NGO approaches to their work with the rural poor in Bangladesh. While a small number of the NGOs went exclusively to one end of the continuum or the other, many organisations sought a balance between the two. At that time, however, conscientisation tended to be the dominant philosophy and credit usually represented only a small part of the overall programme of the organisation. Indeed, some conscientisation NGOs were highly wary of credit giving, because by generating individual income and employment projects it was seen as having a potentially divisive influence on group solidarity. The overall balance between the approaches began to change with the emergence and growth of the Grameen Bank Project.

The Grameen Bank Project started its life in 1976 as an action research project in the neighbourhood of Chittagong University. Much of its approach was reminiscent of lessons which were being learned in the Food and Agricultural Organisation's ASARRD Project (Asian Survey of Agrarian Reform and Rural Development), which was being operated in three areas of Bangladesh. The Grameen Bank focused specifically on the delivery of credit to the rural poor, with the underlying belief that while conscientisation was not unimportant, poor people first needed tangible assistance to work their way out of their poverty. From its beginnings in Chittagong, the Grameen Bank became a Bangladesh Bank sponsored experimental project and expanded, using existing NCB and BKB branches, to operate in Tangail and Rangpur Districts. After encountering difficulties in their working relationship, it disassociated itself from the banking system and set up as an independent organisation with its own branches. As its profile grew and as its coverage expanded in the early 1980s it became a scheduled bank with government representation on its board. In line with its original philosophy, however, its borrowing and saving members continued to hold the majority stake in the organisation.

The Grameen Bank has proven to be a successful and well-known rural development initiative for the poor in Bangladesh and as such it has had a profound influence upon the debates over approaches to rural development in the country. One aspect of this is that over the years credit has come to be regarded as an ever more important dimension of the NGO programmes, while the profile of conscientisation has declined. Many of those NGOs which did not want to operate substantial credit and savings programmes of their own sought to work with the formal banking system. However, reluctance and regulations were often combined by the banks to keep the rural poor and the

NGOs out of their branches. Even where agreements were in place, the banks still did not want the NGOs just to facilitate a relationship, they wanted them to act in the more substantial role of broker. The frustrations which resulted led many NGOs to abandon their attempts to work with the banking system and to set up their own arrangements for credit and savings.

Proshika, one of the largest Bangladeshi NGOs, represents a good example in this respect. During 1980 a detailed agreement was worked out with the BKB to provide credit to Proshika groups for minor irrigation schemes. Despite a comprehensive agreement with the bank and sympathetic officials at high levels in the banking system, it was found that large amounts of time and administrative resources were being spent by Proshika in simply attempting to make the agreement work at ground level. The processing of loans was slow and was subject to unexplained delays. Groups which were attempting to deal with the banks on their own were occasionally faced with corrupt demands for backhanders. What had started out for Proshika as a strategy of facilitation, soon degenerated into a programme of intense brokerage and after a number of years Proshika concluded that the administrative resources spent on attempting to work with the BKB work could be more effectively employed in administering their own credit arrangements. Proshika argued that the inefficiencies of the bank system were immediate and crucial obstacles to the development of their groups and members.

The establishment of their own credit and savings schemes also served to free the NGOs from accepting the rationale of the formal banking sector policy changes on interest rates. In the mid 1980s there was a move to eliminate subsidies from rural lending by disallowing projects or NGOs which worked through the banking system from offering their credit at concessional rates. NGOs such as Proshika, which had parted with the banking system, did not have to accede to this and were able to continue providing their credit at the interest rates, or rather service charges, which they thought were appropriate given the needs of the rural poor. They argued that it was hypocritical of government to aim for full cost interest rates in lending to the rural poor while there continued to be substantial subsidies to industrial borrowers.

NGO involvement in credit and savings activities accelerated in the 1980s, and with the relentless expansion of the Grameen Bank and the more recent emergence of the BRAC Bank, this shows every sign of continuing. The NGOs are now major actors in rural Bangladesh with respect to credit and savings operations for the poor, to the extent that they can almost be regarded as an alternative 'development' banking system. It should always be borne in mind, however, that in aggregate terms the amount of resources available to the NGOs for use as credit funds is small in comparison with the amounts channelled through the banking system.

It can be argued that the success of NGO credit and savings schemes has been achieved only because of the intensive amounts of staff time which are dedicated to them. While staff visits to groups of members, monitoring of borrowers and weekly repayment schedules, cost more in staff time than do normal banking procedures, to insist that this is the definitive reason for their success would be uncharitable and probably inaccurate. We must also seek some explanation of the success of these schemes which does not lie entirely with the NGOs, but also in part with their members. Some insight into this is given by looking at the organisational mechanism which lies at the heart of the Grameen Bank's good repayment record. Each Grameen Bank group consists of five members who save regularly and must conform to the Bank's strict code of discipline. They also take loans which are disbursed on a staggered basis. However, their continued access to Grameen Bank credit depends upon the group's performance; if any one of the five group members defaults on a loan for anything other than emergency reasons, then future credit for all of the group members is threatened. Peer pressure is strong and is used to ensure that all members repay their loans. This engenders a natural process of selection both when groups are being formed and as they go on. The poorest of the poor are not asked to join groups and if a group member has difficulties with repayments and is identified as a potential weakness for the group, they can be replaced. The maintenance of the relationship with the Grameen Bank is a predominant consideration. Not only does this secure continued access to credit, which as has been argued above is of great importance to the rural poor, but membership gives access to a range of other supporting services.

Although the Grameen Bank has credit as its main focus, like the other NGOs it also provides a wider range of assistance to its members. Most of the NGOs involved in credit and savings in rural Bangladesh also provide direct support for the investment activities undertaken by their members. This can include training, the arrangement of supplies of inputs and on some occasions marketing assistance. Over and above that, however, there are other dimensions to the relationship between members and the NGO which makes it of value for the rural poor. Many NGOs provide basic literacy and health training. They also lobby on behalf of their members, notably with local and central government officers. Finally, membership brings local support through the federations of groups within a village and within a locality; in some areas of rural Bangladesh this type of support network has had some effect in strengthening the voice of the rural poor in village decision-making fora.

Most of the NGOs in Bangladesh are very aware of the value of the relationship which they offer to their members. This is illustrated by a dilemma which they have had to face as they have grown throughout the 1980s. Even though they are already stretched by a very high membership to staff ratio and that there are many more poor for them to work with, there has been a reluctance in almost all of the NGOs to terminate people's membership. This has led to a discussion of graduation strategies: most NGOs have been trying to work out some system whereby long-term members continue their membership but make less intensive use of staff time and services than new members. These plans for graduation are based on the understanding that if the NGOs are to be perceived by the rural poor as being a realistic alternative to traditional local patrons then they must offer a secure relationship. This is an important lesson for all development interventions targeting the rural poor; if an organisation is going to present itself as an alternative in some ways to traditional patrons, it must be credible. In Bangladesh, neither the banks nor, indeed, short-term donor sponsored development projects have been credible in this respect. As we have noted, if anything the banks have tended to push the rural poor back into the hands of their traditional patrons.

6.4   THE 1980s: REFORMING RURAL FINANCIAL MARKETS AND THE SHIFT AWAY FROM DEVELOPMENT BANKING

Just as the interventionist policies which had provided the impetus for the SACP were being implemented, a new policy thrust was taking hold. In 1979, the Bangladesh Bank (1979) produced an important volume of papers on agricultural credit and financial markets which signalled a new attitude towards credit and the banking system. Based on the work of McKinnon (1973) and Shaw (1973), and made specific to rural development by economists at the Ohio State University, this analysis emphasised the role of free and efficient financial markets in the development of the economy. In Bangladesh, this 'financial markets' policy position was championed first by USAID, with the World Bank later taking up overall policy coordinating responsibility for the financial sector.

In order to assess a number of the propositions put forward in the financial markets literature, the Rural Finance Experimental Project (RFEP) was undertaken by USAID in Bangladesh between 1978 and 1980. As the 'experimental' of the title suggests, this project attempted to mimic the scientific method. It was designed, with control experiments, to test the viability of a number of alternative models for the delivery of credit to small farmers and it also experimented with a range of interest rates for that credit. A number of branches of each of the NCBs and the BKB participated. The results of this project have never been widely disseminated, reflecting perhaps the essentially inconclusive nature of the experiment. The ex-post evaluations of the different models of delivery tended to conclude that bank performance was variable and was vulnerable to particular social, economic and political relationships at branch level. As such, no clear prescriptions for models of delivery could be drawn readily. On the subject of interest rates, however, more forthright conclusions were advanced.

The different models operated with interest rates ranging between 12 and 36 per cent. From the observation that the interest rates at the top end of that scale did not appear to affect demand or repayment adversely, it was inferred that small farmer demand for credit in rural Bangladesh was relatively price inelastic within this range. One of the main theoretical propositions of the financial markets paradigm is that by eliminating subsidies on rural credit, banks and the rural financial market in general, would be able to operate more efficiently. Amongst other things, this would obviate the need for banks to undertake non-price rationing strategies, which it has been argued have been to the detriment of the poor (Gonzalez-Vega, 1977). The RFEP was cited as providing the evidence that the market, and small farmers in particular, in Bangladesh would be able to bear the necessary high interest rates to set financial markets off on a path towards efficiency.

Following on from this experiment, USAID embarked on the Rural Finance Project. This project, which aimed to commit $75 million over three years from 1983/84 onwards, was both more theoretical and policy oriented than its predecessor. Its stated objective was to induce the Government of Bangladesh to make a number of key financial sector policy changes, specifically to include: 'a) the revision of lending and refinance rates to reduce or eliminate subsidies on rural loans; b) the introduction of incentives and procedures to mobilize additional savings deposits and assure prompt repayment of loans' (Rural Finance Project, 1983, p. 1).

The government set about rationalising the interest rate structure and imposed a standard lending rate of 16 per cent for all institutions operating in the rural sector. This new rate did not eliminate the element of subsidy on rural credit, but it was seen as a step towards the proposed levels. The banks were also required to introduce staff incentive schemes for both savings mobilisation and repayment performance. The 1980s saw a general drive to tighten up procedures and performance in rural banking. It is perhaps ironic that, in the first instance, the 'freeing-up' of the financial markets led to the Bangladesh Bank taking a much greater degree of control over the banking system. One of its immediate tasks was to impose a degree of discipline on the banks, one aspect of which was the elimination of the specific deals for individual projects which donors and their counterpart agencies had been in the habit of negotiating with the banks. This had resulted in a rather chaotic situation where a single bank branch might have been attempting to run as many as ten different credit schemes, each with different eligibility criteria, procedures, and often with different interest rates.

This multi-programme, multi-interest rate burden was undoubtedly a major source of cost inefficiency in the banking system, but it was dealt with primarily from the interest rate perspective, rather than for organisational concerns, because multiple interest rates were seen as generating indiscipline in the financial market. Even after interest rates were made uniform at 16 per cent across the rural banking system, bank branches still found themselves with a costly burden of multiple programmes. Although they all had the same interest rates, different programmes still managed to have different application forms and lending and reporting procedures.

The overall effect of the policy changes which were set in motion in the 1980s was a slow-down in the disbursement of credit to the rural sector. Rural credit disbursements reached a peak in 1985 and thereafter sharply declined. In 1986 the government launched a major credit recovery 'action plan' in an attempt to rescue the already badly damaged rural lending system. Following the floods in 1984 and the instability of jute prices in the mid 1980s, the recovery rate for agricultural credit had fallen to 26 per cent of amounts due. The recovery action plan included the setting of targets for recovery, firmer legal sanctions against defaulters, the expanded use of loan passbooks amongst borrowers, and a programme of interest rate remission for small and medium sized overdue loans. In response to this the banks recognised that they too had to tighten up on rural lending and as such overall disbursements plummeted.

In the early 1980s, some of the banks had come to realise that their encouragement of 'brokerage' had been a major flaw in their approach to rural banking, but their response was largely negative. Rather than try to resolve the problems encountered in 'lending for development', there was a further growth in reluctance to be involved in development credit schemes at all, and especially where these were targeted at the poor. This was reflected not only in the decline in credit disbursement during the decade, but also in a distinct shift in attitude towards involvement in development banking. While in the 1970s bankers had little option but to participate in the development efforts in the newly independent Bangladesh, and were initially content to do so, that pressure was greatly decreased in the 1980s as emphasis was placed on encouraging the banks to become more commercially minded and 'professional' in their banking practices.

In 1990 the Bangladesh Bank embarked upon a second round of policy reform. Apart from (re)introducing a small amount of interest rate flexibility within pre-set bands, in an effort to encourage price competition in the public banking system, one of the most significant aspects of these reforms was a shift from refinancing to rediscounting as a means of channelling funds to the banks. The adoption of rediscounting, whereby the NCBs secure their flow of funds by rediscounting their loan portfolio with the Bangladesh Bank, was a pressure to make the banks pay more attention to the quality of the loans which they made. Under rediscounting, the extent to which the NCBs would be eligible for funds should depend more directly than in refinancing upon the quality of the loan portfolio which they hold. This required the Bangladesh Bank to issue new instructions on the classification of the condition of loans. Loans could be classified as good, overdue, sub-standard, doubtful and bad, and the proportion of each determined the quality of the portfolio. These new classification instructions increased the emphasis upon collateral as a key factor in the determination of the condition of a loan. Loans which are not backed by some recoverable form of security are more likely to fall into the sub-standard category or below. This policy shift confirms that the banks had been correct in their growing reluctance to lend to the rural poor. These are people, after all, who have little to offer by way of security and who usually do not have what, in Bangladesh, is conventionally regarded as the most bankable form of 'security' – land.

6.5 CONCLUSION: THE INCREASING GAP BETWEEN THE RURAL POOR AND THE BANKING SYSTEM

The material which has been presented above suggests that over the past two decades there has been a growing gap between the rural poor and the banking system in Bangladesh. The processes which underlie this have proceeded to the extent that we can regard the greater majority of the rural population now to have been disenfranchised with respect to the national banking system. It is beyond argument that the performance of development credit programmes in developing countries, such as the SACP in Bangladesh, has been disappointing. However, there can be differing interpretations of that failure and these lead to different policy conclusions. The view advanced above is founded upon a detailed analysis of the political economy of credit in rural Bangladesh and is set in opposition to the financial markets analysis which has informed much of the banking policy reforms in Bangladesh since the mid 1980s.

One point on which both analyses agree is that the confusion over the role of banks in development interventions was an important factor in the failure of these programmes. A conclusion which can be drawn from both viewpoints is that banks should not be forced to operate as development organisations, rather they should always be encouraged to operate as banks. This, however, need not be taken so far as to imply that they have no direct role to play in the development process. The confusion of objectives for the banks in development programmes, and the general difficulty of implementing cheap rural credit schemes, combined to make the banks in Bangladesh institute practices which placed a buffer between them and the rural poor. The practices they established, especially the brokerage structure, can be seen as one of the major reasons why development credit programmes failed so badly. The likelihood of recovering loans distributed by brokers as a form of political patronage was remote.

While this problem undoubtedly was recognised by bankers in Bangladesh their response was not to address it directly, but to retreat further from the messy business of development. This response has been more or less condoned by government, since at the same time central policy shifted from promoting the involvement of the banks in development efforts to improving the efficiency of financial markets. The financial markets analysis which has underpinned the new policy discourse encourages a view of direct development involvement as prejudicial to efficient commercial banking. The increased emphasis upon 'commercial' decision-making criteria in the banking system, including upon the importance of collateral, has meant that bankers in Bangladesh can now quite legitimately deploy efficiency arguments to relegate development considerations into a very poor second place.

A further element explaining the growing gap between the banks and rural poor is the success of the NGOs. The emergence of the Grameen Bank and the other NGOs as significant actors in the 'credit for the rural poor' scene can be seen partly as a reaction to the failures of the banking system, but the growing importance of NGOs in lending to the poor has also made it easier for banks to withdraw from even a rhetorical commitment towards the rural poor. As NGOs were bearing the particular burden of providing banking services for some of the rural poor, and as the banks had not been doing this very well anyway, it was perhaps for the best for the banks to withdraw. The successes of the NGOs allowed bankers in Bangladesh off the hook: they did not need to have too bad a conscience about the fact that they were no longer attempting to participate directly in addressing the problems of poverty which beset the great majority of the rural population of their country.

Instead of using observations of credit failures and successes in Bangladesh to institute organisational changes which would be likely to improve the implementation of development credit policy, organisational considerations have been almost completely eclipsed by the policy emphasis on interest rates. The political economy of the reproduction of poverty in rural Bangladesh makes this quite convenient, as the gap between policy statements and implementation, which the brokerage structure of access generates, suits and benefits important actors. This structure of access was popular with bankers and also with existing rural patrons, who represent the bedrock of the political structure of contemporary Bangladesh. Rather than be challenged by development credit programmes, local patrons have been strengthened by them.

The failure to explore these organisational issues has been less convenient for the rural poor. Access to credit is important for the poor in rural Bangladesh, to the extent that they are prepared to make great sacrifices to establish and maintain relationships which offer them that. The NGOs in Bangladesh have recognised this and have offered stable and long-lasting relationships as an alternative to traditional patron-client networks. They have had to do this, however, without the assistance of the banking system.

The retreat of the banks from working with the rural poor increases the burden on the NGOs and leaves an institutional gap in rural Bangladesh in which traditional money-lending practices can thrive. Apart from the question of access to credit, the lack of an appropriate and accessible banking organisation in rural areas also means that opportunities for savings mobilisation are foregone. If, as Schumpeter suggests, the banking system has a vital role to play in the development process, then the institutional gap which currently exists in Bangladesh can be seen to represent a substantial threat to the development prospects of the country.

Despite their successes it is unlikely that the NGOs can take on the full weight of responsibility for development in rural Bangladesh. The fact that they can only offer their services, including credit and savings facilities, to their members means that they are not openly accessible organisations. Moreover, their total membership is only a small proportion of the rural poor of Bangladesh and, as we have noted, the NGOs are already facing difficulties with strategies for expansion. This would seem to suggest that a combination of market and institutional failure once again raises the question of the appropriate role of government in developing countries.

As has been argued in this chapter, credit is central to the alleviation of poverty, especially in rural areas. Furthermore, the health of the banking system is also vital to the long-term development prospects of countries such as Bangladesh. Current orthodoxy sets these two issues in opposition to each other. However, closer observation of the political economy of credit interventions suggests that this need not be the case. The gap which has emerged between the banking system and the poor, who comprise the majority of the population of rural Bangladesh, must first be acknowledged by government and by development donors. It must then be the responsibility of government to embark upon policies which will stimulate the institutional innovation which is necessary to fill this gap in a way which is developmentally progressive. This will require it to undertake an analysis which is not plagued by dogma of either market or state, and which is appropriate to the conditions confronting the people of rural Bangladesh. However, in re-establishing an openly accessible national banking system which is able to serve the general needs of the development process, they would do well to learn from the failures and successes of the past, whether government or non-governmental.

Note

1. One crore equals 10 million. At 1977 exchange rates, Taka 100 crore approximately equalled US$40 million.

References

Adams, D.W. (1988), 'The Conundrum of Successful Credit Projects in Floundering Financial Markets', *Economic Development and Cultural Change*, 36, 355–367.

Ahmad, R.S. (1983), *Financing the Rural Poor: Obstacles and Realities*, Dhaka, University Press.

Bangladesh Bank (1979), *Problems and Issues in Agricultural Credit and Rural Finance*, Dhaka, Bangladesh Bank, Agricultural Credit Department.

BRAC (1980), *The Net: Power Structure in Ten Villages*, Dhaka, Bangladesh Rural Advancement Committee.

BRAC (1988), *Impact of Credit for the Rural Poor*, Dhaka, Bangladesh Rural Advancement Committee, Research and Evaluation Division (mimeo).

Basu, K. (1983), 'The Emergence of Isolation and Interlinkage in Rural Markets', *Oxford Economic Papers*, 35, 262–280.

Bardhan, P. (ed.) (1989), *The Economic Theory of Agrarian Institutions*, Oxford, Clarendon Press.

Bhaduri, A. (1983), *The Economic Structure of Backward Agriculture*, Cambridge, Academic Press.

Cameron, R. (ed.) (1972), *Banking and Economic Development: Some Lessons of History*, Oxford and New York, Oxford University Press.

Gonzalez-Vega, C. (1977), 'Interest Rate Restrictions and Income Distribution', *American Journal of Agricultural Economics*, 59, 973–976.

Grindle, M.S. (ed.) (1980), *Politics and Policy Implementation in the Third World*, New Jersey, Princeton University Press.

Hossain, M. (1988), *Credit for Alleviation of Rural Poverty: The Grameen Bank in Bangladesh*, Washington, DC: IFPRI Research Report No. 65.

Jansen, E. (1986), *Competition for Scarce Resources*, London, Norwegian University Press.

Jones, L.P. (ed.) (1982), *Public Enterprise in Less-developed Countries*, London, Cambridge University Press.

McGregor, J. A. (1989), 'Towards a Better Understanding of Credit in Rural Development. The Case of Bangladesh: The Patron State', *Journal of International Development*, 1, 467–486.

McGregor, J.A. (1991), *Poverty and Patronage: A Study of Credit, Development and Change in Rural Bangladesh*, University of Bath unpublished PhD thesis.

McKinnon, R.I. (1973), *Money and Capital in Economic Development*, Washington, DC, Brookings Institution.

Nevin, E. (1963), *Capital Funds in Underdeveloped Countries: The Role of Financial Institutions*, London, Macmillan.

Proshika (1991), *Proshika Kendra Phase IV: Joint Mid-Programme Evaluation*, Dhaka, Donor Liaison Office (mimeo).

Rural Finance Project (1983), *Project Paper 338–OD37*, Washington DC, USAID.
Shaw, E.S. (1973), *Financial Deepening in Economic Development*, London and Oxford, Oxford University Press.
Thomas, J.W. and Grindle, M.S. (1990), 'After the Decision: Implementing Policy Reforms in Developing Countries', *World Development*, 18, 1163–1182.
Watanagase, T. (1990), *Banks in Distress: The Case of Bangladesh*, Washington, DC, IMF Working Paper (unpublished manuscript).
World Bank (1989), *World Development Report 1989*, Oxford and New York, Oxford University Press.
Yunus, M. (1981), *Rural/Agricultural Credit Operations in Bangladesh*, Dhaka, Grameen Bank Paper No. 14.

7 Distress Sales and Rural Credit: Evidence from an Indian Village Case Study

Wendy Olsen

7.1 INTRODUCTION

Both before and since Independence, concern has been expressed about the plight of India's impoverished smaller farmers. This chapter reports on a village case study of one aspect of their problems: the type of post-harvest 'distress sales' of crops, at low prices, that occur due to farmers' indebtedness to their local moneylenders (see *inter alia* Nadkarni 1980, Rudra, 1983). The study also surveys exchange relations more broadly, taking into account sales of produce, food purchases, and credit relations. Data for the study, obtained from informal discussions and questionnaire interviewing with local inhabitants, is set against both neoclassical and political-economy explanations of economic behaviour.

For our purposes we may define a 'distress sale' as the sale of a foodcrop at harvest time which the household buys back later in the year at a much higher price. The forced sale of assets arising from economic crisis is of related interest, but was not an issue pertinent to the households surveyed in this study. Gore (1978) captures the idea of distress sales nicely, claiming that price discrimination against post-harvest sellers and the high prices these poor indebted households had to pay on purchasing subsistence foods during the rest of the year, was a serious cause of rural inequality. This study is intended to assess whether, how, and to what extent such a process was occurring in 1986/87 in one area of rural Andhra Pradesh, India. The findings, reported in Sections 7.3 and 7.4, are mixed. On the one hand, there were no distress sales of paddy (the dietary staple), and most producers actually stored and ate their own paddy, although generally it was not enough to meet their consumption needs. On the other hand, groundnut (a cash crop) was produced, and here distress sales were prevalent. In particular, indebtedness of small farmers to merchants made them susceptible to several forms of exploitation by the merchant money-lenders. The debt acted as an informal tie between farmer and merchant money-lender, resulting in the post-harvest sale of groundnut production at low prices, higher retail prices for provisions than those charged to untied buyers or in towns, and a reduced freedom to borrow from other lenders because of the risk of losing the tied merchant's favour. Generally, 'tied' relationships with these characteristics were more common in remote areas where competition was weakest.

The findings of this study, and particularly the qualitative differences in credit relationships between classes of individuals in the two villages, reveal much about exchange relations in this part of Andhra Pradesh. Despite their diversity and complexity it is still possible to draw some very interesting conclusions from a one-year study of two villages. These findings tend to support the theoretical claims made by authors such as Bhaduri (1983 and 1986), Basu (1983 and 1986), and Braverman and Stiglitz (1982).

This chapter is set out in the following manner. Section 7.2 gives background to the case study itself, profiling the participants involved in production and exchange. Section 7.3 presents details of the seasonal timing of crop sales, covering both paddy and groundnuts, as well as some related data on credit transactions. In section 7.4 the findings are compared with predictions of relevant theoretical models. Basu's (1983, 1986) model of isolation of economic agents, and of the nature of the power relationships arising in such conditions, appears most appropriate. Bardhan (1989) has labelled such relationships *clientelisation,* pointing out that such behaviour may develop alongside capitalism, having originated in pre-capitalist conditions. Along with her and other authors of village studies (inter alia J. Harriss 1982; B. Harriss 1984, 1990) we find that an emphasis on the power of money-lending merchants in the villages can shed much light on rural social relations. Finally, Section 7.5 summarises the main findings of this case study of distress sales.

7.2   CLASS, PRODUCTION, AND DEBT

The study took place in the dry Deccan plateau of central and southern India in two villages, Tavalam and Nimmanapalle (hereafter TVM and NPL) in western Chittoor District of Andhra Pradesh, about 100 miles northeast of Bangalore, Karnataka. TVM is smaller than NPL and further from the main road and from towns. NPL had many buses and cars going through it and was sufficiently important to boast a bank, a small hospital, several shops and local government offices. Consequently, the two villages represented a mild contrast, with one being more easily accessible, busier and larger than the other. Each village consisted of several hamlets, some along the road and others up to 2 km away from any road. There was a bus serving both TVM and NPL.

The annual rainfall is typically only about 750 mm per year. However, during the period of study (April 1986 to May 1987) there was even less rain than usual. A drought of historic proportions had begun the year before, although by 1988 the rains had returned to their usual level. Rain is concentrated in the months of September to November, with a few showers in June and July that normally allow sowing to take place. The climate is thus unimodal with the main harvest in late December.

Less than one quarter of the villagers' land is irrigated, and most irrigated land is sown with paddy yielding at least one crop per year. A few plots were sown with tomatoes, but this was a rare and risky innovation. The unirrigated land (dry-land) was put under groundnuts. Normally, this main crop was interspersed with sorghum and beans, a drought-resistant, nutritious mix that replenishes the soil with nitrogen. The average landholding in NPL was 2.6 acres, and in TVM 2.2 acres, although average figures like these belie great inequality in owned holdings, and can therefore be misleading.[1]

For the purposes of this study, the households have been classified into seven groups according to the following criteria:

(1) whether or not they owned land;
(2) whether the main occupation of household members was agricultural or not;
(3) what the usual pattern of labour use was (employer, own-farm worker, or employee).

The classes are:

Workers (*kuulies*, in Telugu), who performed manual tasks for cash wages. Landless and landed workers are treated separately within this class in the analysis that follows.
Farmers (*ryotulu*), who performed manual work on their own land but did not normally work as wage labour for others. These households were *petty commodity producers* (PCP in the tables that follow), not peasants. They used their own and others' labour but did not work as kuulies.

Capitalist landlords[2] (*bhuuswamivaari*), who would do no manual labour in the fields. They hire labour for all field operations.

Merchants (*vyaapari* or *shetty*), dealers in goods produced by others including both wholesale and retail trading households.

Salaried, salary-dependent households.

Others, a mixed group including several types of petty commodity producers whose main income was non-agricultural, e.g. barber, clothes-washer, teashop owner.

Tables 7.1 and 7.2 illustrate some important differences between these classes. In particular, the class of petty commodity producing farmers is a very important class of producers (accounting for 46 per cent of paddy and 54 per cent of groundnut production). They nevertheless sold only 11 per cent of their paddy, preferring to keep it for domestic consumption. However, their groundnut sales comprised 53 per cent of reported sales of that crop, with landlord and merchant sales making up the remainder.

The information in these tables indicates the high degree of commercialisation found in the villages. We can summarise the degree of commercialisation by constructing summary measures of market involvement, and these comprise Table 7.3. The measures quantify the purchases of each crop relative to use, sales relative to output, and year-end stocks relative to use for each of the classes. Quantities of paddy and groundnuts have been converted into a monetary value for the purposes of aggregation using a ratio of 9 to 2, reflecting their approximate market values of Rs. 9/kg. for groundnut kernels and Rs. 2/kg for raw paddy.

Table 7.3 indicates that purchases represent a high proportion of use in all categories except the landlord class. The data also demonstrate the reluctance of smaller farmers (workers and PCP farmers) to sell their crop. In fact, small farmers generally consume their own paddy as rice and thus rarely sell any of their production. Sales of groundnut explain why a third of their total output is reported as 'sold' in Table 7.3. As one may expect the landlords and merchants sold far more than they produced; their sales figures included rent and purchased produce. Stock levels as the survey ended were still high for these relatively wealthy producers (over 150 per cent of their output levels, on average), but much lower for PCP and worker-farmers.

This paper focuses on two classes in particular: the PCP farmers and merchants. In exchange relations, these classes interact more frequently and more intensively with each other than with other classes. In particular, landlords did not lend to PCP farmers, or sell them goods,

Table 7.1 *Summary data on sample households by class*

Class	Households in survey	Land owned per Hh (acres)[a]	Proportion irrigated (%)[a]	Paddy harvest per Hh (kg)[b]	Groundnut harvest per Hh(kg)[c]
Landless workers	17	0	—	211	46
Workers with land	11	2.3	15	637	204
PCP farmers[d]	21	4.4	19	1378	594
Capitalist landlords	2	13.8	33	6955	1565
Merchants	6	3.1	32	1300	467
Salaried households	5	1.2	28	360	164
Other/Artisans	9	1.5	26	33	70

Notes
[a] These refer to all households in NPL and TVM, as enumerated in late 1986.
[b] This refers only to sample households.
[c] The groundnut figures here are in 'pods', i.e. groundnut in the shell.
[d] PCP = petty commodity producers. See Crow, et al. (1988) pp. 107–8, 139, for a justification of using this term instead of peasants.

Table 7.2 *Class proportions of total paddy and groundnut output and sales*

Class	Paddy output (%)	Groundnut output (%)	Paddy sold (%)	Groundnut sold (%)
Landless workers	6	3	2	2
Workers with land	11	10	0	6
PCP farmers	46	54	11	52
Capitalist landlords	22	14	76	13
Merchant	12	12	11	22
Salaried	3	4	0	3
Other	0	3	0	2
All classes	100	100	100	100

Table 7.3 *Commercialisation proportions by class (groundnuts and paddy combined), 1986/87*

Class	Purchases as a proportion of use (consumption) and sowings) (%)	Sales as a proportion of output (%)	Year-end stocks as a proportion of use (consumption and sowings) (%)
Landless workers	80	30	4
Workers with land	89	29	55
PCP farmers	72	60	39
Capitalist landlords	42	159[a]	176
Merchant	1238	166[b]	185
Salaried	104	17	52
Other	84	18	10
Average	178	52	46

Notes
[a] Includes de-stocking from previous year's sales.
[b] Includes resale of purchased grain and groundnuts.

as merchants did. In fact there is a social gulf between merchants and landlords in these particular villages which has not been emphasised in the theoretical literature. One reason for this is that in much of northern India landlords are more likely to be the major local money-lenders, whereas the Reddy and Brahmin landlords of upland Andhra are primarily agriculturalists. Where they do lend, it is to their workers, and this relationship was not our focus. Table 7.4 illustrates the debt situation in the villages.

   The debts reported by respondents included all outstanding loans plus each loan taken during the study year. Over Rs. 100,000 of re-payments were recorded, as against Rs. 303,500 in loans. A single merchant in TVM was the source of over one-third of the reported debt there. Loans in-kind were a smaller part of the credit market than expected: there were 100 small kind-loans, with an average total borrowed of 43 kg of paddy and 5 kg of rice per household over the full year, versus 394 cash loans with a total debt averaging over Rs. 4000 per household. Indebtedness rose from 2100 Rs./Hh to 3800 Rs./Hh among agrarian households between the pre-harvest period (December 1986) and the post-harvest period that followed. The break-down of debt by class and by purpose reveals that many loans were for consumption purposes, while PCP farmers, landlords, and a few

Table 7.4   *Principal borrowed* by class of borrower
(*June 1986 to May 1987*)

Class	No. of Sample Households	Total Principal (Rs.)	Per cent of Total Debt	Principal Per Household (Rs.)
Worker	17	15,915	5	936
Worker+	11	30,803	10	2,800
PCP farmers	21	115,245	39	· 5,488
Capitalist landlords	2	31,500	10	15,750
Merchant	6	77,300	25	12,883
Salaried	5	17,105	6	3,421
Other	9	15,655	5	1,739
All	71	303,523	100	4,275

Notes
[a] Figures include principal borrowed before the survey began if still outstanding.
[b] Sample sizes are printed here for reference; they are the same throughout the tables of this chapter.
   The second CF landlord household is a composite.

others also took out larger loans for production or investment purposes. The average size of a provisions loan was Rs. 220, versus Rs. 760 for a cultivation loan, Rs. 6500 for a loan for a house, Rs. 1900 for marriage costs and Rs. 3800 for a pump-set. Apart from a branch of the Indian Bank in NPL and other banks further away, private money-lenders were a major source of loan finance. These money-lenders were also the village merchants and would sell provisions and other goods to the villagers. Petty commodity-producing farmers in NPL got 14 per cent of their principal from merchants and 34 per cent from the Indian Bank; in TVM, by contrast, PCP farmers got 63 per cent of their principal from merchants and only 4 per cent from the Indian Bank (Olsen, 1991). Lending among members of the extended family and friends and from employers, made up the rest of the loans recorded.

7.3   SALES AND SEASONS

With this background in mind we can now consider the seasonality of sales of the two main crops, paddy and groundnuts. The magnitude of landlords' stocks of paddy far exceeds that of other classes, while PCP households had very low stocks (Table 7.3). Landlords and merchants are big vendors of surplus paddy, while PCP farmers sold no paddy during the survey. There were in total only 29 paddy sales among the sample during 1986/87.

Merchants and landlords also dominated the sale of groundnuts, but with two qualifications. First, PCP farmers also sold a lot of groundnuts and there are many more farmer households than there are landlord households. Most of these sales were to local merchants who were in a position to take advantage of seasonal price rises, and indeed they distributed their sales of groundnuts throughout the year. By contrast, all the workers and 22 out of 24 PCP farmers had sold their groundnuts, apart from seed for the next year, within one month of harvest in 1987 (Olsen, 1991, p. 178). The costs and benefits of groundnut storage are very different for the two classes. Neither face significant storage losses, nor any loss in quality, apart from some drying-out of the groundnuts. However, merchants had access to bank credit at roughly 1 per cent interest per month, whereas most PCP farmers borrowed from merchants at the going rate of 2 per cent per month. The cost of tying up cash in stocks is a substantial part of the costs of storage. Whether it is an explicit cost, as in the case of merchants, or an implicit one, as in the case of farmers, who hold their own produce and 'pay' an opportunity cost for lost access to the corresponding cash, the effect on cash-flow is the same.

In summary, merchants could realise substantial profits from groundnut storage whereas PCP farmers were unable to do so and, instead, sold at a time of year when prices were lowest. The claim made here about the different costs of credit to each class is based on detailed measurement and analysis of credit transactions in the villages. One important facet of the credit market is that the seasonal concentration of borrowing by different classes is complementary. Specifically, merchants borrow mostly just after the harvest; PCP farmers mainly during the pre-harvest growing season; and workers (especially those without land) borrow most in the hot season when there are no crops planted on the dry-land.

Even more important, however, is the difference in sources of loans for each class, and hence the interest paid. In all cases local people conceived of interest on a monthly, not annual, basis. They described the banks' lending rate as 1 per cent per month, although there were actually various lending rates such as 11.5, 12.5, and 14.0 per cent per year. Out of 394 loans recorded, 41 were from banks at these rates, and 50 were from merchants at 2 per cent per month. Over 100 loans from merchants carried no interest, as did 114 other informal-sector loans from friends or employer-landlords. In most cases credit was more costly for PCP farmers borrowing from merchants than for wealthy households borrowing from banks or from each other.

Starting from the brief description given above of paddy and groundnut sales and storage, one can develop an explanation of strategies in terms of agents rationally choosing a profit-maximising sale date, given their costs and expected gains from storage. The determinants and constraints differ by class and by crop. In the case of paddy, merchants and landlords stored paddy, releasing it for sale later in the year, realising price gains in so doing. Smaller farmers did not sell paddy; they used it at home and bought rice to make up the gap between production and consumption. The availability of wage labour and cash from sale of groundnuts, along with the availability of cheap rice (about one-third below the market price) from a government rice subsidy scheme, effectively alleviated any need for distress sales of paddy.

In the case of groundnuts, merchants (and to a lesser extent landlords) bought, stored, and sold the surplus. They expected price rises of 2–4 per cent per month for up to seven months after harvest, and were not averse to the risk of unexpected price movements because they had a variety of other income sources which could offset a loss. PCP farmers also anticipated groundnut price increases, but had a higher marginal cost of credit (2 per cent per month) and were averse to taking risks with groundnut stocks, because it was almost their only source of cash income. As a result PCP farmers did not store groundnuts in large quantities. However, this is only part of the story since we have not considered the issue of interlocking transactions, and as a result we have ignored the social side of exchange relations, which play a crucial part in village trade.

7.4 ISOLATION, COMPULSION AND CLIENTELISATION

Most of the village merchants did not operate on an anonymous basis. Instead, offers made were part of on-going relationships. For instance, when a merchant cycled out to a hamlet and offered Rs. 195 per 41 kg bag for a particular farmer's groundnut crop, he had a clear picture in mind of that farmer's past borrowings from him and/or other merchants, and he knew very well to whom the farmer sold his crop in past years. That merchant may well have sold household rice and other goods to the farmer, and may hope in future to sell him fertiliser, concrete and luxury goods. The price offered is unique to this relationship.

The absence of anonymity is critical to the outcomes observed here, as in other studies of distress sales. Bhaduri's (1973) description of the landlord-sharecropper relationship in West Bengal in the 1960s and 1970s (and analysed further in Bhaduri, 1983), emphasised the lack of access to outside markets (i.e. to competitive anonymous offers) as crucial to the power of a landlord-lender over his sharecropper-borrowers. Although Bhaduri's model does not fit the study area very well, it encourages us to examine the possibility that the personal relationship between lender and borrower shapes the kind of influence that the former can have over the latter.

Basu (1983) has described some aspects of such relationships and points out that the relative isolation of people in remote villages of India makes it possible for different prices to reign in different areas. These multiple prices across space are associated with the interlinking of transactions in several markets. The loan to a sharecropper is a classic example where the lender ensures repayment by claiming an extra part of the crop as interest or amortisation (see Braverman and Stiglitz, 1982, and Stiglitz 1986). Applying Basu's model of isolation, the lender reduces the *potential risk of default* by choosing whom to lend to, instead of making a blanket offer to lend (Basu, 1983, p. 265). In such circumstances it may be hard to measure price differentials and price discrimination because of implicit charges and the inclusion of subtle conditions in a particular transaction. In our area, for instance, a few loans to workers involved a promise that the landlord would have first claim to the worker's time in the busy seasons. This would not be reflected in an explicit wage differential, but definitely implied a cost to the worker.

In the villages studied, there was a mixture of competitive forces and isolation. On the one hand, the bank in NPL offered an alternative to merchant credit, and competing merchants would travel to both NPL and TVM from their homes up to 20 miles away at harvest time, looking for groundnuts to buy. On the other hand, particularly in TVM, the competition among merchants was limited mainly to one season and there was strong long-term *clientelisation* of PCP farmers by merchants. In using this term we adopt Bardhan's (1989) description of the way wealthy elites try to protect their very profitable, and superficially helpful, relationships with workers and tenants. In this study, each merchant had certain households to whom he would lend money, sell provisions (such as rice, oil and lentils) and purchase groundnuts. In addition, merchants would offer loans for emergencies and thus earned the reputation of 'protector' among some villagers. However, these personal, long-term relationships did not necessarily imply cheap credit; on the contrary, 2 per cent was the accepted monthly interest rate within the relationship. There was also a feeling that the tied households paid above the usual price for their retail rice and lentil purchases.

Behind this relationship was an implicit threat that if a borrower defaulted, or sold groundnuts to another merchant against their usual merchant's wishes, then the 'tied' merchant would withdraw further loan services. Some respondents also mentioned that the merchant's sons would physically threaten them if there was a disagreement, but matters did not reach such a pitch during the period of study. Instead, there was wide acceptance of the situation. Basu (1986) modelled this type of relationship theoretically and proved that under reasonable assumptions, a landlord (or lender) could coerce a labourer (or, in our case, a borrower) into accepting a deal that made the labourer or borrower worse off, merely by announcing that if the client did not accept his terms, the merchant would no longer trade with that household, *nor with a third party* (or group). Fay (1987) has pointed out in a related context that in such situations, although there may not be any conscious feeling that one party exerts power over the other, there is 'subtle manipulation' and coercion in such relationships. Along similar lines, Basu (1986) demonstrates that utility maximisation does not necessarily imply voluntary exchange. Thus, even in a competitive market, conditions may be such that lenders are in a position of power. Borrowers can be forced to sell their crop, or coerced into selling it at a particular time. Sarap (1988) found precisely this kind of interaction in Orissa, India. After calculating implicit interest rates, including price discrimination against certain borrowers, Sarap found that tied borrowers paid a significantly higher (implicit) interest rate than did untied borrowers. This also occurred in the villages of the present study, though calculation of implicit interest rates was not possible because so many merchants' sales were not complete when the study ended.

Implicit in the foregoing discussion is the phenomenon of 'interlinked transactions' – where exchange in one realm of trade ties the participants to the exchange of other, and most often unrelated, goods and services. Due to some practical difficulties that arose in recording interlinked transactions, the types of linkage reported may appear crude and limited, although the results do indicate the extent and importance of the phenomenon. In particular, tying of loans to groundnut purchases was observed in respondents' reports relating to both the 1986/87 crop year and to past years. Thirty-eight per cent of PCP farmers in the survey sold to their moneylender in 1986/87 and in 1985/86, and 33 per cent reported selling to that money-lender every year. All these cases were in TVM, where 31 loans totalling Rs. 22,000, or 52 per cent of all principal borrowed by PCP farmers, came from the same merchant who bought their groundnuts every year. In a few cases this relationship allowed the farmer to get a loan at no interest, but it also implied a commitment to sell groundnuts to that merchant on demand. As a consequence, the timing of sale was dictated by the merchant, always at post-harvest prices, enabling the merchant to realise a gross profit on the crop upon resale later in the year. This tie was also linked to farmers buying foods and other goods from the same merchant. This practice was common and in NPL a lot of interest-free loans went to retail customers. About 80 per cent of all worker households and 52 per cent of PCP farmer households borrowed on these terms at some point in the year (Olsen, 1991). In three out of every four cases, the borrowings of PCP farmers in TVM from their provisions merchant were at a monthly interest rate of 2 per cent. In the busier and more competitive NPL all such loans were (explicitly at least) interest-free.

The strong exchange ties found in TVM reflect a type of social relation in which the merchant was able to exert influence over the farmers' decisions about groundnut sale timing. This arrangement was advantageous to the merchant on a number of counts. First, the tied PCP farmer could not easily arrange to sell to an outside merchant for fear of losing the local merchant as a creditor and as a source of provisions and inputs in the future. The fact that banks do not offer loans for consumption increased the small farmer's reliance on the moneylender. Once indebted to the moneylender, the PCP farmer is then tied to that lender and must sell the crop of groundnuts whenever the moneylender requests it. Consequently, the moneylender may purchase at low prices and can plan on the flow of groundnuts from all the tied borrowers. Thus, although lending was not in itself a major source of income to every merchant, it created several other profit-making opportunities, both short and long term, and limited the ability of other merchants to compete directly with the tied merchant on provisions, wholesaling or credit.

The views of local people about merchants also varied considerably. At one extreme we met PCP farmers in TVM who had rejected the dominant money-lender's patronage. They had resented his 5 per cent per month interest rate in the past and had broken off relations with him and lost access to all his services as a result. At the other extreme, one PCP farmer in TVM said that the money-lender was his *dikku* (patron, lord, protector), acting as a refuge in bad times because he could approach him for a loan even at odd times or in emergencies. Many families pointed out that the great advantage of merchant-lenders over the banks is that they provide loans for consumption purposes, such as food, festivals, health care, marriages and so on. The local bank had been very lenient about repayments during the drought, so the repayment demands of different lenders were not the main issue.

In the survey year, no lender foreclosed on a loan even though 'bonds' had been written out and kept by merchants for virtually all of their loans to farmers. Merchants did not want to foreclose, partly because of the legal costs involved and the loss of goodwill, and partly because instead of expanding their own landholding they wanted to use a steady stream of profits from trade to finance *other* investments. Only thus could they spread their risk across several activities. Finally, they preferred to exploit labour indirectly through storage and trade, rather than get too involved in the direct employment of wage labour or tenants.

7.5 CONCLUSION

Four main issues arise from this Indian case study of distress sales. First, there were no distress sales of paddy in the villages studied in 1986/7 because of the convergence of several particular circumstances. Specifically,

(a) the availability of cash from groundnut sales in this cash-cropping area;
(b) wage labour possibilities and a rice subsidy scheme which made it easier to pay for purchases of rice;
(c) competitive forces in the credit market, which had pushed the informal interest rate down from 5 per cent per month to 2 per cent per month, inhibiting merchants from blatantly extorting cash from their borrowers,

(d) merchants' unwillingness to coerce PCP farmers into paddy distress sales because they preferred to retain the long-term stream of trading profits from other dealings with clientelised farmers.

Second, although competitive processes were observed, such as the competition between banks and merchants for customers, there were still personalised long-term relationships in which some merchants held power over their clients, mainly petty commodity producing farmers.

Third, distress sales of groundnuts were sufficiently common to be regarded as a major feature of local exchange relations. Some tied farmers sold every year to the same merchant who sold them food and loaned them money. The provision of loans, particularly for consumption purposes, was an effective way of locking lenders into the exchange of groundnuts and provisions at prices that were beneficial to the merchant money-lender. Since there were implicit costs attached to breaking off this relationship, the borrower would reluctantly continue with what may appear to be an inequable relationship. J. Harriss (1987), following Bharadwaj (1974, 1985), suggests that this type of tie leads to *compulsive involvement* in markets and frequently accompanies the clientelisation process, particularly among isolated producers in remote rural areas.

Fourth, the roles, relationships and decision-making processes of respondent households from *each* social class reflected their heavy involvement in, and awareness of, the capitalist economy that has now permeated the villages. Within this partially competitive capitalism, power relations reflected the extremely high degree of inequality. While this village case study has revealed some qualitative and quantitative findings about one area of upland Andhra Pradesh, it has also revealed that the concept of 'remote' or 'backward' villages, totally isolated from wider markets, which figured so prominently in models such as Bhaduri (1973, 1983), did not fit in these villages in the mid-1980s.

Notes

1. Details of the sample and its construction can be found in Olsen (1991, 1992).
2. 'Landlord' is used throughout this chapter to refer to those local farmers who were mainly employers. It should be stressed that by Indian standards their holdings are relatively small (5 to 30 acres). The landlords in the study area were highly entrepreneurial in their economic behaviour. They were by no means semi-feudal as that term has been used by Bhaduri (1973).

References

Bardhan, K. (1989) 'Poverty, Growth and Rural Labour Markets in India', *Economic and Political Weekly*, 25 March, 24:12, pp. A21–A38.

Basu, K. (1983) 'The Emergence of Isolation and Interlinkage in Rural Markets', *Oxford Economics Papers*, Vol. 35, pp. 262–280.

Basu, K. (1986) 'One Kind of Power', *Oxford Economic Papers*, Vol. 38, pp. 259–282.

Bernstein, H., Crow, B., Mackintosh, M. and Martin, C., eds. (1990) *The Food Question: Profits Versus People?*, Earthscan, London.

Bhaduri, A. (1973) 'A Study in Agricultural Backwardness Under Semi-Feudalism' *Economic Journal*, March, pp. 120–137.

Bhaduri, A. (1983). *The Economic Structure of Backward Agriculture*, London, Academic Press.

Bhaduri, A. (1986) 'Forced Commerce and Agrarian Growth', *World Development*, Vol. 14, No. 2, pp. 267–272.

Bharadwaj, K. (1974) *Production Conditions in Indian Agriculture: A Study Based on Farm Management Surveys*, Occasional Paper No. 33, Cambridge, Cambridge University Press.

Bharadwaj, K. (1985) 'A View of Commercialisation in Indian Agriculture and the Development of Capitalism', *Journal of Peasant Studies*, 12:1, pp. 7–25.

Braverman, A. and Stiglitz, J.E. (1982) 'Sharecropping and The Interlinking of Agrarian Markets', *American Economic Review*, Vol. 72, pp. 695–715.

Chambers, R. et al., eds (1981) *Seasonal Dimensions of Rural Poverty*, London, Frances Pinter.

Crow, B., Thorpe, M., Bernstein, H., Byres, T., Elson, D., Harris, L., Humphrey, J., Johnson, H., Rhodes, E., and Wield, D. (1988) *Survival and Change in the Third World*, Polity Press and Blackwells, Oxford.

Fay, B. (1987) *Critical Social Science: Liberation and its Limits*, Polity Press, Oxford.

Gore, C. (1978) 'The Terms of Trade of Food Producers as a Mechanism of Rural Differentiation', *Bulletin of the Institute of Development Studies*.

Harriss, B. (1984) *State and Market: State Intervention in Agricultural Exchange in a Dry Region of Tamil Madu, South India*, New Delhi, Concept Publishing.

Harriss, B. (1990) 'Another Awkward Class: Merchants and Agrarian Change in India' Ch. 8 in Bernstein, et al., eds (1990).

Harriss J. (1982) *Capitalism and Peasant Farming: Agrarian Structure and Ideology in Northern Tamil Nadu*, Bombay, Oxford University Press.

Harriss J. (1987) 'Capitalism and Peasant Production: The Green Revolution in India', Chapter 31 in T. Shanin, ed. (1987), *Peasants and Peasant Societies*, Oxford University Press, Oxford.

Nadkarni, M.V. (1980) *Marketable Surplus and Market Dependence: A Study of a Millet Region,* Delhi, Allied Publishers.

Olsen, W. (1991) 'Distress Sales and Exchange Relations in a Rural Area of Rayalaseema, Andhra Pradesh', Unpublished D.Phil. thesis, Oxford University.

Olsen, W. (1992) 'Random Sampling and Repeat Surveys in South India',

Ch.4 in S. Devereux and J. Hoddinott, eds, *Fieldwork in Developing Countries,* London, Harvester Wheatsheaf.

Rudra, A. (1983) 'Non-Maximising Behaviour of Farmers: Sales', *Economic and Political Weekly*, Vol. 18, No. 2.

Sarap, K. (1988) 'Transactions in Rural Credit Markets in Western Orissa, India', *Journal of Peasant Studies*, 15, pp. 83–107.

Stiglitz, J.E. (1986) 'The New Development Economics', *World Development*, Vol. 14, No. 2, pp. 257–265.

8 Farm Mechanisation and Rural Development in the Philippines

John Lingard

8.1 INTRODUCTION

The green revolution has had a dramatic impact on incomes and food supplies in many less developed countries (LDCs) in Asia. The new technology of modern seed varieties, fertilisers, agrochemicals and irrigation has facilitated change in rural areas providing opportunities for self-sustaining economic growth and reduced poverty. However, the overall effect depends on the economic and political background into which the technology is introduced and, in evaluating the impact of the green revolution, it is necessary to distinguish between the technology itself and the environment into which the technology package is introduced.

The green revolution's impact on food production is a function of the area sown to high yielding varieties (HYVs) and associated yield increases. Shorter growing periods facilitate multiple cropping. About 50 per cent of the rice area in the world (72 million ha) is now sown to HYVs; there are over 50 million hectares of wheat planted with HYVs and improved sorghum, hybrid maize and beans are being planted.

Rice yields for the whole of Asia averaged 3.3 tonnes/hectare in 1988 compared to 1.71 tonnes/hectare in 1946 and the average annual growth rate of output over the period is 1.05 per cent. Output increases can be attributed to input increases, particularly land, irrigation water, fertiliser and labour and it has been estimated that, of the output increase, one-third is due to increased fertiliser use, a third to irrigation and a further third to improved varieties. As a result of higher output, HYVs generally lead to increased labour demand and thus, *ceteris paribus*, exert an upward pressure on rural wages and employment. Nevertheless, these effects can be masked by in-migration, population increases and the use of labour-saving mechanisation. In the absence of technical change, the landless would have been worse off but 'the employment effects of the mechanical technology and its output effects are in general unknown' (Pinstrup-Andersen and Hazell, 1985).

It is certainly the case that the variability of world food production around this upward trend has increased recently and may be due, at least in part, to the sensitivity of HYVs to weather, disease and fertiliser and water availability (Pinstrup-Anderson and Hazell 1985). Indeed, the introduction of HYVs into LDCs has not occurred without criticism. The technology's sternest critics (see for example Griffin, 1979 and Pearse, 1980), have pointed to its large-farm bias. It is argued that large farmers have differential and privileged access to the required inputs compared to smaller producers. In addition, market forces put downward pressure on output prices, upward pressure on input prices and these factors may lead to increased rents and crop-shares, displacement of tenants and reduced rural employment. Economic benefits of HYVs to the poor arise mainly via lower food prices and higher levels of hired employment, rather than via small-farm income. However, the impact of HYVs in poverty alleviation may be of limited help if a rapidly growing population makes the supply of labour real wage elastic and food price restraint then enables employers to keep money wages down. In the absence of higher incomes amongst the poor, there is a lack of effective demand for the extra output from HYVs, and as a consequence there may not necessarily be an improvement in nutrition levels.

The recent counterview to this, backed up by selective evidence, questions the earlier assertions and suggests that the material well-being of the poor has improved. Many studies failed to distinguish between early and subsequent adoption of the new technology (see Herdt and Capule, 1983) – the first adopters were large farmers but small and marginal farmers followed quickly. Consumers have gained through lower prices; multiplier effects were ignored in many studies and the impact of the green revolution was confused with that of other policies, particularly institutional arrangements and labour-saving mechanisation. Low income farmers eventually adopt the technology but it favours specific environments, regions and crops; small farmers were early losers because of failure to control the land and water markets and the constraints they face in other input markets.

It therefore appears that the green revolution's implications for developing countries are far from certain. Indeed, outcomes are to a large extent site specific reflecting the importance of the environment into which green revolution technologies take root. This Chapter begins with a brief review of agriculture in the Philippines and then considers the issues that are central to understanding the effect of mechanisation in the agricultural sector in Section 8.3. Some simple economic theory is introduced in Section 8.4 to aid understanding of the empirical results that are reported in Section 8.5. Section 8.6 is devoted to a case study of a mechanical reaper introduced in the Philippines during the 1980s from which many important lessons may be learnt, not least the need to adopt a holisitic approach to mechanisation in rural economies. The Chapter closes with some conclusions and suggestions for future policy in LDCs.

8.2 AGRICULTURE IN THE PHILIPPINES

Agricultural growth during the 1970s and 1980s in the Philippines was generally satisfactory, production growing by up to 4.9 per cent annually. Output growth derived primarily from higher yields, though some expansion of cultivated land took place in sparsely populated islands such as Mindanao. The four main crops have traditionally been rice and maize for home consumption; coconuts and sugar for export. In recent years pineapples and bananas have also been significant exports.

Agricultural growth took place despite government policies which discriminated against agriculture. That agriculture managed to survive and grow has been claimed as a demonstration of its inherent comparative advantages. While the forms and extent of government intervention varied across sectors, agriculture was discriminated against relative to manufacturing. Direct intervention in agricultural markets took the form of price ceilings, export quotas, export taxes and various levies. Maintenance of government supported monopolies in major crop sectors was an instrument for intervention. Equally important was the maintenance of an overvalued exchange rate which had adverse effects on tradeable agricultural commodities. International agricultural commodity prices declined after the 1973–74 boom, and domestic productivity increases further dampened prices. Not all government interventions were negative, but the positive effects were inadequate to compensate for the strong discriminatory effects. The government funded research and extension and subsidised some inputs, particularly the provision of irrigation water. However, the significant growth achievements in agriculture tended to obscure the negative effects of government policies.

The changes in the rice sector were particularly dramatic and have been well documented. Output rose from 5.3 million tonnes in 1970 to 8.2 million tonnes in 1982 and 9.1 million tonnes in 1988; the Philippines has been self-sufficient in rice since 1977 and exports small quantities. Production grew most rapidly after the government launched the 'Masagana 99' programme in 1973 in the aftermath of a harvest failure and acute rice shortages. The objective was to encourage farmers to adopt a package of new rice technology comprising modern HYVs, inorganic fertiliser and chemicals as well as recommended agronomic practices. To facilitate adoption, the programme supplied low interest credit and subsidised inputs. The government also initiated a floor price scheme to maintain producer prices, to be implemented through state rice purchasing centres buying at guaranteed prices.

Adoption of the new technology was rapid. Between 1973 and 1978, output growth averaged 6 per cent per year. By 1980, over 85 per cent of the irrigated area and 70 per cent of the rain-fed area were planted to HYVs. Fertiliser use rose from 73 to 147 kg per hectare between 1970 and 1979. Though increased multiple cropping took place, cultivated area increases contributed only 15 per cent of total output growth, which came primarily from yield increases. The vigorous extension campaign and the subsidised input package of the programme contributed to initial rapid adoption. However, direct coverage declined rapidly. In 1973–74, at its peak, the Masagana 99 programme covered 40 per cent of rice area: by 1977–78 it covered less than 10 per cent.

While the new technology raised output and yields, this green revolution has not brought all the anticipated benefits. In its initial period, the technology was poorly adapted to rain-fed conditions, which constitute 60 per cent of the Philippine rice area. Even on the irrigated farms, farm level performance was well below that achieved in experimental stations. Thus nearly three decades after the introduction of new rice technology, average Philippine rice yields are below those achieved in comparable tropical countries (Table 8.1).

Irrigation expansion slowed appreciably in the 1970s and despite subsidies to fertiliser importers and domestic producers, the fertiliser:rice price ratio in the Philippines is among the highest in the region (see Table 8.1), owing to low output prices.

Because of inadequate government procurement, floor prices were not maintained and the government's foreign trade monopoly in rice enabled it to maintain domestic prices at levels substantially lower than world prices. The artificially depressed price became a mechanism

John Lingard

Table 8.1   *Rice yields and the fertiliser: rice price ratio in Asia*

Country	Yield (1988) (tonne/ha)	Fertiliser: Rice Price Ratio (1981) (kg N:kg paddy)
Bangladesh	2.2	1.76
Myanmar (Burma)	3.2	1.80
India (Coimbatore)	2.1	2.71
Indonesia (Java)	4.0	1.62
Japan	6.3	0.45
Korea (South)	6.4	1.19
Malaysia	2.9	1.77
Pakistan	2.4	3.61
Philippines	2.7	3.68
Sri Lanka	2.9	1.08
Thailand	2.0	3.35

Sources: Palacpac (1982); *IRRI Rice Facts 1988*.

for transferring many of the benefits of technical change to consumers. Rice producers faced unfavourable terms of trade and productivity gains were not adequate to compensate for unfavourable price movements: hence profitability of rice production has not risen in line with productivity.

While the new rice technology raised labour demand in its initial stages, labour absorption has been declining substantially in recent years due to the adoption of labour-saving mechanical, chemical and agronomic innovations. Even where cropping intensity has increased, aggregate annual labour use has been declining. Hence, it is difficult to sustain the thesis that a higher rate of technical change in rice agriculture would raise agricultural wages by increasing labour demand. On balance, the green revolution, despite clear benefits – particularly greater output – has not been a complete solution to the problems of the rural sector because of distributional effects and the complicated nature of mechanisation. It was unrealistic to expect it to be.

8.3   THE ISSUE OF FARM MECHANISATION

It is into this setting that the question of farm mechanisation must be viewed. Technological change is an important vehicle for development but its full potential for achieving growth and equity can only be achieved by integrating it in some overall development strategy.

Otherwise it can amplify inequality. Rural societies in LDCs are characterised by unequal distribution of productive assets, lack of uniform access to health care and education and differential access to both factor and product markets. Such features inevitably interact with the technology. Technical change helps to generate economic surplus to facilitate growth and reduce poverty. LDCs need a long-term commitment to agricultural research and development; there are no quick-fix solutions, but what part will machine technology play in solving their problems?

The development, introduction and use of agricultural machines in developing countries has produced a large, controversial literature describing technical, economic and socio-anthropological attempts to measure and evaluate its impact on output, employment and incomes. On balance, there appear to be few rigorous studies which demonstrate conclusively and convincingly the net effect of mechanical techniques. One school of thought maintains that mechanisation is a necessary condition for sustained agricultural and economic development. Another maintains that machines, have replaced labour that has few alternative employment opportunities, further accentuate problems of income distribution and benefit only those with the largest holdings or greatest wealth.

There appears, however, to be one inescapable finding from these studies; farmers are mechanising their operations, even in situations where research indicates it to be unprofitable or where the social benefits are less than private returns. This trend can be expected to continue. The issue for engineers and social scientists should not be use or non-use of machines, but the selection, development and introduction of technologies which maximise the production potential of farm resources such as land and labour and which minimise social and economic negative side-effects on the distribution of income and access to employment opportunities.

Machines come in many different shapes and sizes and fulfil different functions. There are small manual-powered and large gasoline-powered water pumps, tools for oxen and buffaloes as well as for tractors, two-wheel tractors, four-wheel tractors of various sizes, threshers, reapers, transplanters, etc. It is facile to generalise about mechanisation *per se*. Rather, each separate item of equipment must be assessed on its own merits, taking into account whether it substitutes or complements labour, its farm size requirements for optimal operation, and whether it raises farm output.

Addressing some of these issues, Binswanger (1984) lists five key questions:

1. What is the contribution of mechanisation?
2. What is the most efficient pattern of mechanisation?
3. Should governments support mechanisation? If so, how (subsidies and trade policy) and at what stage (machine development, testing, production)?
4. What, if any, are the harmful side-effects of mechanisation?
5. Should governments influence the choice of techniques directly, by regulating imports, restricting the number of brands sold or even banning some machines?

This chapter considers some of the above questions in relation to the author's involvement with the *Consequences of Small Farm Mechanisation Study* at the International Rice Research Institute (IRRI) in the Philippines. Some theoretical issues particularly the induced innovation model of the mechanisation process are first examined. Results of a comparison made between Philippine rice farms 'with' and 'without' machines for yields, cropping intensities and employment are presented. A case study of the IRRI reaper is briefly discussed and more overall conclusions drawn.

8.4   SOME ECONOMIC THEORY

The economics literature on technical change in agriculture is large, embracing a range of theoretical issues and empirical applications. It is necessary to specify what is meant by the term 'technical change', distinguish between this and change in technique and explain how technical change arises within the economic system.

Technical or technological change is characterised by additions to the set of inputs used in production and by changes in available techniques of production. Use of new or improved inputs is implied; improved in the sense of embodying more or better quality attributes or characteristics. New inputs are the vehicle whereby technical change is introduced into the production system; they embody technical change and it is questionable whether disembodied technical change actually exists. Figure 8.1 is used to distinguish between technique and technology. If the isoquant Q_0 represents the alternative combinations of two inputs used to produce a given level of output, then a shift from combination A to combination B (along the existing isoquant) is a change in technique of production.

A change in technology, on the other hand, involves a shift in the

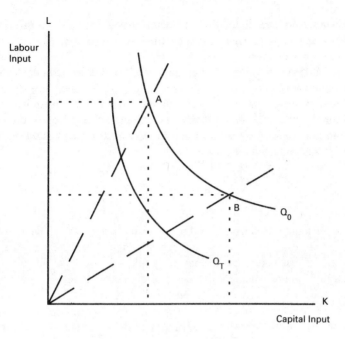

Figure 8.1 Change in technique and change in technology

isoquant itself such as that shown by Q_T where the same output as Q_0 can now be produced by smaller combinations of the two inputs. Change in technique (or factor substitution) occurs as a result of changing relative factor prices and cost-minimising behaviour. Technical change, in contrast, means a reduction in the quantity of resources required to produce a given output; or, alternatively, more output for the same level of inputs. In practice, technical change is usually defined and measured as the proportional decrease in costs of production achievable by the innovation when both old and new techniques operate at their optimal input combinations where factor prices are held constant (Binswanger, 1978).

The distinction between factor substitution and technical change is important. If we take an example like the purchase of a tractor on a farm which previously used manual labour, it makes a considerable difference to the assessment of the impact of this change whether it (a) results in the same production cost for a given level of output (factor substitution), or (b) results in a decrease in production costs for the given level of output (technical change). In practice, with unknown isoquants, it is difficult to discern which of these effects has taken place; input prices shift over time as well as techniques and the underlying isoquants.

In addition, technical change can be classified as either neutral or biased to one factor of production or another. If it results in a parallel movement of the isoquant inwards towards the origin, implying that at given factor prices the ratio of the inputs (L/K) is the same before and after the change, then the technical change is called neutral. If technical change is 'biased' in favour of using more of one input than another, then different social and economic implications follow.

Generally, the bias of technical change is defined according to whether the income share of a factor rises, stays the same, or decreases, for constant factor proportions. Where w is the wage rate of labour and r is the interest rate or return to capital, then if the income share of labour, wL, rises relative to that of capital, rK, we have labour-biased or capital-saving technical change; if the income shares of factors stays the same, we have neutral technical change; and if the share of labour, wL, falls we have capital-biased or labour-saving technical change. Labour-saving technical change implies a lower share of total income accruing to labour and a higher share to non-labour resources.

The biological and chemical technologies are thought to be scale-neutral with respect to differing farm sizes. Seeds, fertiliser, pesticides and other complementary inputs of the technology package are divisible and hence appropriate and available to all farmers irrespective of the area farmed. In principle they can be purchased and acquired in large or small amounts with no real advantages in the form of bulk discounts to the larger operators. In practice market distortions and institutional bias often result in differential access to these purchased inputs between differing groups of farmers, in which case, the intrinsic technical characteristics of scale neutrality associated with divisibility are lost. Tractors, on the other hand, may be biased with respect to both technical change and scale. They may have a labour-saving bias in technical change, and a scale bias towards larger farm sizes due to their indivisibility. Rental markets or custom-hiring arrangements may go some way to removing this large farm bias and 2-wheel tractors and other design modifications could also mould machinery technologies to different farm sizes.

Induced Innovation and Farm Mechanisation

Whilst some sources of technological change, such as the aid agencies and state-run research institutes, may introduce technologies that are independent of market forces, in the main it is factor prices that direct the thrust of research and development, in either the public or private sectors. Engineers and machinery manufacturers respond to changing relative factor prices in farm production and design equipment which provide cheaper methods of producing the same output. More generally, emerging relative resource scarcities manifest themselves in changing relative factor price levels which all agencies, both private and public, respond to. Thus relative prices induce public and private research into innovations which save on the most expensive resource. This is the basis of a theory of technical change known as induced innovation which seeks to explain paths of technological development in terms of changing relative factor scarcities over time (Hayami and Ruttan, 1985). This school emphasises the demand pull version to explain the process of mechanisation. Input and product price relationships *induce* investment in research in a direction consistent with a nation's resource endowment. Technology can thus be developed to facilitate the substitution of relatively abundant and hence cheap factors for relatively scarce and expensive factors of production.

Kislev and Peterson (1981) describe how mechanisation increases the capital-labour ratio in two stages. As shown in Figure 8.2 we first observe a change in technique along a given isoquant to input price changes which are possibly distorted (the move from A to B). The second stage involves a change in the technology (an asymmetric shift in the production function) following the change in relative factor prices (a move from B to C). A new production method is devised causing the isoquant to shift inwards and this is the basis of the induced-innovation model.

Biased Technology and Factor Market Prices

Factor prices in LDCs can often be distorted due to a variety of forces; government intervention in the form of subsidy/tax and credit policies, monopoly and monopsony behaviour and other imperfections associated with imperfect information, immobilities and unequal distribution of resources, particularly land and water, mean that farmers face widely different prices for both inputs and output. In a dualistic

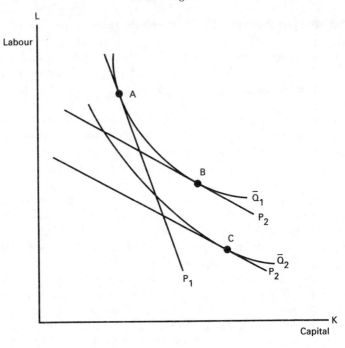

Figure 8.2   Induced technical change

agriculture, small and large farmers confront different factor scarcities and different relative factor prices. This means that large farmers often press for access to technologies, like mechanisation, which are inappropriate for rural society as a whole. The appropriate path of technological progress in agriculture is induced in a socially efficient direction as predicted by the induced-innovation model provided that the relative factor prices properly reflect underlying factor scarcities. The policy implication is that factor market distortions should be removed, and 'democratic' avenues of farmer participation instituted, otherwise market bias and institutional bias will direct technology down inappropriate avenues. Unequal access to novel, bought-in inputs of the new technologies will lead to predictable uneven adoption/non-adoption of new methods and this form of bias can be illustrated with the aid of Figure 8.3.

Linear production theory is assumed in this model with fixed proportion production processes or techniques available to two types of farmers (small and large, say). Initially only the three techniques, I,

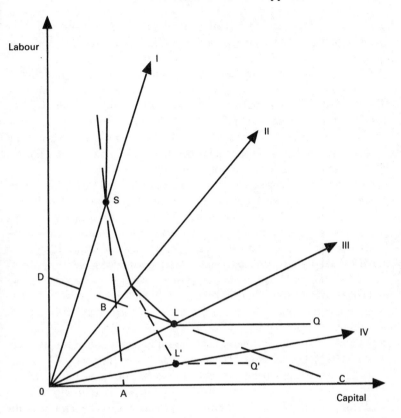

Figure 8.3 Bias and factor-price ratios

II, III are available and the linear segmented isoquant Q shows a constant level of output (1 tonne of rice) for each of the techniques. Intermediate sections between the separate technique rays can be interpreted as producing Q using combinations of two techniques and the combination between I and III is clearly an inefficient one. We further assume that the farmers face different factor prices with the large farmer operating along isocost line BC and the small farmer along line SA. Labour is relatively cheap to the small farmer, capital expensive, whilst the large farmer has privileged access in the capital and credit market.

As a consequence, cost-minimising behaviour implies that they use different techniques of production; the small farmer produces Q of output at S using technique I adopting a labour-intensive system; the larger farmer operates at L using technique III producing the same level of output Q but using a capital-intensive system. If a new production technique IV arises with the characteristic that the isoquant shifts to Q', clearly it will only be adopted by the large farmer who will relocate his production of Q' output at L' using the new method. His/her costs per unit output will fall, output will tend to rise and possibly market price will fall if a significant number of large farmers follow suit. The new technique is however irrelevant to, and unavailable to, the small farmer who continues to operate at S with his/her traditional technique possibly with a reduced income.

This conclusion applies to any technology located in the area BAC which is biased to the large farmer. Small farmer bias occurs if new techniques fall within the area BSD and techniques superior for both types of farmers arise in area DBAO. It is held by some critics of the Green Revolution technologies (see for instance Griffin, 1979) that the HYV seeds, fertiliser and chemicals packages, whilst being divisible and scale-neutral, are in practice biased towards large farmers because of market and institutional imperfections which deny equal access to the inputs. This compounds their inherent bias to irrigated farms, regions and crops reinforcing inequality in the rural sector. The capital requirements of much machinery plus the lumpiness of such inputs probably results in them being biased towards larger farmers.

Large farmer bias of machines can also be shown using the analysis in Figure 8.4. Assume that a thresher for rice is introduced into a small farm system, and that the individual farm household can use the thresher on a custom-hire basis. The isoquant for the farm shifts from I_1 to I_2, representing a labour-saving bias in technical change. It pays the household to use the thresher since it reduces total costs for threshing. Equilibrium thus moves from point A to point B at prevailing factor prices. This causes a substantial reduction in family farm labour from L_1 to L_2, and an increase in capital from K_1 to K_2 representing the hire of the thresher.

At point B, there is unemployment of family labour. For full employment of family labour to occur, output would need to expand to I_3 giving an equilibrium at C with labour use back to L_1. This would require an increase in the scale of output by increasing capital use to K_3, and an increase in farm size in order to achieve economies of scale. However, peasants do not always have access to mechanised technology on a custom-hire basis, and the nature of their farms are not suitable for large machine operation. Thus a possible impact of an innovation like a thresher or tractor is a movement from point A

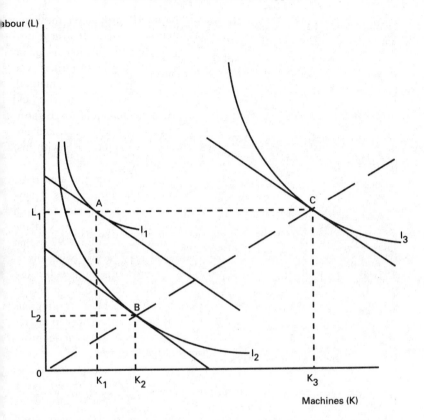

Figure 8.4   Farm-level impact of labour-saving technical change

to point C. The small farm disappears, at the expense of a large farmer. McInerney and Donaldson's (1975) study of tractorisation in Pakistan mirrors this process; tractors set in train a process of farm size expansion and displacement of small tenant farmers by larger farmers.

8.5   EMPIRICAL EVIDENCE

Agricultural mechanisation in the Philippines commenced with the introduction of four-wheel tractors into the sugar-cane industry in the 1960s. Imported power tillers or two wheel tractors were first available by 1962 but widespread adoption only occurred between 1966 and 1968 following the First Central Bank/ IBRD Rural Credit Project

($5m) signed in November 1965. Further rural credit projects were approved in 1969 ($12.5m), 1974 ($22m) and in 1977 ($36.5m) and there is evidence suggesting that the mechanisation process was a credit driven one. Devaluation of the peso reduced sales of imported tractors and power tillers in 1970, and increased sales of power tillers in 1972 were primarily a result of the invention of low-cost IRRI designs. Four-wheel tractor sales improved between 1971 and 1974 because of favourable world prices for sugar which was, however, followed by the 1973 oil crisis. Peak sales for both tractors and tillers occurred in 1975 when a serious outbreak of foot and mouth disease severely reduced the carabao (water-buffalo) population.

Sales improved in 1977 because of the release of funds from the Fourth Central Bank/IBRD Rural Credit Project and there was an increasing demand for mechanical threshers and driers. Since 1978 however sales of power tillers and tractors have declined. Increased costs, the second oil crisis in 1979 and a secular decline in sugar prices have all contributed to this downward trend and with the 1983 peso devaluation the agricultural machinery industry in the Philippines was clearly at a crossroads. In 1985 there were 78,000 power tillers in use and 19,500 tractors (Duff et al. 1988).

Output Effects of Mechanisation

The issue of whether mechanisation increases yields and cropping intensity is difficult to answer. Data is often inadequate and site specific and there are difficulties in isolating the effects of mechanisation from the confounding influences of complementary inputs particularly irrigation and fertilisers. The Consequences of Mechanisation Study at IRRI collected cross sectional data in 1979/80 from selected households in eight villages in Nueva Ecija Province, Central Luzon, the Philippines, in both rain-fed and irrigated areas. Households were classified on the basis of land preparation technique and the type of irrigation, Table 8.2 shows the number of households in each class.

Because of the cell sizes, the study focused on the differences between non-mechanised and partially mechanised farms in the rain-fed areas and between partially and fully mechanised farms in the gravity irrigated class. The basis for inclusion in mechanisation classes was the land preparation technique used in both wet and dry seasons. Non-mechanised farms used draught animals in both seasons, fully mechanised farms tractor and/or power tillers in both seasons and the partially mechanised category used both animal and machine power. All farms

Table 8.2 *Distribution of sample households among irrigation/mechanisation classes, wet season*

Irrigation		Mechanisation		
	Non-Mech.	Partial Mech.	Full Mech.	All
Rain-fed	77	46	1	124
Pump irrigated	39	15	0	54
Gravity irrigated	7	79	54	140
All	123	140	55	318

used modern rice varieties, transplanted rather than broadcasted and the average farm size was a little over two hectares.

Studies measuring the effects of mechanisation on cropping intensity appeal to the timeliness issue but frequently the dominant variable is irrigation rather than power supply. High levels of cropping intensity are often achieved without tractors although in rain-fed Philippines environments, for example Iloilo Province, shorter turn-around times and earlier crop establishment can mean the difference between double and single-cropping. Mechanical threshers may play a part in reducing the turn-around period. Evidence from the Consequences Study on cropping intensity (the ratio of the total land planted in both seasons to farm size) shows the importance of water availability. Cropping intensity in the gravity irrigated areas was close to 2; in the rain-fed areas it was much lower, 1.17 on non-mechanised farms, 1.24 on partially mechanised farms, although the difference is not statistically significant. Using regression analysis and dummy variables to explain cropping intensity on rice farms in the Philippines, Lingard (1984) demonstrated that, as expected, irrigation dummies are positive and highly significant while the mechanisation dummies are positive, small and insignificant. The results indicate that irrigation dominates cropping intensity effects in the sample, with mechanised land-preparation playing a minor supportive role.

Yield effects were significantly different between rain-fed and irrigated groups with dry season yields much higher than wet season yields. There were however no significant differences between mechanisation classes within each irrigation group for the wet season and few rain-fed farms cultivate in the dry season. Regression analysis was used to test whether mechanisation had any effect on yield when differences in other inputs are taken into account. The results obtained indicate that fertiliser, pesticides and pre-harvest labour all had positive and significant effects on yields as did irrigation. However, once again the effect of mechanisation was small and statistically insignificant, suggesting that mechanisation had little effect on yield. On the basis of this analysis we conclude that, for the sample, in the year 1979/80 the major determinant of yield and cropping intensity is irrigation. There is no discernible evidence of output effects which are directly attributable to mechanisation.

Employment Effects of Mechanisation

In the absence of increased output, adoption of machinery will shift earnings from one group to another. If a machine replaces labour then the wages formerly paid to labourers will accrue to the owner of the machine. When machinery has no output effects, adoption simply redistributes income. It is important therefore to measure the degree of substitution between capital and labour. However, it is difficult to partition changes in labour input over time and across different farm types into separate components since mechanisation is often associated with the adoption of additional yield augmenting inputs, so that the observed gross effect on employment may outweigh the net effects of any capital–labour substitution. Inferring and measuring from cross-sectional data based on the sample of Table 8.2 has major limitations as one attempts to disentangle and decompose aggregate data into separate identifiable effects. The 'with' and 'without' mechanisation data were collected to infer the dynamic 'before' and 'after' effects, yet the forces that operated on the mechanisation process in the 'before' situation cannot be recreated and some differences are not reflected in the static 'with' and 'without' mechanisation data. Despite these shortcomings, it is illuminating to examine differences in labour utilisation on farms with different land preparation methods at one point in time. Labour use figures for the farms of Table 8.2 are shown in Table 8.3.

Total per hectare labour use is higher on rain-fed than irrigated farms and within the rain-fed area, non-mechanised farms used 15 per cent more labour and 50 per cent more land preparation labour per hectare than partially mechanised farms. Other differences within the rain-fed class were small and there are few significant differences within the irrigated class between mechanisation states. Irrigated farmers obtained considerably higher yields yet harvesting labour was similar to that of rain-fed farmers, partially due to the greater use of mechanical threshers within the irrigated area. Mechanisation results in a reduc-

Table 8.3   *Average labour use (hours per ha) by crop activity,*
Nueva Ecija, Philippines, wet season

| | Rain-fed | | Irrigated | |
	Non-Mech.	Partial Mech.	Partial Mech.	Fully Mech.
Land preparation	146	98	66	47
Seedbed preparation and planting	176	154	191	214
Fertilising	6	6	9	9
Spraying	9	6	13	15
Weeding	15	18	5	2
Harvesting/Threshing and post-harvest	261	243	247	225
Total:	613	525	531	512
% Hired labour	56	48	74	84
Yield (kg)	1902	1826	3860	3803
% using threshers	40	48	42	56
% transplanting	95	93	94	98
Sample size	77	46	79	54

tion of land preparation labour, however, some of the labour time saved is redeployed in additional seedbed preparation, transplanting and crop care activities which may contribute to the higher yields. In the rain-fed areas the potential displacement of labour by machines is great at the prevailing low levels of mechanisation.

A further feature of these labour figures is the breakdown into family and hired categories. In both absolute and percentage terms, hired labour use is considerably greater on irrigated farms and the substitution of machines for labour appears to be one for family as opposed to hired labour. Machines may release family labour to work in the non-farm sector since the irrigated villages are relatively close to Cabanatuan City, a source of urban employment. Econometric analysis reported in Lingard (1984) indicates that mechanisation of land preparation operations is labour displacing and that displacement tends to affect family labour rather than wage labour, thereby freeing family labour for managerial activities, off-farm employment and leisure. Increased tractor use in the rain-fed areas will result in substantial reductions in employment and in the absence of rising real wages, should be discouraged.

Landless Labourers

Within the Philippines industrial expansion has been capital-intensive and despite migration to the urban informal sector, a significant proportion of landless labourers remain in rural areas dependent on small rice farms for wage employment. Some 40 per cent of the agricultural labour force falls in this category and with population growth they account for up to four million people. Small farmers likewise depend on wages for the continued existence of their peasant livelihood and recent advances in rice technology have affected both labour use and shares.

Landless labourers as a group are distinguished by their inaccessibility to the means of production land and complete dependence on farm work to earn an income. The common perception is that they are plagued by problems of low income, hunger, infant mortality, low educational attainment and little upward mobility. To test that view some 47 landless labourer households were included in our survey and a supplementary study considered a further 64 landless labourers and 36 small farmers who hired out their labour. Landless labourer households comprise between 5 and 18 per cent of the total households in the eight sample villages, average age of household head was 40 years with up to four years' schooling and household size averaged 5.6 persons. Migration of a seasonal or permanent nature from households was minimal and, unlike farmers, they had little access to public agencies. Asset valuations averaged 1580 pesos including houses and half the households were in debt with loans averaging 430 pesos in the wet season and 230 pesos in the dry season. Most loans were for consumption purposes in both seasons. Almost all the landless households derived their income solely from agriculture, working on average 243 man-days per year split equally between the seasons with an average income per household of 2,400 pesos. Females contributed little directly to family income, allocating most of their time to housekeeping and child-rearing.

Harvesting and threshing arrangements are crucial to the earnings of the landless. Some 50 to 60 per cent of their income comes from crop shares of the rice harvest; harvesting, threshing and transplanting are tasks traditionally carried out by hired labour. Opinion surveys of the landless revealed that they thought introduction of small mechanical threshers had improved their situation due to reduced hauling and faster threshing, which enabled them to harvest additional fields and receive their crop share earlier. A decline in sharing rates from one-sixth to one-eighth for both manual harvesting and threshing down to one-tenth using mechanical threshers was outweighed by these advantages. In addition, under the new threshing technology more women and children had access to an income source in less physically demanding tasks. Workers were however aware that machines had led to an excess supply of harvesting labour and feared further declines in sharing rates might occur, particularly if mechanical reapers were introduced into labour-surplus areas.

8.6   A CASE STUDY – THE IRRI REAPER

Harvesting rice is labour intensive; cutting by hand and hauling the *palay* (roughly, the unprocessed rice husk) to a thresher may take up to 150 hours per hectare and threshing labour must be added to this figure. Shortages of labour at harvest delays getting a ripe crop off the field and results in an increased turn-around time and possible grain losses. Such losses may rise to 11 per cent for a 10-day delay. Multi-cropping of rice may be inhibited by labour constraints. Mechanisation can even out fluctuations in labour supply and demand, matching available resources to crop requirements. With this peak labour aspect in mind, collaborative research between IRRI and the Chinese Academy of Agricultural Mechanisation Sciences was initiated in 1980 to adapt a Chinese reaper to fit the IRRI power tiller. The aim was to produce a small, cheap, machine appropriate for the small Asian rice farmer.

Subsequent design developments proved successful and both 1 metre and 1.6 metre reapers were tested and released in the Philippines. The design characteristics permitted manufacture in small local, fabrication shops and by developing two sizes of reaper, appropriate technologies could be made available to a range of rice farming situations. In areas where there is no labour shortage at harvest time, it was not expected that an energy and capital-intensive technology would replace traditional manual harvesting; substitution was expected to only take place in response to relative factor prices and resource availabilities and adoption rates would vary between countries and within regions of countries. This presumption however neglected the other factors affecting the mechanisation decision such as prestige, easing toil and drudgery, easier management and preferential access to credit.

Field trials on the reaper were carried out in 1981 at sites in the Philippines as part of the machine's development and durability tests.

Data collected and analysed shed some light on the question of labour displacement, grain losses etc. and these were compared with manual harvesting methods. While a general picture failed to emerge, (rice varieties, degree of lodging, parcel shape, size and topography, water depth, mud consistency, hauling distance to thresher and team numbers affected the results in important ways) the field tests pointed to a manual cutting time of 85 hours/ha and a hauling time of 53 hours/ha. In comparison the reaper could reduce the cutting time to 10 hours/ha (allowing for manual harvesting of inaccessible corners and lodged areas) and hauling could be reduced to 25–35 hours/ha since collecting/gathering time for the wind-rowed palay was lowered. In addition, easier land preparation the following season and improved rat catching were secondary benefits of using the reaper.

Further calculations on the reaper along with private profitability estimates were carried out giving required break-even rates of 4.7 and 8.1 ha/year for different investment options (reaper without/with power tiller). Such market research type studies shed little light on the wider social issues, but indicated a low break-even utilisation rate should custom-hire reaping become prevalent. The reaper was released in 1982.

A general case could not be made then either to promote or prevent its release. Whilst it appeared that introduction of the reaper would reduce labour requirement at harvesting it would, in addition, reduce field losses. Distributional aspects of the reaper's introduction were largely overlooked despite the importance of harvesting from the social/institutional viewpoint. While land preparation and threshing can be done by family labour alone, harvesting usually needs to be supplemented with hired labour. On many farms more than 50 per cent of the post-production labour requirements is carried out by hired labour. Of these, harvesting is the most expensive, accounting for 10 per cent of total production, whilst the fee for a mechanical thresher is about 6 per cent. Harvesting is thus a major source of income for most landless labourers and this implied that some income transfers could result if the reaper were to be widely adopted.

From 1982 onwards small IRRI type reapers mounted on two-wheel tractors began to appear in localised areas of the Philippines: 68 were produced in 1982, 363 in 1983 and 140 in 1984. Imported Kubota reapers were also available. A survey carried out in 1984 (Juarez et al., 1988) subsequently found declining sales due to technical problems. These included easily-blunted cutter knives, the inability to operate in wet, muddy fields, and labour force problems such as threatened boycotts by harvesting labourers and, in some cases, sabotaging reapers by placing metal objects in fields to damage cutter bars.

Interviews with 78 farmers comprising reaper users and non-users revealed efficiency gains for gathering and hauling palay when using mechanical reapers, although many non-reaper-using farmers claimed not to have adopted the machines out of pity for harvesters who might lose their jobs. In practice, a substitution of capital for labour was observed. Manual harvesting required an average of 17 man-days/ha compared to only 2 man-days/ha when using the mechanical reaper. A net labour displacement of 15 man-days/ha thus resulted. A number of farmers (18) indicated decreased private grain losses associated with the use of the reaper, although this probably represents a redistribution of the harvest formerly going to gleaning gangs primarily women. Reaper owners typically used their machines on their own farms and for custom-hire, on average, harvesting 45ha per machine within a 5km radius of the owner's village. At such utilisation rates the imported reapers were not an economically worthwhile private investment.

A sample of 58 harvesters of low educational levels revealed an average annual household income of peso 10,600 for a family of six of which 72 per cent came from rice production-related hired work. Over 90 per cent of these households reported a decline in income from harvesting due to competition from the reaper; some family members were no longer required at harvest and others worked fewer hours. One hundred and nineteen individuals indicated a lowering of income as a result of the competition and manual harvesters were the obvious losers from the introduction of mechanical reapers.

The initial success of the reaper between 1982 and 1984 was however not a result of the free interplay of competitive market forces with labour becoming more expensive relative to capital due to seasonal labour shortages. It was due to the policy-induced cheapening of capital. Reapers were acquired at artificially low prices due to manufacturers not having to recoup the publicly funded research, design and development costs. Blueprints were provided free to manufacturers and fabricators. Imported reapers were inexpensive due to the overvalued peso and interest rate policies favoured capital-intensive technologies at the expense of labour.

It can be concluded that development and promotion of the reaper was not successful in the Philippines, a country with nearly 50 per cent of its labour force engaged in agriculture and where over 10 per cent of Filipino households are headed by landless labourers.

The technical development of the reaper could have been left to the private sector. Output did not increase as a consequence of the use of reapers; earnings tended to be transferred from workers to the owners of machines. Seasonal labour displacement meant several landless families were unable to afford school fees; grain formerly gleaned by labourers or ducks was redirected to the owners and operators of machines and the income distribution effects were adverse. Thus short-term benefits to the few were obtained at the expense of the long-term interests of the many and in future a more cautious approach to technological change in agriculture in less-developed economies is needed.

Since its initial introduction however, the reaper has faced unfavourable economic conditions. Factors which have changed since 1983 include inflation, devaluation, interest rate rises and a continuing decline in the real cost of labour. As a consequence the reaper is no longer privately profitable in most parts of the Philippines and sales are minimal. Technical and socio-economic factors combine to influence the path of adoption of new technologies, but it is not socially desirable to artificially promote capital-intensive technologies in surplus labour economies. It will be some time before the reaper regains increasing acceptance in the Philippines, requiring as it does both an upturn in the economy and a rise in agricultural labour costs in a country with a population growth rate of 2.5 per cent per annum.

8.7 CONCLUSIONS

The desirability of farm mechanisation in surplus labour economies of Asia has been the focus of debate and controversy for some time but adoption and use of machines on small farms in Asia is continuing to increase. A lack of data and the difficulty of generalising findings has hindered the debate but firm evidence is now beginning to emerge. Earlier predictions of excessive labour displacement and inequitable income redistribution consequent upon mechanisation were perhaps misplaced, but the relationship between mechanisation and increased yields, cropping intensities or expanded area under cultivation is also weak. Substitution effects are the major incentive to mechanisation as farmers attempt to switch techniques and reduce costs.

Often this substitution takes place in response to prices determined by government policies. The use of machines has been made privately profitable through subsidies for credit or on their purchase price (David, 1983). However because such machines have potentially significant adverse effects on employment and income distribution, subsidies are socially undesirable. Exchange rate policy, credit availability, minimum wage policies, foreign aid and research and development strategies all help shape the path of mechanisation. In other words, the profitability of mechanisation depends largely on government policies, but in countries like the Philippines with a shortage of cultivable land per rural worker, constant or falling real rural wages, an adequate draught animal population, moderate paddy yields and a limited capacity to support mechanisation, there is no case to artificially stimulate mechanisation by government policy. Future projects or programmes considering the possible mechanisation of small farm agriculture must consider all the technical, economic and political aspects to avoid further misallocation of resources.

References

Binswanger, H.P. (1978). *The Economics of Tractors in South Asia*. A.D.C., New York.

Binswanger, H.P. (1984). *Agricultural Mechanisation: A Comparative Historical Perspective*. World Bank Working Paper No. 673. Washington DC.

David, C.C. (1983). 'Government Policies and Farm Mechanisation in the Philippines'. *IRRI/NEDA* December Workshop Paper.

Duff, B., Catanus, F. and Shin, L.S. (1988). *Agricultural Modernisation. Mechanisation and Rural-Based Industrial Development in Asia*. IRRI Agric Economics Dept Paper No. 88, 10.

Griffin, K. (1979). *The Political Economy of Agrarian Change*. London, Macmillan.

Hayami, Y. and Ruttan, V.W. (1985) *Agricultural Development : An International Perspective*, Baltimore, Johns Hopkins University Press.

Herdt, R.W. and Capule, C. (1983). *Adoption, Spread and Production Impact of Modern Rice Varieties in Asia*. IRRI.

IRRI Rice Facts 1988, Manila, IRRI.

Juarez, F., Te, A., Duff, B. and Stickney, R.E. (1988). *The Development and Impact of Mechanical Reapers in the Philippines*, Agric Econ Paper No. 88/1, 88–23, IRRI.

Kislev, Y. and Peterson, W. (1981). 'Induced Innovations and Farm Mechanisation'. *American Journal Agricultural Economics*, Vol. 63, No. 3.

Lingard, J. (1984). 'Mechanisation of Small Rice Farms in The Philippines: Some Income Distribution Aspects'. *Journal of Agricultural Economics*, Vol. 35, No. 3, 385–393.

McInerney, J.P. and Donaldson, G.F. (1975). *The Consequences of Farm Tractors in Pakistan*. World Bank Staff Paper, No. 210.

Palacpac, A.C. (1982). *World Rice Statistics,* IRRI.

Pearse, A. (1980). *Seeds of Plenty, Seeds of Want*. Oxford, Oxford University Press.

Pinstrup-Andersen, P. (1983) *Agricultural Research in Economic Development*. London, Longman.
Pinstrup-Andersen, P. and Hazell, P. (1985) 'The Impact of the Green Revolution and Prospects for the Future'. *Food Reviews International* 1(1), 1–25.

9 Agribusiness, Peasant Agriculture and the State: The Case of Contract Farming in Thailand

David Burch[1]

9.1 INTRODUCTION

The increasing significance of contract farming in Third World agriculture has attracted a good deal of interest in recent years, resulting in a substantial body of literature on this topic (see de Treville, 1987). This literature has addressed a wide range of concerns, from business and policy studies which serve to guide agribusiness activity in extending the contract system, to radical studies which have criticised that system for (among other things) intensifying the exploitation of peasant farmers and encouraging the substitution of cash crops for food crops (Glover and Kusterer, 1990). It is not possible, in the space available, to address all of the important issues raised by this literature, although many of these do form a significant component of a wider research programme currently underway. This chapter is concerned with the role of the state in promoting the contract farming system in the Third World. This issue is seldom analysed in a literature which usually focuses on the relationship between the agribusiness companies, the main proponents of contract farming, and those farmers who produce commodities under contract. We focus on Thailand, which has put considerable emphasis on export-oriented agri-processing industries in recent years and has, as a consequence, experienced an increasing emphasis on contract farming and a growing role for the state in agricultural development.

We wish to identify the factors accounting for the expansion of contract farming in Thailand, in particular the role of the state, and the social and economic implications of such a pattern of agricultural development. Section 9.2 outlines the nature of contract production and its place in the changing structure of global agriculture. Section 9.3 addresses the role of the state in promoting contract farming in

Thailand while Section 9.4 considers the relationship between the state and agribusiness. Some concluding reflections, which consider the implications for rural development and poverty, are provided in Section 9.5.

9.2   THE CONTRACT SYSTEM IN AGRICULTURE

Contract farming, or vertical co-ordination in agriculture, can be defined in a variety of ways but it usually involves an agreement between a farmer and a 'first handler' of agricultural produce, such as a processing or exporting company, for the production of a specified commodity. The terms and conditions of contracts may vary, but they are usually instigated by the processor/exporter and will typically specify the quantity of the commodity to be produced and the price to be paid, and may often specify the quality requirements. The processor/exporter will normally provide credit and/or inputs, such as seeds and chemicals, the cost of which will be deducted from the payment to the farmer. In addition, the contract may require the farmer to follow prescribed procedures, such as those relating to the frequency of weeding and fertiliser application or the use of a particular variety of seed. Failure to comply with the terms of the contract may result in cancellation or the loss of contracts in subsequent years (Glover and Kusterer, 1990).

Contract production is becoming increasingly widespread as a consequence of the transformation of food production systems in recent years. The restructuring of agriculture which has accompanied the adoption of 'appropriationist' and 'substitutionist' strategies by agribusiness necessarily implies an increased reliance upon contract production at this stage (Goodman et al., 1987). Appropriationism, defined as the process by which particular elements of the rural labour and production process have been taken over by industrialists and transformed into manufactured inputs, has resulted in increasingly integrated packages of technology-embracing, high-yielding, fertiliser-responsive seeds; plant protection chemicals; mechanisation and advanced management practices (Goodman, 1991, p. 40). Contract farming is especially significant in this context because such innovations are most effectively utilised under a system which allows for the close specification of the inputs to be applied and the manner and timing of their application. Substitutionism refers to a system in which farmers act as suppliers of raw materials for further processing into significantly transformed end products rather than as suppliers of final foodstuffs to consumers. In such a system, contract farming is necessary to maintain a constant supply of raw materials and to ensure optimal use of the capital equipment employed by food processors. In this context, contract production has obvious advantages over spot markets, which are uncertain and variable, and over full vertical integration, which involves the processor in direct cultivation and higher risks.

According to Friedmann (1991), the adoption of appropriationist and substitutionist strategies implies that the traditional distinction between the agricultural and industrial sectors no longer holds. Since both inputs to, and outputs from, agriculture are so closely integrated with industrial production, it is now more relevant to refer to 'agri-food' systems which combine both sectors. Equally, it follows that the old international division of labour based on the traditional distinction between agriculture and industry, with the colonial territories exporting bulk, unprocessed tropical goods and importing manufactured industrial goods from the richer nations, is also no longer tenable (Friedmann, 1991). This has far-reaching implications for producers and consumers in both the developed and underdeveloped regions. The adoption of appropriationist strategies means that the site-specific agriculture governed by climate and season has given way to an integrated agri-food sector in which new seeds, chemicals and other inputs ensure that global agribusiness corporations engaged in production and trade can now source their raw materials inputs from anywhere in the world. At the same time, the industrial processing and transformation of these inputs into canned goods, frozen meals, fast foods, snacks and other significantly transformed food products, ensures a capacity to deliver produce for consumption anywhere in the world. In short, production and consumption in the agri-food sector are now global activities which transcend conventional categories of analysis.

In this situation, the role of Third World countries is being radically changed. What is being imported into the richer countries from the Third World and elsewhere are not the simple staple or unprocessed goods which were the basis of trade in an earlier era but are 'luxury' items such as cut flowers, citrus fruits, snack foods, off-season vegetables, frozen poultry, canned meats, seafood, tropical fruits, jams and preserved fruits, breakfast cereals, canned vegetables and fruit juices, i.e. non-traditional exports which are not specifically tropical and which compete with first world exports. Moreover, increased production of luxury commodities in the Third World is not simply additional to developed country production, but in many cases comes to supplant it. Seen in these terms, agricultural transformation in the Third World is based on the capacity to produce goods which can no longer be efficiently sourced from former production sites in the developed countries, either because of higher costs, environmental degradation, or for some other reason. Southeast Asia is particularly significant, and a number of researchers have pointed to the changing pattern of agricultural exports by Malaysia, Indonesia, Thailand and the Philippines, involving a growing emphasis on the production of luxury items such as those detailed above (Doner, 1974; Ping, 1980; Hawes, 1982). Thailand is of particular importance in this regard, and has been referred to as 'Asia's Supermarket' because of the extent of its involvement in export-oriented agri-processing (Goldstein, 1988). By 1988, Thailand was already the world's largest exporter of canned tuna and canned pineapple, and later emerged as the leading exporter of canned baby corn and frozen tiger prawns. Its share of world trade in poultry products grew from 3.9 per cent in 1987 to 5.8 per cent in 1991, by which date it had emerged as the world's fourth largest exporter of broiler meat (Foreign Agricultural Service, 1992).

This pattern of agricultural development and diversification in Thailand has implied a growing reliance on contract production over a wide range of commodities. Few precise data are available, but in exports of frozen chicken, nearly one hundred per cent of production is made under contract. In vegetables, such as canned baby corn, bamboo shoots and tomatoes, production is also largely under contract, as is much of the output of canned fruits. In order to evaluate fully the impacts of such developments, it is necessary to turn to a more detailed analysis of recent agricultural change and consider this in the context of the wider political economy.

9.3   CONTRACT FARMING AND THE STATE IN THAILAND

In the 1950s, Thailand was basically an agricultural economy. Industrial development became marked with the adoption of a policy of import-substituting industrialisation around 1960. Eventually, under the influence of local capital and the World Bank, Thailand switched to export-oriented industrialisation and manufacturing output grew at a fairly rapid rate (see Hewison, 1989). The share of agriculture in GDP fell from 30 per cent in 1970 to some 16 per cent in the late 1980s although agricultural output continued to expand. While rice remains a cornerstone of agricultural production, its relative importance has declined with the emergence of new cash crops. Rice output grew by about 3.8 per cent per annum over the period 1964/5 to 1989/90, whilst cassava output grew by 16.4 per cent per annum, maize by 12.2 per cent, sugar-cane by 10.7 per cent and rubber by 13.1 per cent (Office of Agricultural Economics). These five commodities not only account for the largest component in agricultural production, but are also Thailand's major export crops. In recent years, however, the most dynamic activity has occurred in the production and export of highly processed, value-added goods in the agri-processing industries. For example, over the nine years 1981–89 exports of frozen poultry products grew at an annual average of 35 per cent in volume and 45 per cent in value, while canned vegetables grew at an annual average of 54 per cent in volume and 66 per cent in value. In particular commodities, export growth was even stronger; canned baby corn, for example, expanded at a rate of 290 per cent per annum in volume and 262 per cent in value over the same nine-year period (Office of Agricultural Economics). As noted earlier, all of these commodities depend, to a greater or lesser degree, on contract production, and as the significance of this system has expanded, so has the involvement of the state.

The use of contracts in Thai agriculture dates back at least twenty-five years, and possibly longer. Karen (1985) refers to the use of contracts in tobacco production as early as 1969. In 1970, the Charoen Pokphand (CP) company, Thailand's largest conglomerate with major agribusiness interests, utilised the contract system when it established a vertically-coordinated poultry enterprise with the aim of exporting to Japan (Ping, 1980). Laramee (1975) refers to a joint Thai-Israeli company which, from 1972, established the contract production of vegetables in Chiengmai Province. Some of the pineapple canning plants established in the 1960s and early 1970s initially attempted to operate on the basis of contract farming but, as Siamwalla (1978) and Abbott (1988) note, these early attempts were largely unsuccessful because of competition from the fresh market.

In most of these cases, it was the private sector which laid the groundwork for such developments. However, the state very soon came to play a major role in terms of both setting the broad policy directions for diversification into agribusiness and in underwriting private sector activity in a variety of ways. The state performed this role by the establishment of an institutional and legislative framework which facilitated intervention at a number of points. One of the earliest institutions it employed for this purpose was the Board of Investment (BOI).

The BOI was established in 1954 as the Board of Industrial Promotion, and assumed its present form, policies and powers in 1977. The BOI offers a wide range of tax exemptions, investment incentives and promotional privileges and, more particularly, has targeted particular industries for promotion, such as industries encouraging the use of agricultural products or natural resources as raw materials. Although it had no particular brief to foster contract farming, this has been an inevitable by-product of its activities, given its involvement in sectors in which contract production predominates, such as frozen or canned fruits and vegetables, aquaculture, poultry production and processing (Board of Investment, 1990).

The National Economic and Social Development Board (NESDB)

Among the most powerful of state instruments in Thailand is the National Economic and Social Development Board (NESDB), which is the body mainly responsible for economic planning and implementation in Thailand. With the growing significance of agribusiness in Thailand's overall performance, contract farming came to be of particular interest to the powerful bureaucracy which operated through the NESDB. The first official reference to agribusiness and export-oriented agricultural diversification occurred in the NESDB's Fourth National Economic and Social Development Plan (1977–81) which referred to the growth potential of agribusiness, the need to ensure adequate supplies of inputs to these industries, the benefits in crop diversification and the gains to provincial areas in establishing decentralised agri-processing facilities (NESDB, 1978).

The focus on contract farming as an organisational model for agribusiness became more defined in subsequent national planning documents, although initially this appeared to be related to concerns about the impact that contract farming was having on farmers. In the Fifth Development Plan (1982–86), the NESDB noted that policies in agricultural marketing and pricing needed to be reviewed as 'the development of the private sector's contract trading system has progressed very far in creating trade contracts between farmers and factories, resulting in greater injustice in some cases' (NESDB, 1982, p. 46). Subsequently, the NESDB instigated a number of research projects designed to evaluate the contract farming system. One such project, jointly sponsored by the NESDB and the Ministry of Commerce and funded by the World Bank, commissioned the Social Research Institute of Chulalongkorn University to undertake a wide-ranging study on ways to improve agricultural marketing in Thailand. Among the terms of reference was a requirement to study the contract farming system, to evaluate its advantages and disadvantages to the participants (farmers, private sector companies, state organisations), to recommend crops or products to which the contract system could be applied in such a way that all parties could benefit, and to consider a range of issues pertinent to the contract farming system, such as product standardisation and quality control, dispute settlement procedures, information systems, and so on.

In general terms, the Chulalongkorn study perceived no inherent problems in contract farming that would lead to any participating group being permanently disadvantaged. Particular problems in individual sectors were noted, however. For example, broiler production under contract was categorised as a high-risk occupation as increased production costs were not always reflected in higher prices for broilers, and a large part of production costs were accounted for by animal feed which was usually provided by the processing companies. In addition, overproduction and a lack of freezer storage on the part of small poultry growers led to fluctuating prices and uncertainty in returns. However, the study recommended a number of policy changes to overcome such problems and advocated an extension of contract farming into crops such as soybeans, cotton, lychee and longan (Social Research Institute, 1984).

Another study, also commissioned by the NESDB with support from the World Bank, was carried out by the Asian Institute of Technology in Bangkok and formed part of a major policy study on agricultural development and related activities (Tang, 1985). In a generally uncritical evaluation, this study also suggested that contract farming was an effective system for overcoming the problems experienced by farmers in terms of marketing and managerial skills and their access to finance. Tang (1985) suggested the establishment of contract farming schemes on a tripartite basis, with the private sector providing financial, management and marketing services, the government providing finance and land, and the farmers providing the resources to work the land. Following these suggestions, the Guidelines for Development of Agro-Industries, part of the Sixth National Economic and Social Development Plan 1987–91, laid down a number of general objectives (Manarungsan and Suwanjindar, 1992, p. 12):

1. To develop and support agro-industries which have potential for export promotion and import substitution;

2. To expand into new forms of agro-industrial production which have potential for further development, such as food processing industries;

3. To create linkages and improve production techniques, marketing, research, as well as management and investment of the public and private sectors;

4. To support farmers in production planning with emphasis on ensuring a consistent supply of high quality raw materials to meet the requirements of agro-industrial processing plants;

5. To assist agro-industrial plants in transferring appropriate technology to farmers.

The Guidelines stated explicitly that contract farming would be one of the production systems to be promoted by the government, and the institutional framework for the development of this policy was laid down in the Four-Sector Co-operation Plan to Develop Agriculture and Agro-Industry, approved by the Council of Economic Ministers in January 1987. Under this plan, co-operation between the four sectors – government, agribusiness, financial institutions and farmers – was to be encouraged in order to promote contract production of selected commodities (*The Nation*, 20 January 1987). A programme of assistance was formulated, covering import-substituting crops (dairy cattle, paper pulp, wheat, barley, rapid-growing trees for use as fuel, cotton, oil crop, cocoa and silk) and export-promotion crops (vegetables, fruits, flowers, decorative plants, basmati rice, mali-fragrant rice, beef cattle, goats, sheep, poultry, cashew nuts, maize products, herbs, pepper, sealing wax, honey and vegetable seeds).

Under this programme, private sector companies formulate project proposals covering one or more of the above products and invite farmers to participate under contract arrangements. The private sector would be eligible for a range of investment incentives such as those provided by the BOI, and would in turn, provide appropriate technology for farmers and assist them with production and marketing. The public sector would provide farmers with low-interest loans through the Bank for Agriculture and Agricultural Cooperatives and would provide other subsidised inputs and extension services. Farmers were expected to form co-operative groups in order to carry out their respective operations, and to make full use of 'modern and appropriate technology' (*The Nation*, 20 January 1987). The contract was the key to the programme, a fact which was acknowledged at the highest political level following the meeting of the Council of Economic Ministers which adopted the programme: 'Prime Minister Prem Tinsulanonda ... noted that projects between the private sector and farmers would inspire more confidence on both sides if they took the form of contract farming' (*Bangkok Post*, 20 January 1987).

Up to 1989/90, twelve projects were approved (Table 9.1); six in the export-promoting sector and six in the import-substituting sector. In a matter of two or three years, the Four-Sector Co-operation programme covered over 100,000 farmers and some 877,000 rai of land (6.25 rai = 1 hectare), which is evidence of quite rapid diversification into new crops. Undoubtedly, there were strong financial and other incentives for farmers to enter into contract production under this arrangement. Not only was the programme sanctioned and monitored by the government, but in addition the financial inducements were very attractive. In May 1991, farmers with contracts under the scheme were being charged a rate of nine per cent for loans, three per cent below the normal lending rate. Of course, contract farming also continued to expand outside of the Four-Sector Co-operation Plan, in commodities including beef, vegetables, shrimps, silk, chicken, soybean, baby corn, sweet corn, tomato, and sweet grass.

In the latest five-year plan covering the period 1992–96 (NESDB, 1992, pp. 37 and 117), the government reaffirmed its commitment to contract farming and announced a range of measures designed to extend the use of contracts to new crops and new areas. Following the election held in September 1992, the reform government of Chuan Leekpai also endorsed these programmes in its policy statement to Parliament on 21 October 1992. Clearly, the Four-Sector Co-operation Plan remains a central element in the programme to establish contract production relationships between producers and processors. Another is the use of Thailand's land reform programme and the attempt to ensure that land coming under the control of the Agricultural Land Reform Office (ALRO) is incorporated into the state's plans for diversification and agro-industrial development.

The Agricultural Land Reform Office (ALRO)

Land reform emerged as an issue of official concern in the mid-1970s as a result of a number of factors. The first was an emerging landlessness which, according to ALRO, accounted for ten per cent of agricultural households in 1982 (Judd, 1989, p. 121). Second, the rate of tenancy, involving high rent payments by poor farmers, was substantial. A third factor was growing farmer indebtedness which led to mortgage

Table 9.1   *Projects promoted by the Government under the Four-Sector
Co-operation Plan 1987/88 - 1989/90*

Crop	Period (years)	Targeted area ('000 rai)	Progress (by 1989) area ('000 rai)	farmers (persons)
Export Oriented Crops				
1. Basmati rice	1987–89	649	229	37,135
2. Maize and millet	1987–90	480	409	31,502
	1989–91	291	–	–
3. Asparagus	1987–88	6	5	1,375
4. Cashew nuts	1985–89	260	199	22,938
5. Eucalyptus	1988–92	100	1	60
6. Swine	1988–91	–	–	–
Import Substitution Crops				
1. Bamboo for paper pulp	1988–91	25	0.4	150
2. Castor beans	1988–90	15	6	438
3. Sunflower seed	1987–89	43	8	1,009
4. Jute grass	1987–88	6	0.9	434
5. Barley	1988–91	150	11	3,815
6. Wheat	1988–91	24	7	3,680
Total		2049	877	102,536

Note: 6.25 rai = 1 hectare.

Source: Center for Public-Private Cooperation on Agricultural Development
(1989), *Progress Report: Crop Year BE 25 32/33*, Royal Thai
Government, Bangkok, pp. 13–15.

foreclosures and loss of land. Finally, there was illegal squatting on
state land and the need to deal with such claims with a minimum of
conflict (Cohen, 1990). The catalyst to land reform legislation to address these issues was the civil unrest arising out of the student upris-
ing of October 1973. This led to farmer demonstrations which demanded
action over issues such as high rents, indebtedness and the confiscation
of land by unscrupulous lenders. As a result, the ALRO was established in 1975 and by 1989 it had distributed some 1.5m rai of land
to 76,389 farm families (*Bangkok Post*, 30 March 1989). Significantly,
much of this land was specifically targeted for contract farming. 'ALRO
is committed to developing agribusiness on [land reform areas] and
no doubt ALRO sees contract systems as an acceptable compromise
between agribusiness promotion and its mandate to preserve smallholder owner-operators' (Cohen, 1990, p. 28). Also, contract farming

schemes organised under the Four-Sector Co-operation Plan were targeted to land reform areas:

> Growing interest is being shown by both domestic and foreign agro-industrial enterprises in investing, particularly in areas partly controlled by government, such as settlement and agricultural land reform areas. The Office of Agricultural Land Reform [ALRO] has adopted a vigorous policy for integrated agro-industrial development and has announced a series of schemes in silk rearing, cashew, asparagus, cocoa, wheat, beef and milk cattle, ginger and eucalyptus, which seek to have local farmers in the land reform areas enter into contract with agro-industrial companies.
>
> (Economist Intelligence Unit, 1988, p. 21).

These commodities are, of course, among those that have been targeted by the Four-Sector Co-operation Plan for priority in production, which demonstrates the extent of co-ordination of state policy in underwriting contract farming and agribusiness. Indeed, a number of agricultural developments have succeeded in attracting state support from all institutional sources discussed so far. For example, cashew nut cultivation has been organised in several locations by the Mahboonkrong Sirichai Group, a major conglomerate with interests in agricultural production, commodity trading, production, retailing, property and several other sectors. The company has received BOI privileges in both the production and processing of cashew nuts, as well as the benefits made available by contracting with farmers in land reform areas to produce under the Four-Sector Co-operation Plan.

It is clear that state support for contract farming and agribusiness development has revolved around a range of financial and other incentives directed at both agribusiness companies and, to a lesser extent, the peasant growers. However, in recent years, the state has become more directly interventionist and has, on occasions, even considered measures to make contract production mandatory. The clearest manifestation of this trend has been the proposals for a National Agricultural Council.

The National Agricultural Council (NAC)

The proposal for a National Agricultural Council (NAC) was initially approved by the Cabinet in January 1987, only one week after the Council of Economic Ministers had established the Four-Sector Co-operation Plan for Agriculture and Agro-Industry. In an obviously related decision, the Cabinet agreed to set up the Council to serve as its key adviser on agricultural policy and supervise the implementation of the policy on the production, processing and marketing of crops. The Council was to comprise representatives from the government, farmers and the private sector, and was to be responsible for formulating production, processing and marketing plans for *all* crops. It also had responsibility for working out directions on production, processing promotion, marketing and pricing measures so that agricultural development would be 'systematic and in line with market demand both in terms of quantity and quality of the crops' (*The Nation*, 28 January 1987). The Council was also to lay down policy guidelines for government agencies with an interest in agricultural development, which would take into account the interests of all parties concerned, would promote the establishment of farmer groups and cooperatives, and would provide advice on suitable crops for specific terrains and technology to reduce production costs (*Bangkok Post*, 4 July 1987).

The proposal to establish the Council at this time lapsed with the fall of the Prem government in 1988. The idea was subsequently taken up by the Chatichai government and a Bill establishing the Council passed a first reading in Parliament. However, this also was aborted by the military coup of February 1991, and the establishment of a caretaker government by a military junta. The caretaker government, headed by Mr Anand Panyarachun and largely composed of businessmen and technocrats, revived the proposal for a National Agricultural Council in March 1991. The new Council was to have seventy-four members: twenty-two representatives from each of the three main groups (farmers, bureaucrats and agribusiness companies) and eight politicians. The Council was to be given wide-ranging powers, the most significant of which gave it the authority to: determine the areas of production, types of produce, targets and the type of marketing system or monopoly; determine the amount of produce a business would buy from farmers and set quality standards; set rules that require farmers or companies to do or refrain from doing certain things, or to cooperate with each other for the common interest (*Bangkok Post*, 28 May 1991).

In this form, the proposal for the Council was far more interventionist than the 1987 legislation proposed by the Prem government. These new provisions implied an extensive degree of state direction and control over agriculture and generated a good deal of opposition from farmer groups, non-governmental organisations, social activists and academics who saw the NAC as a threat to peasant producers. The concern was that the Council would be biased in favour of the agribusiness companies since the bureaucratic representatives would normally align themselves with the business groups to form a majority. In particular, critics of the proposal expressed concern that the powers of direction and control vested in the Council could lead to peasant farmers being compelled to enter into contract farming, and being told what to grow, for what company and at what price (Economist Intelligence Unit, 1991).

As a consequence of this persistent opposition, the proposals were suspended in December 1991. Political instability, culminating in the early demise of the Suchinda government following the slaughter of civilian demonstrators in May 1992, effectively immobilised all such policy initiatives. However, legislative proposals for a new Council or something similar will undoubtedly reappear at some time in the near future. The Seventh National Economic and Social Development Plan contains a commitment to establish a 'national committee on agro-industrial policy to formulate plans and coordinate agro-industrial development, together with clear designation of responsible agencies and their respective duties' (NESDB, 1992, p. 47). Clearly, the bureaucrats in the NESDB are still strong advocates of centralised control and the repeated attempts to establish the NAC are a manifestation of the deep commitment of the state to contract farming as a model for agribusiness development. It is also a symptom of the contradictions faced by the state in attempting to push this particular model, for it implies a commitment to intervention and centralised control in the agro-industrial sector which is in stark contrast to its policy orientations in other spheres of the economy. Thailand has long been held up as a model of a market-oriented and outward looking economy which, as a result of liberal economic policies, has reaped the rewards of consistently high rates of economic growth. Yet, in dealing with peasant farmers, successive governments have sought to impose policies which would not be out of place in a command economy.

9.4 THE STATE AND AGRIBUSINESS IN THAILAND

A full analysis of the relationship between the state and agribusiness in Thailand would have to include a discussion of many issues which can not be considered for reasons of space. Chief among these is the role of the military and of the monarchy in stimulating agribusiness development. This section will focus on the bureaucracy in an attempt to understand its role as the major advocate of an interventionist policy in support of contract farming and agribusiness development. In this context, it has been suggested that one of the main reasons for bureaucratic support of contract farming stems from the belief that it provides a solution to continuing poverty in rural areas. By integrating small farmers with world markets through the production of value-added processed goods it is believed that greater returns can be generated for farmers. The Four-Sector Co-operation Plan, discussed above, was justified in terms of the need to address the problem of low rural incomes. In framing its proposals, the government stated that projects under this programme must have clear goals of raising the income of farmers and providing jobs to rural people (*The Nation*, 20 January 1987).

The proposal to establish a National Agricultural Council with wide powers of direction and control has also been justified as a way of increasing rural incomes. Commenting on this proposal at the time of its introduction, Agriculture Minister Harn Leenanond said that the Council would solve the problem of rural poverty by ensuring better prices for products and assistance with marketing loans (*Bangkok Post*, 4 July 1987). However, although supported and advocated by politicians, the proposal for a National Agricultural Council was largely the brainchild of the planning officials and bureaucrats who believed they could 'solve rural poverty through better management in the farm sector and systematic marketing planning offered by contract farming ... According to this rationale, rural poverty is caused by poor production per unit of land and labour due to lack of modern farm inputs, technology, access to credits, and planned marketing based on information. [The bureaucrats] believe that these drawbacks, along with price uncertainties, can be overcome by contract farming' (*Bangkok Post*, 28 May 1991).

Certainly, the issue of rural poverty has re-emerged in recent years, following an apparent decline in both relative and absolute terms between the early 1960s and early 1980s. This resulted from the opportunities opened up by Thailand's first wave of agricultural diversification from the 1960s, combined with a range of welfare-oriented measures introduced after the civil disturbances of 1973 (Krongkaew, 1985). However, from the early 1980s, income inequalities increased so rapidly that by 1986 the relativities between the richest and poorest were even more pronounced than they had been before this period of im-

provement. For example, the lowest 40 per cent of households received 16.6 per cent of income in 1962, but only 13 per cent in 1986.
By contrast, the top 10 per cent of households increased their share
from 34.3 per cent to 38.4 per cent (Ikemoto, 1991, p. 17).

In this context, contract farming was seen as one of the ways of
increasing rural incomes without implying the radical social change
that had been advocated by a variety of domestic commentators who
criticised policies, such as the export tax on rice, which ensured that
urban consumers enjoyed cheap food at the expense of rural producers.
Thus, contract farming was thought to hold out the prospect of solving rural poverty without challenging the *status quo*, thereby ensuring
the stability of civil society and the state. It also emerged as a vital
element in the planning role and functions of the state, because the
bureaucrats who were responsible for consolidating and extending Thailand's status as an industrialising country came to see contract farming as essential to the agro-industrial sector which was so important a
part of this strategy.

Seen from this perspective, the state is not simply or even primarily concerned to increase rural incomes through contract farming.
Rather, in the provision of subsidies and incentives, the state has come
to assume responsiblity for the wider organisation of the system in
its attempts to guarantee supplies of raw materials to processing companies at prices which enable them to compete in local and world
markets. In short, the role of the state has also to be understood in
terms of underwriting contract farming as a way of promoting capital
in this sector. Certainly, the long-standing alliance between the bureaucracy and the business sector in Thailand indicates a good deal of
state support for both local and overseas capital, with state funds being used to assist with the establishment of enterprises approved by
the Board of Investment, with the financial and institutional support
of NESDB and ALRO, and in the support offered in the Four-Sector
Co-operation Plan. But if this is the case, why has it proved necessary for the state to move towards such a strongly interventionist position, represented by the repeated attempts to establish the National
Agricultural Council?

One answer to this lies in the suggestion that contract farming cannot be seen as a way of increasing rural incomes on a sustained and
long-term basis, although in the early phase of production of a commodity under contract demand for a new product is likely to be high
and this might generate large returns to processor and grower. However, if demand falls or if consumption reaches saturation point, there

is less scope for maintaining high returns. Again, if input costs increase through inflationary pressures which are not reflected in farm
prices, rural incomes will fall. Any such fall may be exacerbated by
processor attempts to renegotiate the terms of the contract in order to
ensure better profits or to relocate to cheaper production sites. More
important than this is the fact that the processes of appropriationism
and substitutionism, of which contract farming is currently an integral
part, inevitably serve to redistribute the returns to agriculture from
the farmer to the processor. As Friedmann (1991, pp. 72–3) notes in
the US context, the farm share of the value of all foods in the US is
now 31 per cent, while the other 69 per cent goes to the corporations
that process, distribute and sell food. Of course, the total value of
agro-industrial output in the US has grown significantly and it may
be that total rewards going to rural producers are larger than before.
On the other hand, under conditions of appropriationism and
substitutionism, smaller and marginal producers are likely to be increasingly squeezed, leaving only a handful of large farmers who are
able to maintain viable operations and share in this larger cake.

If this is the case, then many marginal farmers in the less developed countries will be unwilling to operate under the conditions established by global agribusiness and may seek to withdraw from contract
operations. This has certainly been the case in Thailand where farmers have, on many occasions, been subjected to cost pressures as a
result of entering into contract production with agribusiness companies. Ekachai (1990) has reported on the falling returns to farmers for
baby corn in recent years. While experiencing rapid growth and good
returns from canned baby corn over the 1980s, Thailand now dominates the world market and production has reached a peak. There are
no more gains to be made by expanding production for global markets and the price paid to farmers has been stable for several years.
However, the costs of fertilisers and other inputs continue to increase,
with the result that farmers receive less income and will switch to
alternative crops if possible (but, because of debt and/or contractual
obligations, they may face difficulty in doing so).

Similar problems have occurred in Thailand's poultry industry. In
the case of the Charoen Pokphand group, for example, there is little
doubt that their contract farmers earned a good income in the early
years. However, from the early 1980s, returns were highly variable
and many farmers were left with heavy losses and high debt levels.
Farmers who ran at a loss for several successive lots of chicken were
subjected to penalties ranging from criticism to suspension of sup-

plies to suspension from the project. Many farmers have opted out of contract production and the turnover rate has been as high as 50 per cent. Plans for a 10 per cent annual increase in output have been suspended as a result of farmer withdrawals. The number of farmers contracting with this company has remained steady, at about 150, and output has stabilised at two million chickens per flock (Manarungsan and Suwanjindar, 1992, p. 45).

Under these circumstances, it is understandable why the state has moved towards increased regulation in an attempt to exert control over what is grown, where, by whom, for whom, and at what price. For, unlike contract farmers in the developed countries who are so highly specialised that they experience little flexibility in their operations, peasant producers in the Third World may still have room to manoeuvre in their dealings with processing and/or exporting companies. When confronted with attempts to reduce prices paid for output goods, or to increase the costs of inputs, many Third World producers still have the option of retreating into subsistence farming or, possibly, alternative cash crops. The main factor limiting such action by peasant farmers is the need to continue to earn a cash income in order to service debts owed to the BAAC or the agribusiness companies. These debts have to be repaid, even where falling real returns or lower than expected yields mean a diminished capacity on the part of peasant farmers to meet these commitments. As a consequence, farmers become locked into a cycle of cash crop production which offers little guarantee of a higher standard of living or an end to continuing poverty.

Whether farmers withdraw from contract production or are forced to continue as a result of debt pressures, there are obvious difficulties for the agribusiness companies in maintaining a guaranteed supply of high quality inputs. The companies could respond by increasing the prices paid to farmers, but this is unlikely if it means reduced profits in a situation where world demand will not bear a price increase. Another option for the company in the medium term is to relocate to cheaper overseas production sites, such as Charoen Pokphand is doing in establishing feed mill operations in Vietnam. But, importantly, this option would be unacceptable to the state, which sees *Thai*-based operations as vital to its overall development strategy. Given this, it is not surprising that legislation along the lines proposed for the NAC is seen by both agribusiness and the state to be necessary, in order to keep peasant farmers in the contract farming system and producing on terms, and at prices, acceptable to the agribusiness companies. There is little doubt that in taking an increasingly interventionist role the state is responding to the demands of the these companies. For example, the proposals for the Four-Sector Co-operation Plan for Agriculture and Agro-Industry came out of the consultative processes established through the Joint Public–Private Consultative Committees. The most import-ant committee in this system has businessmen and cabinet ministers as members; the Prime Minister presides while the Secretary-General of the NESDB serves as secretary (Laothamatas, 1992). While in theory a consultative committee, in practice it is an avenue for business to forward complaints or requests to the government. The prestige and power of the committee ensures that implementing agencies take its resolutions seriously.

Within this consultative process, committees have also been estab-lished to cover specific areas of interest. Of particular relevance is the Joint Public–Private Consultative Committee for Agricultural De-velopment, established to work out plans and strategies for develop-ing the agricultural sector. This committee, on which there are no farmers' representatives, initiated the Four-Sector Co-operation Plan which, as noted earlier, gave a major government commitment to agribusiness expansion and contract farming. It was very influential in getting the state to underwrite contract farming in a wide range of crops, by subsidising farmers, by making land available in land re-form areas, and by a range of other means. Equally, private sector agribusiness had a significant, if less formal, role in the framing of proposals for the National Agricultural Council, and the Charoen Pokphand group in particular is reported as having had a direct influence on this legislation. For example, Dr Ajva Taulananda, one of two deputy Ministers of Agriculture in the Anand government was, before his appointment to the ministry, vice-president of the CP group, while Dr Suchart Thada-Thamrongvech, a senior ministerial adviser, was also economic adviser to the CP group.

Clearly, the agribusiness sector has had a dominant role in the for-mation of policy for peasant production of cash crops, and has util-ised this to try to organise farmers into contract production on the basis of government regulation rather than economic incentives. Given this, it is doubtful whether contract farming will result in any sus-tained improvement in rural incomes. Importantly, the contract farm-ing system also serves to redistribute the risks in cultivation and shifts a larger part of the burden onto peasant farmers. It is they who carry the increased volume of debt, which must be serviced out of a cash income which may be good for a few years but which is unlikely to be maintained in the long term.

9.5 CONCLUSIONS

In recent years, the state in Thailand has established a substantial degree of control over the small-scale agricultural sector. It has justified its promotion of contract farming as a way of increasing rural incomes and addressing the issues of poverty and inequality, but it appears more likely that its extensive capacity for intervention is exercised on behalf of private capital. While it has not yet succeeded in establishing the National Agricultural Council, the repeated attempts to do so suggest powerful motives which, it has been argued, are related to the extent to which peasant farmers are prone to reject the contract system. If this is the case, proposals for the Council or some alternative way of achieving the same ends, will undoubtedly re-emerge as a way of attempting to control the numbers of peasants required to maintain the commitment to agro-industry. In the longer term, of course, questions relating to the future role of contract farming in the Third World will depend upon the nature of the technological developments which emerge as a consequence of the continuing application of appropriationist and substitutionist strategies by global agribusiness (Goodman, 1991). In the meantime, contract farming continues to be important and for this reason state intervention in an agricultural sector locked into the world system will continue to be exercised in ways which result in continuing instability and poverty in the rural sector.

Note

1. This paper is based on research conducted while the author was Australian-Southeast Asian Research Fellow at the Institute of Southeast Asian Studies, Singapore, in 1992. The author would like to express thanks to the Institute for the opportunity to undertake research in Singapore and Thailand, and is especially grateful to those civil servants, academics, journalists and activists in both countries who gave their time and much valuable information.

References

Abbott, J.C. (1988), *Agricultural Processing for Development*, Aldershot: Avebury.
Board of Investment (1990), *Thailand Investment 1991–2*, Bangkok: Cosmic Enterprises.
Cohen, P.T. (1990), 'Land Reform and Agribusiness in Thailand: Are they

Compatible?', *Proceedings of the Fourth International Conference on Thai Studies*, Institute of Southeast Asian Studies, Kunning, China, 11–13 May 1990.

Doner, R. (1974), 'The Development of Agribusiness in Thailand', *The Bulletin of Concerned Asian Scholars*, 6, 8–15.

Economist Intelligence Unit (1988), *Country Report: Thailand, No.3*, London: Business International Limited.

Economist Intelligence Unit (1991), *Country Report: Thailand, No.3*, London: Business International Limited.

Ekachai, S. (1990), *Behind the Smile: Voices of Thailand*, Bangkok: Thai Development Support Committee.

Foreign Agricultural Service (1992), *The World Poultry Situation*, Washington, DC: US Department of Agriculture.

Friedmann, H. (1991), 'Changes in the International Division of Labour: Agri-Food Complexes and Export Agriculture', in W.H. Friedland *et al* (eds), *Towards a New Political Economy of Agriculture*, Boulder, Colorado: Westview Press.

Glover, D. and Kusterer, K. (1990), *Small Farms, Big Business*, London: Macmillan.

Goldstein, C. (1988), 'Asia's Supermarket', *Far Eastern Economic Review*, 29 December, 48–51.

Goodman, D., Sorj, B. and Wilkinson, J. (1987), *From Farming to Biotechnology*, Oxford: Basil Blackwell.

Goodman, D. (1991), 'Some Recent Tendencies in the Industrial Re-organisation of the Agri-Food System', in W.H. Friedland et al. (eds), *Towards a New Political Economy of Agriculture*, Boulder, Colorado: Westview Press.

Hawes, G.A. (1982), 'Southeast Asian Agribusiness: The New International Division of Labour', *Bulletin of Concerned Asian Scholars*, 14, 20–29.

Hewison, K. (1989), *Bankers and Bureaucrats: Capital and the Role of the State in Thailand*, New Haven: Yale University Press.

Ikemoto, Y. (1991), *Income Distribution in Thailand: Its Changes, Causes and Structure*, Tokyo: Institute of Developing Economies.

Judd, L.C. (1989), *In Perspective: Trends in Rural Development Policy and Programs in Thailand 1947–87*, Research Report Series No.41, Payap University Centre for Research and Development, Chiengmai.

Karen, R. (1985), 'Adams International: Tobacco Growing and Marketing in Northern Thailand', in S. Williams and R. Karen (eds), *Agribusiness and the Small-Scale Farmer*, Boulder, Colorado: Westview Press.

Krongkaew, M. (1985), 'Agricultural Development, Rural Poverty and Income Distribution in Thailand', *The Developing Economies*, 23, 325–46.

Laothamatas, A. (1992), *Business Associations and the New Political Economy of Thailand*, Boulder, Colorado: Westview Press.

Laramee, P.A. (1975), 'Problems of Small Farmers under Contract Marketing, with Special Reference to a Case in Chiengmai Province, Thailand', *Economic Bulletin for Asia and the Pacific*', 26, 43–47.

Manarungsan, S. and Suwanjindar, S. (1992), 'Contract Farming and Outgrower Schemes in Thailand', in D. Glover and Lim Tek Ghee (eds), *Contract Farming in Southeast Asia: Three Country Studies*, Kuala Lumpur: Institute for Advanced Studies, University of Malaya.

NESDB (1978), *The Fourth National Economic and Social Development Plan 1977–81*, Bangkok: Royal Thai Government.

NESDB (1982), *The Fifth National Economic and Social Development Plan 1982–86*, Bangkok: Royal Thai Government.

NESDB (1992), *The Seventh National Economic and Social Development Plan 1992–96*, Bangkok: Royal Thai Government.

Office of Agricultural Economics, *Annual Agricultural Statistics of Thailand*, Bangkok: Royal Thai Government, various years.

Ping, Ho Kwon (1980), 'Profits and Poverty in the Plantations', *Far Eastern Economic Review*, 11 July, 53–57.

Siamwalla, A. (1978), 'Farmers and Middlemen: Aspects of Agricultural Marketing in Thailand', *Economic Bulletin for Asia and the Pacific*, 29, 38–50.

Social Research Institute (1984), *Project on the Improvement of the Agricultural Marketing System: Southern Region*, Bangkok: Chulalongkorn University.

Tang, J.C.S. (1985), 'Contractual Farming in Thailand: Role of Government and the Private Sector', *International Journal for Development Technology*, 3, 57–61.

de Treville, D. (1987), *An Annotated and Comprehensive Bibliography of Contract Farming*, Binghampton, New York: The Institute for Development Anthropology.

10 Small-Scale Banana Growers in the Windward Islands: External Implications of the Single European Market

Robert Read[1]

10.1 INTRODUCTION

The economies of the Caribbean islands of Dominica, St Lucia, St Vincent and Grenada (the Windward Islands) are heavily dependent upon the banana industry in terms of its contribution towards GDP, employment and export earnings. This dependency is further accentuated by their complete reliance upon the European Community (EC) market, principally the UK, for their banana exports. As former British Colonies and signatories of the Lomé Convention, the Windward Islands have long enjoyed preferential access to these markets, currently enshrined in the Community's Banana Protocol. The advent of the Single European Market (SEM) however, has important external implications for LDC exporters of products such as bananas. The SEM legislation necessitates the elimination of nationally-administered trade barriers within the EC, including those sanctioned under the Banana Protocol. In the absence of the implementation of an equivalent import scheme, the SEM is likely to create severe difficulties for many LDCs. In the case of the Windward Islands, these difficulties threaten the social and economic structure of the smallholder agricultural sector (primarily banana growing) with worrying implications for rural poverty and inequality.

This chapter addresses the impact of the SEM, and the consequent changes to the EC import regime for bananas, on the economies of the Windward Islands: the issues relate directly to rural development in these economies. Section 10.2 reviews the global banana export industry and identifies the particular problems facing small producers. Section 10.3 analyses the contribution of the banana industry to the industry and identifies the particular problems facing small producers. Section 10.3 analyses the contribution of the banana industry to the economies of the Windward Islands, including a discussion of its organisation and structure. Section 10.4 appraises the competitive position of the Windward Islands and Section 10.5 outlines the EC Banana Protocol, paying special attention to the UK market. Section 10.6 provides an overview of the internal market for bananas, while Section 10.7 analyses the implications of the SEM for the Windward Islands. Section 10.8 offers conclusions and draws out the implications for rural development prospects.

10.2 THE GLOBAL BANANA EXPORT INDUSTRY

The banana export industry has arisen because cultivation is generally confined to tropical LDCs while the main consuming markets are found in the temperate industrialised countries. Export-oriented production is concentrated in Central America, the Caribbean, northern South America and the Philippines; these were responsible for 83 per cent of world exports in 1990 but accounted for only 29.3 per cent of world production (FAO, 1990a; 1990b). International trade in bananas was worth $4.5bn in 1990, $3.7bn (over 82 per cent) of which was accounted for by the North American, Western European and Japanese markets (FAO, 1990a). The general pattern of trade in bananas is strongly influenced by barriers in consuming countries. Protection has been particularly important in the EC where there have been special arrangements for imports from the Départements d'Outre-Mer (DOMs) and some LDCs.

The export trade is complicated by the inherent perishability of bananas which necessitates the close co-ordination of production and distribution. Bananas require specialised shipping facilities, including refrigeration and ventilation, for transportation and distribution to final markets. Their susceptibility to disease led to the introduction of disease-resistant, but more fragile, strains in the late 1950s. Boxes to protect the fruit from damage during shipping and distribution have since become the norm. Boxing has also facilitated the use of quality control to increase the returns from product differentiation through branding.

Competitive advantage in the industry arises principally from the ability of suppliers to deliver high quality low cost brand-differentiated bananas which command premium prices in consuming markets (Read, 1985; 1988). As a consequence, the structure of the banana export industry differs from that of most other tropical agricultural products in that it is dominated by three highly vertically-integrated multinational enterprises (MNEs) – United Brands, Castle & Cooke and Del Monte. These firms are responsible for almost 60 per cent of world trade in bananas and the greater part of imports in the markets of the major industrialised countries.

Banana cultivation techniques are relatively simple but there are significant risks of possible disruptions to supply caused by natural catastrophe and disease as well as strikes and expropriation. To minimise these risks, the leading firms have diversified the location of their plantation activities. Although export-oriented banana production is usually associated with large-scale plantations, a significant proportion of MNE output has been contracted-out to smaller growers to diversify inherent production risks. Open market purchases are made by the MNEs only in the event of shortfalls in plantation and contract supplies. The supply strategies of the MNEs provide a 'window of opportunity' for higher cost smaller scale growers, who continue to flourish. Several successful smaller companies are also active in particular exporting countries and consuming markets.

10.3 THE BANANA EXPORT INDUSTRY IN THE WINDWARD ISLANDS

The Windward Islands comprise the former British Colonies of Dominica, Grenada, St Lucia, and St Vincent and the Grenadines, which lie off the north east Caribbean coast of South America. These four independent island states cover a total area of around 2,100 square kilometres and have a combined population of less than half a million (Table 10.1). Their economies are small and poorly diversified with a relatively underdeveloped infrastructure, partly as a consequence of their mountainous topography, and they continue to be highly dependent upon the agricultural sector. Unemployment and under-employment are both pervasive, particularly in rural areas, and the islands have low average levels of per capita income.

The Windward Island economies were originally highly dependent upon sugar grown on large plantations located on the most fertile and accessible land. The abolition of slavery in 1833 deprived the sugar plantations of much of their former labour force and created a whole new class of subsistence smallholders farming more marginal and inaccessible agricultural land. Large-scale sugar cultivation slowly

Table 10.1   *The Windward Islands: basic economic indicators*

	Dominica	Grenada	St Lucia	St Vincent	WI
Population ('000, 1991)	71.2	91.0	153.0	114.6	429.8
Area (sq km)	750	345	616	388	2099
GDP ($m, 1991)	147.4	164.3	336.5	178.0	826.3
GDP ($ per capita)	2070	1805	2200	1555	1925
Unemployment (%)	13.0	30.0	14.5	40.0	23.0
Exports ($m, 1991)	51.2	19.7	100.4	66.6	237.9
Sectoral Shares of GDP (1981–83 average)					
Agriculture	29.9	21.3	13.9	15.5	18.6
Manufacturing	7.8	2.6	9.7	11.0	8.2
Tourism	1.2	4.4	7.6	2.3	4.7
Government	3.6	21.1	22.1	18.9	17.9
Other	57.5	50.6	46.7	52.3	50.6

Source: IMF *International Financial Statistics* (various years) and Winban statistics (various years).

declined in importance during the nineteenth and early twentieth centuries. The commercial cultivation of bananas first began during the 1920s, strongly encouraged by the Colonial Government because it promoted diversification, reduced dependence upon sugar production and both large- and small-scale production were feasible.

The island smallholders had already been compelled to diversify out of sugar because of the large amounts of capital required to produce it efficiently. They diversified, partly through inter-cropping, into a variety of export crops, including bananas, which provided small cash incomes. Bananas continue to be very popular with smallholders because they are a short-term crop which provides a regular (weekly or fortnightly), rather than a single annual, cash income. Large-scale banana cultivation in the Windward Islands did not begin until 1948 when Antilles Products Ltd initiated its own banana production on Dominica. It also secured an exclusive sales contract with the Banana Growers Association (BGA) on each island. The company shipped its fruit to the nearby US market but found itself unable to compete effectively with bananas produced by the MNEs on their extensive Central American plantations. In 1952, its interests, including the exclusive sales contracts, were acquired by Geest Industries, a UK fruit and vegetable producer and distributor (Thomson, 1987).

Table 10.2 *The contribution of the banana industry to the economies of the Windward Islands*

	Dominica	Grenada	St Lucia	St Vincent	WI
Output ('000 tonnes)	60.9	8.2	118.2	62.0	249.3
Share (islands, %)	24.4	3.3	47.4	24.9	100.0
Change (%, 1983–91)	96.6	−21.9	87.5	132.5	91.9
Employment ('000)	12.5	2.0	20.0	13.0	47.5
Share of active pop. (%)	50.0	6.7	45.5	54.2	39.9
Banana Exports ($m, 1991)	30.0	3.7	54.2	33.1	121.0
Banana exports as a share of:					
Total Exports (%)	58.5	18.6	54.0	49.7	50.9
Agricultural exports (%)	91.6	28.4	87.4	63.6	75.8
Exports to EC (%)	94.2	47.7	95.5	89.8	90.7
Exports to UK (%)	96.1	79.9	96.6	98.4	96.3
GDP (%)	20.3	2.2	16.1	18.6	14.6

Note: Output is measured as the average over the period 1987–91.

Source: Eurostat (1992) and Winban statistics (various years).

The Contribution of Bananas to the Windward Island Economies

The Windward Islands are of minor significance in the world banana trade with a share of around 5.6 per cent of world exports (FAO, 1990a), 6.3 per cent of the EC market and 49.3 per cent of the UK market in 1991 (Eurostat, 1992). From Table 10.2, it can be seen that the banana industry is of critical importance to their economies with the partial exception of Grenada. The industry contributed almost 15 per cent of Windward Island GDP in 1991 and more than 20 per cent in the case of Dominica. Banana exports were worth $121m in 1991, down from $148m in 1990 (FAO, 1990a), and accounted for 50 per cent or more of total export earnings in all but Grenada. The industry is also a significant source of employment, averaging almost 40 per cent of the active population in the islands and 50 per cent or more in Dominica and St Vincent.

The dependence of the Windward Islands upon the banana industry means that their economies are highly susceptible to the vagaries of the weather. Severe hurricanes in 1979 and 1980 had a devastating impact upon agricultural production, particularly that of bananas, with adverse effects upon export earnings and farm incomes. This dependence is intensified by their total reliance upon the EC market for their banana exports, principally the UK (87.8 per cent) and Italy (10.2 per cent) (Eurostat, 1992). This dependency has grown steadily during the last decade, except in Grenada, as total banana exports have risen significantly. This increase has been facilitated by several factors: the greater area being devoted to banana cultivation; higher effective yields; and continued preferential access to the UK market within the designated quota as Jamaican output declined. In Dominica, dependence has been further heightened by the collapse of the lime industry in 1983 with the land being switched to banana cultivation. The continued switching of land to bananas in the Islands has also had an adverse impact upon local food supplies and so aggravated their visible trade deficits.

The Windward Islands have struggled to diversify their productive base. Policies promoting industrialisation were initiated during the 1970s and 1980s, both before and after Independence, but these attempts have, at best, only been partially successful, most notably in Dominica and St Vincent. Dominica's only other major source of export earnings is Dominica Coconut Products which grows and processes local coconuts into oil for soap production. Relatively low wage rates have been successful in attracting labour-intensive manufacturing such as textiles and electronic components to St Lucia and St Vincent, and US investment has expanded under the Caribbean Basin Initiative. Tourism has also become an important source of foreign exchange and now makes an increasing contribution to GDP, especially in St Lucia. The industry has been of less importance in Grenada as a result of its more diversified agricultural base and its poor production and quality performance in bananas. Between 1979 and 1983, Maurice Bishop's New Jewel Movement initiated infrastructural investment, further land reform and, unsuccessfully, promoted both agricultural and industrial diversification.

The Windward Islands Banana Growers Association (Winban) was established in 1958 to co-ordinate the activities of each island's Banana Growers Association and to represent the growers in all negotiations with Geest. Winban is responsible for negotiating and monitoring market and shipping contracts; purchasing inputs, including pesticides and fertilisers; providing technical assistance, undertaking research and statistical support; and representing Windward Island growers on the UK Banana Trade Advisory Committee. The leading role of Winban superseded that of the individual island BGAs in dealing with Geest and providing scientific and technical support. The BGAs were instrumental in the development and support of the industry and their function has been to co-ordinate the activities of the numerous, generally very small, banana farmers. They continue to be responsible for purchasing bananas of exportable quality from individual growers; boxing, delivering and selling bananas to Geest; disease-control and organising and administering agricultural extension, including credit. They comprise a combination of both government appointees and local farmers and represent the island growers in dealings with governments and Winban.

Geest Industries has played an extremely important role in the development of the banana industry in the Windward Islands since its entry in 1952, supplying bananas to the UK market. Geest bears exclusive responsibility for the sale of all Windward Island bananas. This both assures the company of continued supplies of bananas and has enabled it to support the development of its market share in the UK through the encouragement of the gradual but sustained expansion of Windward production. Geest ceased production on its own account in 1983, converting its former estate in St Lucia into 'model farms' along the lines of those associated with Central American banana plantations. Although its banana business is concentrated in the Windward Islands, Geest's commercial interests are widely diversified; it is estimated that bananas accounted for only around 25 per cent of the company's turnover in 1990.

The relationship between Geest, Winban and the Windward Island growers has to be viewed in the general context of vertical relations between producers and distributors in the industry. The 18,000 growers in the Windward Islands effectively produce bananas for Geest on exclusive purchase contracts. To the extent that these contracts assure Geest of continued supplies and reduce their risks in production, they resemble those between the MNEs and their Central American associate producers. There are however, several important differences which partly explain the poor competitive position of the Windward Islands and, by implication, that of Geest relative to Dollar Area production. These differences relate to key characteristics in the structure and organisation of the industry in the Windward Islands.

Peasant smallholder banana growers in the Windward Islands cultivate land under a variety of different tenure arrangements. Apart from freehold family plots, land is rented both for cash and in kind (sharecropping) and some is farmed by squatters. Farming is the sole occupation of most small growers although this varies between islands; dual employment is more common in Dominica (Henderson and Gomes, 1979). Most farmers are self-employed and generally rely upon assistance from their families and work-sharing arrangements with other growers rather than on rural labour markets. The larger banana estates in Dominica and St Lucia offer employment for agricultural labour but at low wages. Banana cultivation provides a regular cash income where there are few alternative sources of income for small-holders; in the absence of the opportunities from cultivating bananas, they could be expected to revert to virtual subsistence farming. This suggests that many peasant small-holders have become 'locked-in' to banana production and, by implication, to marginal incomes. A study of St Lucia found that the majority of farm households, comprising a significant proportion of the total population, were below the poverty line of $400 (LeFranc, 1980). Because many essential foodstuffs are imported at prices beyond the reach of the rural poor, this lack of purchasing power has also meant inadequate nutrition.

The dualistic ownership and tenure structure of land in the Windward Islands, characterised by large estates and peasant smallholdings, is a legacy of the original sugar plantation economy. The agricultural smallholder sector developed in the wake of the abolition of slavery but the large sugar estates have, with the exception of Grenada, never been subjected to land reform. In addition, many of the smallholdings have experienced repeated sub-division and fragmentation over time. In St Lucia, this trend has been more rapid because of the retention of Napoleonic law under which an estate is divided upon its owner's death. Data on the size distribution of land holdings devoted to bananas in the Windward Islands is presented in Table 10.3. The overall average size of holding is just under 0.8 hectares but it is evident that the distribution is heavily skewed by the large number of very small plots. Some 63 per cent of all banana holdings were less than 0.42 hectares (1 acre), varying between 70 per cent in Dominica and only 33 per cent in Grenada, and around 9 per cent were greater than 2.1 ha (5 acres). The great proportion of bananas however, are grown on larger holdings, including small plantations; in St Lucia, around 1,500 growers produce between 80 and 90 per cent of the island's total output of bananas (World Bank, 1985). The statistics are likely to underestimate the actual number of plots however, in that many of the smallholdings themselves are fragmented rather than consolidated. The average size of holding is considerably smaller than in other producer countries except for the Canaries and Madeira (see Table 10.4 below).

Robert Read

Table 10.3 *Land distribution in the Windward Islands*

	Dominica	*Grenada*	*St Lucia*	*St Vincent*	*WI*
Area ('000 hectares)	5.26	1.42	4.86	2.63	14.17
Growers ('000)	5.10	1.91	6.32	4.89	18.23
Average holding (hectares)	1.03	0.74	0.77	0.54	0.78
Distribution by Holding Size (%):					
< 0.42 ha (< 1 acre)	70	33	69	· 61	63
0.42 ha < 2.1 ha (1 – 5 acres)	25	40	23	31	28
> 2.1 ha (> 5 acres)	5	27	8	8	9

Source: Food and Agriculture Organisation (FAO, 1986).

The Determination of Growers' Prices

The price formula for Windward Island growers has been modified several times. Antilles Products' original annual fixed-price contracts were retained by Geest until 1955 when they were replaced by the Green Market Price (GMP) system. This was based upon prices obtained by Geest for green bananas in the UK which were subject to almost daily fluctuation. The growers received the GMP net of deductions for Geest's shipping and handling margins and the services provided by the BGAs. Since 1984, the prices paid by Geest have been based upon the Green Wholesale Price (GWP) which relate growers' prices more closely to market conditions than the GMP (Thomson, 1987). Growers receive around 25 per cent of the gross GWP, Geest's deductions account for 35–45 per cent and the remainder is deducted by the BGAs (calculated from World Bank, 1985; Thomson, 1987). The price received by the Windward Island banana growers is a function of market conditions and the margins deducted from the gross GWP. Net GWP receipts are therefore determined by the institutional relationships between individual growers and the BGAs, the BGAs and Winban and between Winban and Geest.

The BGAs represent all banana growers although most are dominated by the larger producers responsible for the bulk of output. Smallholders therefore tend to be at a disadvantage in the determination of the deductions in spite of their large numbers. Winban is comprised of representatives from each of the BGAs and is financed by their contributions. This close relationship provides little incentive for the minimisation of Winban's costs. Although it has a monopoly over banana exports, Winban has relatively weak bargaining power in its negotiations with Geest. The Windward Islands are highly dependent upon exports of bananas, almost completely reliant upon sales in the UK market and wholly dependent upon Geest for their market access. Although there might appear to be a problem of bilateral monopoly, the bargaining power of Geest is much stronger than that of Winban. Geest has a diversified product base and its vertical control of the shipping, ripening, distribution and marketing of bananas offers the potential to switch its source of supply at little cost. The institutional structure therefore favours Geest over Windward Island banana growers, and smallholders in particular, in the determination of prices and the allocation of profits.

10.4 COMPETITIVENESS OF WINDWARD ISLAND BANANA INDUSTRY

It has been acknowledged implicitly by Geest's Managing Director that their competitive position, and by implication that of the Windward Island producers, is weak in consuming markets where there is direct competition from Dollar Area bananas (*The Independent*, 22 July 1990). Their lack of competitiveness can be ascribed to several factors, notably the yields obtainable and productivity of factor inputs, but also relating to supply disruptions and consumer preferences on the demand side.

Yields

The average output of bananas per hectare in the Windward Islands is generally higher than in other ACP countries but lower than in the DOMs, regardless of the size of average holding (Table 10.4). Actual yields achieved in the Windward Islands, however, exhibit significant variation between islands and because of the skewed size distribution of holdings within islands. Yields on large farms in St Lucia have been found to be twice the average, and in Dominica they vary greatly according to the size of holding (Caribbean Centre for Action Research, 1978). The lower yields of smallholders however, are at least partly offset by inter-cropping with subsistence food crops and other export crops, principally cocoa.

Since 1986, Geest has actively encouraged Windward Island growers to undertake field-packing whereby bananas are boxed on the farm

Table 10.4 *Efficiency in the banana export industry*

	Total output ('000t)	Average holding (ha)	Yield (t/ha)	Labour productivity (t/worker)	Labour intensity (worker/ha)
EC and DOM:					
Canaries	394	0.88	37.5	15.8	2.38
Crete	20	n/a	n/a	n/a	n/a
Guadeloupe	159	4.60	24.5	27.4	0.89
Madeira	53	0.17	32.0	3.4	9.47
Martinique	202	6.00	25.9	31.1	0.83
ACP:					
Belize	28	1800	15.6	n/a	n/a
Cameroun	44	19.08	15.6	10.2	1.52
Côte d'Ivoire	115	10.49	21.0	4.3	4.94
Jamaica	80	2.61	14.0	6.7	2.11
Somalia	103	n/a	16.0	7.4	2.17
Suriname	32	1725	19.9	22.9	0.87
Windward Islands	249	0.78	17.6	5.2	3.35
Dominica	61	1.03	11.6	4.9	2.38
Grenada	8	0.74	5.8	4.1	1.41
St Lucia	118	0.77	24.3	5.9	4.12
St Vincent	62	0.54	23.6	4.8	4.94
Dollar Area:					
Panama (p)	192	5094	37.6	43.7	0.92
Panama (ap)	48	140	25.2	46.5	0.63

Notes: Data are for various years. Dollar Area production refers to Armuelles plantation (p) or Armuelles associate producers (ap); labour productivity and intensity figures also include Bocas del Toro operations.

Source: Calculated from: Winban statistics (various years) and Ellis (1978).

immediately after harvesting. The responsibility for boxing, including the additional labour requirement, is thus transferred to farmers in return for an allowance previously deducted by the company. By raising farmers' revenue, the introduction of field-packing has provided an incentive to increase banana production. The response of growers to this change has been most marked in St Lucia: increased output has been the result of both the expansion of the cultivated area and higher effective yields, the latter due to reduced damage to fruit en route to port and the direct incentive to improve quality. Economies of scale in field-packing however, have favoured the larger banana growers over smallholders.

Average yields in the Windward Islands do not appear to be greatly inferior to those achieved by Fyffes on their plantations in Belize, Cameroun and Suriname, nor United Brands' associate producers at Armuelles. The yields achieved in the DOMs, particularly in the Canaries and to some extent Madeira, are not far below those of the Armuelles plantation. It is important to note however, that yields on the corporate plantations incorporate a downward bias because of their more stringent quality control since they measure effective yields (exports per hectare rather than just output per hectare).

Capital and the Productivity of Labour

The establishment of the banana industry in the Windward Islands was originally encouraged because smallholder production was feasible without significant inputs of capital. Labour continues to be the main input in production but high yields are dependent upon expenditure on complementary inputs of costly chemical fertilisers and sprays. All banana farmers make contributions to BGA finances but low incomes and very high rates of rural illiteracy mean that many small-scale growers are unable to take full advantage of BGA credit and technical services. The opportunity cost of small-holders' labour and of their families is likely to be low and, therefore, relatively supply-elastic over a certain range. Farm income is an increasing function of output so that there is an incentive for additional labour effort to be used as a substitute, to some extent, for technical inputs. The marginal productivity of such labour must be positive but it is likely to be significantly below the local money wage rate.

The comparatively high yields achieved by small-scale producers, such as those in the Windward Islands, can be seen to be the result of the intensive use of labour in spite of its low productivity (Table 10.4). Labour intensity is significantly lower and output per worker significantly higher in those countries characterised by larger-scale production, with the exception of Guadeloupe and Martinique. The comparative data suggests that the lack of capital is a key constraint on the efficiency of smallholder banana cultivation.

Supply Shortfalls and Disruption

Like most agricultural products, banana cultivation suffers from the risks associated with supply shortfalls and disruption. Bananas, however, are very susceptible to such problems for two reasons: cultivation is concentrated in locations prone to unpredictable and severe weather and, because of their perishability, stocks cannot be held in reserve. Firms are better able to assure their supplies of bananas than are countries because they can diversify their risk by producing in several locations. The banana MNEs have geographically diversified production bases so that further supplies can be obtained from alternative sources in the event of problems. This form of diversification is not open to individual producing countries. The supply-elasticity of the MNEs is also extremely high because they can increase their exports rapidly by lowering their quality requirements to reduce the rate of rejection.

Quality Control and Consumer Preferences

Windward Island bananas, particularly those of smallholders, suffer from quality problems which put them at a disadvantage relative to the MNEs. These problems arise because of both their lack of technical inputs and the difficulties of monitoring and controlling the output of a large number of small-scale growers. The introduction of delicate disease-resistant varieties by the MNEs led to the development of boxing to improve their quality control over all aspects of production and distribution. This has enabled the MNEs to maintain quality *and* consistently high effective yields without punitive rates of rejection. Geest controls its bananas only after their delivery at the dockside prior to shipment. This hinders its scope in the Windward Islands for emulating the MNEs' rigorous quality control. The introduction of field-packing in the Windward Islands has improved the quality of their banana exports by reducing the damage prior to shipping. The incentives for improving quality control, however, have been diluted by limited quality competition in consuming markets and the acceptance of low rates of rejection for economic, political and social reasons. These factors have favoured a strategy of maximising export volume rather than quality.

The emphasis on quality raises the issue of consumer preferences. Banana MNEs have devoted substantial resources to developing varieties which embody specific uniform visual characteristics, notably length, straightness and unblemished appearance. Arguably, they have concentrated upon appearance to the detriment of taste. Bananas produced by smaller growers, such as in the Windward Islands, come in an assortment of varieties and sizes with a generally poorer appearance but have a reputation for a superior taste. Winban's recent 'Taste of the Islands' advertising campaign in the UK attempted to highlight and exploit this difference. It is generally believed that consumers are more concerned with price and appearance than taste.

10.5   THE WINDWARD ISLANDS AND THE EC BANANA PROTOCOL

The Windward Islands have preferential access to the EC market under the Lomé Convention which provides especially favourable trade and aid treatment for some LDCs. In the case of bananas, EC imports from ACP States enter the Community tariff-free, while Third Country (Dollar Area) imports face the Common Commercial Tariff (CCT) of 20 per cent. This enables favoured producers to charge higher prices and/or bear higher costs.

The preferential access of ACP bananas is governed by the Banana Protocol, a special protocol (Number 5) of the Lomé Convention. The Protocol is the result of restrictive trade policies having been applied to banana imports by some Member States with the objective of preserving the access of particular producing countries. The key sections of the Protocol relate to: no ACP exporter being treated less favourably in its traditional Community markets than it has been used to (Article 1); Community assistance for improving ACP competitiveness with respect to production, harvesting, handling, internal transport and trade promotion (Article 2); and Community support for financial and technical assistance (Article 3). EC aid to the banana sector has been largely through the Stabex scheme to stabilise primary commodity export earnings. Payments were made to the Windward Islands after hurricanes, for regional disease control and for the model farm in St Lucia (*The Courier*, 1983).

Before the completion of the SEM, the Banana Protocol sanctioned the imposition of additional discriminatory measures on banana imports over and above the CCT by six EC Member states. Greece operated a system of import licences to protect growers in Crete, the only producing area inside the EC. Portugal and Spain had derogations to restrict market access to protect their DOM growers in Madeira and the Canary Islands respectively. Italy had special provisions for imports from Somalia, with an overall quota on imports. France granted free market access to DOM growers in Guadeloupe and Martinique and to francophone ACP states, while requiring licences for imports from all other sources including other ACP states. The UK operated a quota on total imports and issued import licences to Third Countries only when ACP imports failed to meet the quota. A special derogation was applied to the German market for historical reasons whereby all banana imports had tariff-free access regardless of origin, so making it the only truly free market within the Community.

The Banana Protocol segmented the EC market according to the prevailing national import regime by restricting the free internal circulation of bananas. This created considerable scope for supply and demand conditions, and by implication prices, to vary significantly between EC markets although explicit price discrimination is contrary to EC Competition Law. In addition, the Protocol maintained the price of bananas in many EC markets (excluding Germany) significantly above the world price. Virtually the whole of the cost of the transfer to preferential producers was borne by consumers in the most protected markets of France, Spain and the UK.

The Windward Islands and the UK Banana Market

Under the Lomé Convention, all ACP banana exporters were granted access to the UK under general licences. Prior to the SEM, the provisions of the Banana Protocol had two specific interrelated effects in highly protected EC markets such as the UK. By restricting the supply of bananas, it stabilised the price at a level significantly above the world market price. The average unit value of UK banana imports in 1991 was 655 ecus per tonne compared with 463 from the Dollar Area, a margin of 41 per cent at cif prices, and 556 including the CCT, an 18 per cent margin (calculated from Eurostat, 1992). UK imports from the Windward Islands averaged 709 ecus per tonne in 1991, 53 per cent higher than the dollar cif price and still 30 per cent higher after the CCT. In addition, the system of protection also guaranteed market access and share to exporters otherwise uncompetitive on cost and quality grounds. In spite of their higher import unit values, preferential suppliers took almost 80 per cent of the UK market, and the Windward Islands 49 per cent, by volume, in 1991.

Although the UK market afforded a significant degree of protection to preferential suppliers, it could be argued that their premium prices were a consequence of protection rather than reflecting any real cost disadvantage. This argument is not borne out by the evidence of their failure to penetrate more competitive EC markets. In addition, preferential suppliers were consistently unable to take full advantage of the available UK quota, mainly because of persistent supply irregularities and poor quality but also high production and transportation costs (McQueen and Read, 1986). In spite of the production boom in the Windward Islands, the expansion of exports from Belize, and the eventual recovery by Jamaica, the ACP were still unable to supply the whole of the UK market. These difficulties enabled Dollar Area banana imports to establish a growing bridgehead in the UK market during the 1980s. The low unit value of Dollar Area imports in the UK might suggest pure cost advantage and/or very high distributor and retailer mark-ups.

10.6   THE INTERNAL EC MARKET FOR BANANAS

The provisions of the Single European Act require member states to permit Third Country imports to circulate freely upon entering the EC, unhindered by internal barriers. This has had important implications for exporters of products which had traditionally enjoyed privileged access to the EC market under nationally-administered trade barriers. The legal obligation to the SEM therefore conflicted with, but had precedence over, the Community's prior commitment to preferential exporters under the Banana Protocol. The EC recognised that the elimination of these barriers posed a considerable external threat to the economies of those exporting countries particularly dependent upon bananas for employment and foreign exchange earnings, such as the Windward Islands.

The cost to preferential suppliers of creating a single market in bananas, together with the Community's commitments under the Banana Protocol, necessitated the formulation of a revised Community-wide import regime. The proposed structure of this regime provoked prolonged debate between those member states in favour of a free market, notably Germany, and those seeking some form of protection, such as France and the UK. The European Commission published its final proposal for the establishment of an internal market for bananas in August 1992 (European Commission, 1992). It remains subject (at the time of writing) to ratification by EC member states and GATT approval in the Uruguay Round negotiations.[2] The proposal is based upon 1990 consumption levels in the Community and distinguishes between three key sources of bananas; the EC and DOMs, the ACP and the Dollar Area.

Banana production within the EC and the DOMs of up to 854,000 tonnes is eligible for compensation under the Common Agricultural Policy (CAP) based upon an internal reference price. This allocation includes provisions for a reduction of 10,000 tonnes per annum in 1993 and 1994 through the withdrawal of inefficient producers. Each EC and DOM producing region has its own quota within the overall quota. The arrangements for ACP and Dollar Area imports are more complex. ACP imports up to an effective quota of 622,000 tonnes (the 1990 level) have been defined as 'traditional' and only require import certificates. ACP producers will also receive aid to improve the quality of their exports, linked to provisions for marketing and vertical integration, and compensation for declining revenues caused by lower prices and falling market share. 'Non-traditional' ACP imports, those above the traditional level, together with Dollar Area imports have a consolidated annual quota of two million tonnes and require special import licences. A supplementary quota may be implemented, if necessary, to maintain Community prices at a 'reasonable' level. The EC is also providing finance to Dollar Area producers to fund co-operation on development and diversification. The ACP continue to have tariff-free access to the EC market while all Dollar Area imports incur the now harmonised 20 per cent CCT.

The scheme also encompasses a revised marketing arrangement within the Community. This is intended to improve the competitiveness of EC, DOM and ACP producers by enhancing their vertical integration through links with established importers. Seventy per cent of the consolidated and supplementary quota is primarily reserved for 'traditional' importers marketing Dollar Area and non-traditional ACP bananas on their own account. The remaining 30 per cent is open to any Community-based importer under a partnership arrangement whereby traditional EC and ACP bananas are marketed in parallel with non-traditional ACP and Dollar Area imports.

10.7 THE SEM AND WINDWARD ISLANDS' BANANA INDUSTRY

The revision of the EC import regime for bananas in the wake of the SEM raises a number of important issues, notably the distributional effects upon particular groups of producers and consumers. These can be assessed by investigating the static and dynamic effects of changes in absolute and relative preference. The former is a non-discriminatory change in the degree of protection which affects the distribution between producers and consumers. The latter is a discriminatory change in the degree of protection which favours some producers and consumers at the expense of others. The static effects are the once-and-for-all effects of these changes while the dynamic effects are the long-term effects.

With respect to the change in absolute preferences, the issue is whether the revised EC import regime is more or less open to suppliers than it was prior to the SEM. The new system does not appear to be any more or less restrictive than previously so long as consumption in the quota base year of 1990 is taken as 'typical'. Of key importance are the impact of the supplementary quota mechanism and the marketing arrangements. In the event of a projected shortfall in preferential supplies, Articles 16 and 17 of the import regime provide a corresponding increase in the supplementary quota. If Community demand rises above the 1990 level, the effective supply elasticity of additional imports is determined by the response of the supplementary quota. The system of administered imports has, by means of this quota, been extended to the EC market as a whole with an ambiguous impact upon the absolute degree of preference. The new partnership arrangements within the consolidated quota are intended to improve the access of preferential suppliers such as the Windward Islands. Their impact is also unclear in that they may not prove feasible, given the problems of supply disruptions, high cost and poor quality, and so may only inhibit Dollar Area imports.

The aggregate impact of the new Community regime on the absolute level of protection therefore would appear to be small in magnitude and ambiguous in its direction. This implies that Third Country suppliers, including the Windward Islands, have experienced little change in their degree of access to the EC banana market. Any significant benefits for EC consumers as a whole from the internal market for bananas will therefore arise only from the long-run dynamic competition effects.

Regarding the change in relative preference, the reorganisation of the EC internal market for bananas represents a move from a system of national controls, including discriminatory quotas, to a Community-wide system. Changes in relative preference therefore have two distinct effects: within the EC as a whole, a discriminatory change favours certain consuming markets over others; within any particular EC consuming market, a discriminatory change favours certain producers over others. There has been no change in the markets of Belgium, Denmark, Ireland, Luxembourg and the Netherlands because they remain subject to the CCT alone and had no derogations under the Banana Protocol.

The six national markets which previously imposed restrictive con-

trols on banana imports have increased their degree of openness so
that there has been a relative fall in banana prices. There has been a
rise in relative preference in the German market with a corresponding
increase in prices, due to the removal of the tariff derogation. The
principal gainers have therefore been consumers in France, Spain and
the UK, where the import regime has been liberalised, while the German consumers have lost unambiguously from the abolition of their
tariff derogation.

Effects on Banana Producers

The revised import regime has had an asymmetric effect upon the relative
preferences of the three main groups of producers, the EC and DOM,
the ACP and the Dollar Area. The EC and DOM producers have suffered a reduction in their margin of preference in the six markets where
national derogations on imports have been superseded. Their relative
preference has only improved in the German market where the CCT
is now levied on Dollar Area imports. The loss of preference in their
domestic markets indicates that their position has deteriorated.

The impact upon the ACP is more complex since the pre-SEM arrangements under the Banana Protocol favoured particular states. The
relative preference of the ACP has improved relative to EC and DOM
producers in Greece, Portugal and Spain. In France, the margin of preference of the francophone ACP has deteriorated relative to all other
ACP suppliers, while the ACP in general have also gained at the specific
expense of Somalia in Italy. The ACP margin of preference, however,
has not improved relative to the Dollar Area in any of these markets.
In the UK, the relative preference of the ACP, particularly that of Jamaica and the Windward Islands, has also declined. Germany is the
only market in which the ACP margin of preference has improved with
respect to the Dollar Area. The aggregate impact of the changes in
relative preference on the ACP is determined primarily by the changes
in France and the UK which accounted for almost 90 per cent of all
EC imports from the ACP in 1991. In both of these markets, the relative preference of the ACP has declined significantly such that their
position in the EC market has unambiguously deteriorated. The impact
of the revised import regime upon Dollar Area exporters is generally
favourable. Their relative margin of preference has improved in the six
previously highly restrictive national markets although it has been adversely affected by the imposition of the CCT in Germany.

Dynamic Implications of the Internal Market in Bananas

The dynamic impact of the revised EC import regime for bananas is particularly important because the EC, DOM and ACP producers have been relatively weak in markets where they have faced direct competition from Dollar Area bananas. The principal reasons for their competitive disadvantage have been identified in Section 10.4. These give rise to significant differences in the average cif unit values of EC banana imports: in 1991, DOM imports were 753 ecus per tonne; the ACP, 662 ecus per tonne; and the Dollar Area, 480 ecus per tonne. Some of this variation can be ascribed to differences in quality, competition, demand conditions and transport costs between EC markets.

Dollar Area bananas are better able to compete in the now more open markets in terms of both price and quality and can therefore be expected to achieve a high degree of penetration. This will be at the expense of higher cost, lower quality bananas from EC, DOM and ACP sources, including the Windward Islands. Preferred producers have had little success in penetrating markets other than the most heavily protected ones. This suggests that they will find it difficult to gain significant market share from the Dollar Area in Germany despite the imposition of the CCT. The revised EC import regime strongly favours Dollar Area bananas in the long-run, particularly those distributed by the integrated MNEs. In so doing, it further undermines the position of EC, DOM and ACP suppliers in the Community market. Consumers will benefit to the extent that better quality bananas are available at significantly lower prices in previously protected markets. Arguably, this also means that homogenous bananas have replaced the pre-SEM assortment of varieties, sizes, tastes and prices, so reducing consumer choice. The further accretion of market power by the MNEs in the Community market, leading to the diminution of competition, has adverse implications for future prices and consumer welfare. The rate at which these dynamic competition effects are realised, however, is dependent upon the resistance of the Community to growing pressure for the revision of the traditional and consolidated quotas in favour of the Dollar Area.

10.8 CONCLUSION: PROSPECTS FOR THE WINDWARD ISLANDS

The economies of the Windward Islands are highly dependent upon the export of bananas to the EC. This acute dependence means that the changes in the Community as a consequence of the SEM are of critical importance to the future of the banana growers and the economies of the Windward Islands. The creation of the EC internal banana market has necessitated a change in the UK import regime from a nationally-administered quota to an open market subject to Community-wide protective measures. This change provides for the unrestricted access of Dollar Area bananas to the UK market as part of the EC's commitment to the free internal circulation of goods. The replacement of the UK national quota with a Community-wide one therefore represents a significant adverse change in the preference for the ACP relative to the Dollar Area.

The greater degree of price and quality competition in the UK market, partially avoided under the previous import regime, has increased the pressure on higher cost suppliers, such as those in the Windward Islands. There is little potential for a compensating expansion in those other EC markets where relative preferences have moved in their favour given the strength of competition from the Dollar Area. This indicates that many marginal growers will be forced to exit from the industry. The skewed structure of banana production in the Windward Islands means that this will affect a large number of highly labour-intensive smallholders with few alternative sources of income. The long-term prospects of those remaining in the industry are good to the extent that the larger growers are more likely to be able to enhance their competitive position. The social and economic impact of such a large-scale exodus could have a devastating impact on GDP, exports and employment. It would certainly further aggravate already high levels of unemployment and hidden unemployment, and exacerbate the problem of rural poverty.

The change in the Community's import regime for bananas as part of the SEM programme will have adverse implications for preferred sources of supply such as the Windward Islands. The increased intensity of competition in the Community market casts grave doubt upon the future of preferential suppliers to the EC as a whole. It could be argued that the Windward Islands and other preferred sources have a case under Article 1 of the Banana Protocol, which is intended to preserve their preferential position. In the context of the legislation of the Single European Act prohibiting internal barriers to trade, however, it is unlikely that the provisions of the Article can be satisfied simultaneously.

The banana export industry in most DOMs and ACP States, including the Windward Islands, is at a competitive disadvantage with respect to Dollar Area producers, especially the MNEs. This disadvantage is principally a consequence of the structure of their production, characterised by small-scale labour-intensive peasant smallholdings, which gives rise to high cost and relatively low quality output. In addition, nation states, unlike firms, cannot diversify the location risk of an industry which is highly susceptible to adverse weather conditions. Increased competitive pressures will mean the enforced exit of higher cost preferential growers, most of whom are peasant smallholders with few alternative sources of income. Preferential access to the EC market will only favour those growers of a scale sufficient to improve their competitive position through the production of higher quality bananas at a viable cost. The enforced restructuring in the Windward Islands will therefore have a significant social and economic impact given the preponderance of smallholders and the industry's critical importance to the economies of the islands.

The crucial issue for the Windward Islands is therefore the formulation of an appropriate policy response to the impending decline of the smallholder sector and possibly the whole of the industry. These policies need to minimise the extent of social and economic dislocation of restructuring. This is likely to include crop diversification, the provision of alternative sources of employment and, possibly, the consolidation of land holdings. The EC could use the revised import quota system combined with a resource transfer to promote gradual adjustment in the Windward Islands banana industry. This would moderate the detrimental effects upon small growers who have few immediate alternatives.

10.9 POSTSCRIPT

Since the completion of this chapter, the EC has finalised its rules for the internal banana market (February, 1993). These encompass some amendments to the proposals outlined and analysed here.

The most important change so far as the Windward Islands are concerned is the introduction of specific quotas for each ACP exporter based upon its pre-1991 peak. This has meant an upward revision of the ACP general quota to 857,700 tonnes within which Dominica has a 'traditional' quota of 71,000 tonnes, Grenada 14,000, St Lucia 127,000 and St Vincent 82,000.

The 20 per cent tariff on Third Countries has been replaced by a fixed levy of 100 ecus per tonne – equivalent in 1991 to an *ad valorem* tariff of 20.8 per cent, with a substantial penalty levy on all imports above the total quota.

There have also been slight modifications to the marketing arrangements so that there is now no longer a requirement for parallel marketing.

The regulations for the internal banana market continue to generate considerable controversy, both from within the EC (which included an unsuccessful case brought to the European Court by the German Government) and from the Latin American exporting countries. In June 1993, a GATT panel ruled in favour of the Latin Americans that the EC's pre-SEM regime for banana was illegal, a decision which has opened the way for a legal challenge against the new rules. The story of bananas and the Single European Market is far from over.

Notes

1. The author wishes to thank Mr Bernard Cornibert, UK Representative of Winban, for providing data on the banana export industry in the Windward Islands, and the editors, for their helpful comments on an earlier draft.
2. See the postscript in section 10.9 for an update on the proposals.

References

Caribbean Centre for Action Research (1978), *Action-Oriented Research into the Production & Marketing of Bananas in Dominica: A Preliminary Investigation*, mimeo (location of CCAR unknown).

The Courier (1983), 'The banana trade and the ACP States', No. 78, pp. 64–91 (Brussels: EC-ACP).

Ellis, F. (1978), *The banana export activity in Central America 1947-76: a case-study of plantation exports by vertically-integrated transnational corporations*, unpublished PhD thesis, University of Sussex.

European Commission (1992), *Proposal for a Council Regulation (EEC) on the Common Organization of the Market in Bananas*, Brussels: EC, Com (92) 359.

Eurostat (1992), *Import Statistics 1991*, Luxembourg: Eurostat.

FAO (1986), *The World Banana Economy 1970-84*, Rome: Food and Agriculture Organisation.

FAO (1990a), *Trade Yearbook 1990*, Rome: Food and Agriculture Organisation.

FAO (1990b), *Production Yearbook 1990*, Rome: FAO.

Henderson, T. and Gomes, P. (1979), *A Profile of Small Farming in St Vincent, Dominica and St Lucia: Report of a Baseline Survey*, St Augustine: UWI, Department of Agricultural Extension.

LeFranc, E. (1980), 'Small farming in Grenada, St Vincent and St Lucia', in *Small Farming in the Less Developed Countries of the Commonwealth Caribbean*, Barbados: Caribbean Development Bank.

McQueen M. and Read, R. (1986), *The Effects of the Second Enlargement of the EC on the Exports of the ACP States*, Unpublished Report for the UK ODA.

Read, R. (1985), 'The banana export industry: oligopoly and barriers to entry', in M. Casson and Associates, *Multinationals and World Trade: Vertical Integration and the Division of Labour in World Industries*, London: Allen & Unwin.

Read, R. (1988), *The determinants of intra-firm trade: case studies of the copper, synthetic fibre and banana export industries*, unpublished PhD thesis, University of Reading.

Thomson, R. (1987), *Green Gold: Bananas and Dependency in the Eastern Caribbean*, London: Latin American Bureau.

World Bank (1985), *St Lucia: Economic Performance and Prospects*, Washington DC: World Bank.

Index

208

Index